Young
Mr. Roosevelt

For
Mark & Judith
David & Carie Lee
Erica & Bruce

Young Mr. Roosevelt

FDR'S INTRODUCTION TO WAR, POLITICS AND LIFE

Stanley Weintraub

DA CAPO PRESS
A Member of the Perseus Books Group

Design and Composition by Trish Wilkinson
Set in 11 point Goudy Old Style

Library of Congress Cataloging-in-Publication Data

Weintraub, Stanley, 1929–
    Young Mr. Roosevelt : FDR's introduction to war, politics and life / Stanley Weintraub.
        pages   cm
    Includes bibliographical references and index.
    ISBN 978-0-306-82118-9 (hardcover)—ISBN 978-0-306-82235-3 (e-book)
1. Roosevelt, Franklin D. (Franklin Delano), 1882–1945. 2. Presidents—United States—Biography. 3. United States. Navy Department—Officials and employees—Biography. 4. United States—Politics and government—1913–1921. 5. World War, 1914–1918—United States. I. Title.
E807.W425 2013
973.917092—dc23
[B]   2013014328

Published by Da Capo Press
A Member of the Perseus Books Group
www.dacapopress.com

Da Capo Press books are available at special discounts for bulk purchases in the U.S. by corporations, institutions, and other organizations. For more information, please contact the Special Markets Department at the Perseus Books Group, 2300 Chestnut Street, Suite 200, Philadelphia, PA 19103, or call (800) 810-4145, ext. 5000, or e-mail special.markets@perseusbooks.com.

10 9 8 7 6 5 4 3 2 1

Contents

Come, gather children by my side
And listen well to me
How fortune de[a]lt
With Roosevelt
The pride of our Navee.

—Louis McHenry Howe

'Tis the curse of the service,
Preferment goes by letter and affection,
Not by the old gradation, where each second
Stood heir to the first.

—Othello, General of the Venetian Navy

We cannot anchor our ship of state . . . We must go
forward, or flounder.

—FDR accepting the Democratic
vice presidential nomination, Hyde Park,
August 9, 1920

Preface
The Beginnings of Promise

WORKING ON *FINAL VICTORY*, about the wartime 1944 presidential campaign in which Franklin Delano Roosevelt won an unprecedented fourth
term, abbreviated by his sudden death in April 1945, I planned to include a chapter on the service vote. Millions of Americans in uniform at
sea or on distant fronts were eligible for absentee ballots. In the first decade of the new century, many former servicemen I contacted, however
elderly, recalled where they were and how they voted. By mail, in person,
and through helpful questioners on my behalf across the country, I
recorded their responses. In each case I asked why the veteran voted for
the candidate chosen then. Former sailors and their officers frequently
answered, "I voted for Roosevelt because he was a Navy man."

A Navy man? Young Roosevelt was, indeed, Assistant Secretary of the
Navy during World War I, and into 1920. I determined, once the 1944
book was completed, to examine what kind of Navy man he was, and how
those wartime years of political apprenticeship foreshadowed his future.

THE ONLY CHILD of a young mother and a father in late middle-age, both
wealthy, patrician and bred on venerable rustic estates long predating the

nation's independence, Franklin Delano Roosevelt could look forward to an untroubled future as a country squire. He might interrupt his moneyed leisure with golfing, boating, gentlemen's clubs, cocktails, cards, connoisseurship, and oversight of family properties and investments. Perhaps, too, through an undemanding Ivy League law background, he might endure the occasional preparation of briefs in a prestigious Wall Street firm. An arranged marriage with a well-to-do society beauty also seemed inevitable, and very likely an honorary and unexacting position in politics and public life arranged through lending his Roosevelt signature to corporate letterheads and through his liberality to party funds. After an estimable, blameless, boring passage of years, he would be remembered in a modest obituary in the New York press, but hardly beyond—and then quietly forgotten.

None of the above would happen. Owning an inherited fortune and recognizable surname might push someone into unwarranted prominence, then prove poor springboards, as the disappointing successors to famous names have repeatedly demonstrated. Yet exceptions to such handicaps happen. Robert McCormick, implacable publisher of the *Chicago Tribune*, called FDR scornfully "one-half of one percent [Theodore] Roosevelt"— but Bertie McCormick lived to see his words haunt him. Although vastly overshadowed at first by a flamboyant elder cousin, his wife's "Uncle Ted," who had made the White House his "bully pulpit," a callow FDR would overcome the mixed blessing of his background. He would explore paths into government; run for political offices, and win and lose; survive a potentially devastating extramarital scandal; come close to death in a pandemic, then prevail over crippling paralysis that left him wheelchairbound; energize recovery from the greatest economic depression in the nation's history and oversee its greatest war; and campaign and win four tumultuous terms as President.

SUPPORTED BY DOCUMENTATION beyond lists and names and places and dates, biographers are inevitably prompted by their recognition of how lives turn out. As readers, we possess that delicious sense of dramatic irony that we know not only what the figure at the center—here, the young Franklin Delano Roosevelt—could not have known, but how and why what happened did happen. We possess a growing awareness of how unforeseen disasters were averted or surmounted, and how successes were frustrated by *hubris* or followed up by even further achievement. And how routine associates on the margins of his early experience would turn up later as vital supporting players on a larger stage.

Young Franklin's first and unpromising acquaintance with that stage occurred when he was four or five, and his father, already nearly sixty, gained entrée to the White House, where a president of his own party, whom James Roosevelt had financially supported, sat, burdened with political troubles. "I have one wish for you, little man," said burly Grover Cleveland, "that you will never be President of the United States." When Roosevelt died on December 8, 1900, his only child was eighteen. A distant cousin, Theodore, from the rival and dominant party, had just been elected vice president. A freshman at Harvard, Franklin had briefly joined the college's Republican Club to promote TR's candidacy. The next year an assassin's bullet would elevate the elder Roosevelt, who had won with William McKinley, to the presidency.

THE TEENAGE ROOSEVELT had hoped to go to the Naval Academy at Annapolis, but James had not wanted Franklin away at sea during his father's declining years. The closest he would get to Annapolis would be as an unseasoned young man on the make, when he would relocate to Washington on a minor peacetime political appointment at the pleasure of another Democratic president he hardly knew, Woodrow Wilson. Despite Franklin's heady dreams, he was hardly confident, except in friendly brag, that he would later return as President himself, defying the sudden and unanticipated burdens of being physically handicapped—that he would live out his greatest years in that relentlessly competitive capital, thwarting what might have been terminal disability and premature retirement.

Young Mr. Roosevelt is about how the expectations of an unremarkable patrician future unraveled and the FDR that we, and history, remember began to emerge. On October 24, 2012, at the southern tip of Roosevelt Island in the East River between Manhattan and Queens, a Four Freedoms

Park was dedicated as a memorial to President Roosevelt. It is the last completed design of Louis Kahn, one of the most influential architects of the twentieth century. He died in 1974, long before his vision took shape. Did he intend in part to suggest FDR's beginnings in national office? "A pointillist carpet of grey and white granite bricks [leads] towards the apex," an observer wrote, "which parts the waters like the prow of a great ship."

Stanley Weintraub
BEECH HILL
NEWARK, DELAWARE

1

The Shadow of "Uncle Ted"

D OFFING HIS DERBY, the debonair young Franklin Delano Roosevelt, smartly suited in English tweeds and with pince-nez in place, entered the fusty suite of the Secretary of the Navy ready to go to work. Across a narrow street from the White House was the huge, ornate State, War & Navy Building, at 17th Street and Pennsylvania Avenue, built in 1871 in what was thought to be French Second Empire style—a muddle of mansard roofs, turrets, and Victorian clutter. A third-floor office next to that of the Secretary was available, but Franklin quickly learned that he couldn't occupy it. His appointment as Assistant Secretary of the Navy had not yet been confirmed. He exchanged some pleasantries and retrieved his hat. Roosevelt had expected "to enter upon his duties," Navy Secretary Josephus Daniels noted in his diary on March 15, 1913, "but the Senate, not having acted, he returned to New York."

Woodrow Wilson had been inaugurated on March 4, succeeding William Howard Taft, once a Theodore Roosevelt protégé. When Daniels first learned from Wilson of his own designation, he recalled, "I immediately determined upon having Mr. R. as assistant if it was agreeable to the President. It is singular that I never thought of any other man in that connection." Daniels told his wife that he had Roosevelt in mind, and that "his

NATION'S MEN OF AFFAIRS IN CARTOON

FRANKLIN D. ROOSEVELT.
Lawyer, Clubman and Statesman.

Cartoon from the *Washington Herald*, March 23, 1913,
satirizing young Franklin's appointment as Assistant
Secretary of the Navy. FDR LIBRARY

distinguished cousin TR went from that place to the presidency. May history repeat itself!"

Theodore Roosevelt's rise had been dramatic but not quite that direct. He had been Assistant Secretary of the Navy at thirty-nine (in 1898), resigning to raise a regiment of Western cowboys and Eastern elites remembered as "Rough Riders" to fight the Spanish in Cuba. (As an instant lieutenant colonel, TR ordered his custom-made fawn-colored uniform with canary trim from Brooks Brothers.) Returning in magnified glory after victory at San Juan Hill—actually nearby Kettle Hill, but that did not sound as romantic—he was elected Republican governor of New York.

Nominated for vice president in 1900 and taking office when William McKinley won a second term, Roosevelt succeeded to the presidency on McKinley's assassination by an anarchist in September 1901. Elected for four more years in 1904, Roosevelt proved as flamboyant as his predecessor had been reserved. The stout, stodgy William Howard Taft, his hand-picked successor, disappointed TR and was struggling through his single term.

Being a Roosevelt in politics in the aftermath of "Uncle Ted's" lively presidency was both a boon and a bane for Franklin, only thirty-one when Taft's unremarkable presidency expired in early 1913. Although Theodore Roosevelt was actually Eleanor's uncle, and only a distant cousin to her husband, TR's over-the-top presence loomed over their lives. That James Roosevelt, Franklin's late father, had been a lifelong Democrat, and that his son had followed into the rival camp, seemed almost a betrayal. Theodore's outspoken elder daughter, Alice, and his four sons, Franklin's near-contemporaries (Theodore, Jr., was five years younger), considered their Hudson Valley namesake a patrician amateur and pilferer of the Oyster Bay family's reputation. Not so Uncle Ted. At his fatherless niece's marriage to Franklin in New York in 1904 he had given Eleanor away, and had even offered the White House for the ceremony.

Then a young swell at Columbia Law School,* where TR also had gone but had dropped out before the bar exam, FDR had no need for a bohemian walk-up. After living with Eleanor at 125 E. 36th Street in Manhattan, a townhouse rented for him by his managerial mother, Sara, he would relocate to what he called "a fourteen-foot[-wide] mansion" purchased by her at 49 E. 65th Street. Adjacent was Sara's house, in which the main ground-floor rooms communicated with Franklin's residence, ostensibly for convenience but obviously so that "Mrs. James" could continue her dominance of her only child at every turn. When James Roosevelt had died while Franklin was at Harvard, Sara moved to Boston to be nearby—much as, at about the same time, Douglas MacArthur's formidably possessive mother, "Pinky," moved to a hotel close to the Military Academy at West Point.

---

* When TR went to Columbia Law, the school consisted of one professor.

Late in 1907 young Roosevelt joined the firm of Carter, Ledyard & Milburn in Manhattan, treading water in routine practice—and unpaid during his first year—until he could find a role in politics. One of six law clerks, each at a cluttered rolltop desk, Franklin had no desire, unlike the others, for a career path into a serene partnership there or somewhere. Like TR, who was then midway into his boisterous second term, he looked for opportunities in elective office, recognizing that the Roosevelt name had become magic. He hoped to begin modestly, with a seat in the State Assembly, New York's lower house. (His Uncle Ted had also begun in the legislature, in 1884.) After establishing a small reputation there, Franklin intended campaigning for the election of a president from his party, then procuring an appointment, as did Uncle Ted, as Assistant Secretary of the Navy. He would then, he envisioned rather than calculated, succeed to the governorship of New York, as did TR in 1898. "Once you're elected Governor of New York," he explained to a less enterprising law colleague, "if you do well enough in that job, you have a good show to be President."

Franklin ruled out accidental office. Although TR had made the leap to the White House from the vice presidency after William McKinley was shot, as, following assassinations, had Andrew Johnson and Chester Arthur, lesser men than the flamboyant Uncle Ted, the office had to be competed for, and won. Grenville Clark, a fellow law clerk who would become a prominent Wall Street lawyer, and then a congressman, recalled FDR's quite serious revelation of intent as "proper and sincere," and moreover, as Clark put it, "entirely reasonable." Franklin was a Roosevelt. He could dream big.

Bored by legal procedure after nearly three years at Carter, Ledyard & Milburn, FDR saw opportunity in an approaching statewide election in 1910 for which no Democratic candidate in his overwhelmingly Republican district seemed forthcoming. He might well lose, but his party would owe him something. While stumping for the GOP candidate for governor, the "Colonel" (TR had long elevated his Rough Rider rank a grade) learned that Franklin was interested in running as a Democrat for the Assembly seat that included "Springwood"—FDR's mother's thousand-acre estate, and informally his own—in Hyde Park. Hoping that Uncle Ted would forgo campaigning in Dutchess County, Franklin inquired indirectly to TR's sister, Bamie Cowles (Eleanor's "Auntie Bye"). Undismayed by party affiliation, the Colonel wrote to Bamie, "Franklin ought to go into politics without the least regard as to where I speak or don't speak. . . . He is a fine fellow." Uncle Ted would not electioneer in Franklin's district, which seemed not to need his intrusive star power.

The run for the legislature was young Roosevelt's first try for public office. At the time of TR's letter to Bamie Cowles, dated August 10, he had been considering a run for the local Assembly seat. At the Democratic state convention in Poughkeepsie on October 6, only a month before the election, Franklin's name was placed in nomination—but, disappointingly for him, it was not for the seemingly more accessible lower house. The Republican incumbent in the Assembly had changed his mind about retiring—and seemed unbeatable. No Democrat, however, had risked a run for the upper house, the Senate. After a long pause by the leadership to encourage an alternative candidate to FDR to come forward, none had emerged. There was no contest. The convention secretary was directed to cast one ballot for Roosevelt, all that was technically necessary.

Following tradition, a committee of three was named to escort the winning candidate to the podium, where, accepting his nomination, FDR made his first political speech. Preparing it required him to think about why, beyond his own future, he was seeking office. Suddenly he had to begin considering the kind of impact on the public that was expected of an elected official. He realized that he was not only running for himself. The hostile Republican *Daily Eagle* in Poughkeepsie would editorialize that the Democrats "have made a new and valuable discovery, Franklin D. Roosevelt, younger son* of the late James Roosevelt of Hyde Park. This is one of the exceptional branches of the Roosevelt family that is Democratic in politics. . . . Presumably his contribution to the campaign

---

*Franklin had a much older step-brother, James ("Rosy") Roosevelt Roosevelt, the elder James's son from an earlier marriage. The elder James disliked "Jr." and instead repeated the Roosevelt surname.

funds goes well above four figures—hence the value of his discovery. . . . Senator Schlosser, we imagine, will not be greatly disturbed by Mr. Roosevelt's candidacy."

The *Daily Eagle*'s guess at Franklin's net worth was as fanciful as his likely vote-getting future. He could bear the small expense of losing the campaign, after which the party would owe him a nomination the next time around if the Assembly seat again became available. Both Eleanor and Franklin possessed what were then very comfortable annual incomes from paternal trust funds, about $7,500 and $6,000. He also had his small salary from Carter, Ledyard & Milburn, and could anticipate generous birthday checks each January 30 from his wealthy mother, Sara, who had inherited $1.3 million from her father, and even more, at forty-six in 1900, from James Roosevelt. When not in Manhattan, the Roosevelt couple continued to live in Hyde Park with the matriarchal Sara at spacious Springwood. "I guess several people thought I would be a gold mine," Franklin recalled much later, but little gold was needed in a largely rural upstate area in pre-inflationary years. The entire four-week campaign would cost little more than $2,500 at a time when sugar was four cents a pound and eggs fourteen cents a dozen.

To get around his district Franklin rented a bright red, open two-cylinder touring car, complete with driver, who festooned the sputtering Maxwell with flags and bunting. Clad in a duster, with a broad gray mustache under his goggles, Harry "Hawkey" Osterhoudt was the local piano tuner, and a Democrat. Still rare on country roads, and so expensive to purchase and maintain that Franklin did not own one, an auto could call undue attention to his privileged background, and its clatter might frighten local horses. On the other hand, the striking vehicle emphasized his youthful audacity—he was twenty-eight—and his matinee-idol attractiveness. Besides, he was a Roosevelt, as he stressed, a dozen or more times a day, at markets and at crossroads, shaking hands and overcoming his shyness. Like an earlier candidate with whom he happened to share a name, if not a party, he claimed to be against bossism and corruption in politics. Although there was bossism aplenty in upstate Republican towns, both liabilities were attributed to the notorious Tammany Hall Democratic machine in New York City and upstate.

In his notes for campaign speeches was an unidentified clipping with lines from Lincoln, which Franklin may have quoted: "I am not bound to win, but I am bound to be true. I am not bound to succeed, but I am bound to live up to the light I have. I must stand with anybody that stands right, and part with him when he goes wrong." It may have suggested to him his thin chances against John F. Schlosser—yet who could go wrong, even a Democrat, by quoting Lincoln? And to what would he be "true"?

In that off-year election—New York governors then served only two-year terms—Franklin surprised even himself, polling an upset win. Ahead of the Democratic statewide ticket, he tallied 15,708 votes to his opponent's 14,568. Another Roosevelt was in office.

SENATOR ROOSEVELT HAD barely taken his seat in January 1911, days before his twenty-ninth birthday, when a *New York Times* reporter covering Albany asked him, "Are you an admirer of your uncle-in-law?" And was he covertly the ex-president's political agent? The barbed questions arose from FDR's open opposition to William F. Sheehan, once boss of the corrupt Buffalo Democratic machine, who had moved to Manhattan as director of lucrative, Tammany-controlled, public utility companies, notably the trolley trust. Billy Sheehan was now Tammany's candidate for U.S. senator—a seat still filled by the legislature. Uncle Ted was not only vocally anti-Tammany, but a proponent of a constitutional amendment for election to the Senate by popular vote.

"Who can help but admire him?" young Roosevelt claimed, predicting that his Uncle Ted would make a political comeback as President Taft's disappointing term ended, and that TR would be difficult to beat. "It is only a question of time before people generally will appreciate what he has done in arousing the public conscience and in driving corruption out of politics." As for being anyone's agent, "That's absurd," he scoffed to the man from *The Times*. "Why, I haven't seen my distinguished cousin since the first of the year. We've had absolutely no communication on this subject." The disclaimer was a stretch. New Year's Day was earlier that month, and only a week before the reporter had come to interview young Roosevelt, TR had written, "Just a line to say that we are all really proud of the way you have handled yourself. Good luck to you!"

Also congratulating him on his election was Langdon Marvin, who had clerked at Carter, Ledyard & Milburn before becoming a junior partner at Jerome & Rand. Despite his own "affiliation with the party of your illustrious kinsman," Marvin wrote, he was "much pleased at your election. You will be quite the boy wonder and certainly the pride of Albany. May this first big step lead on to the heights attained by the aforesaid illustrious kinsman, and the White House again resound with Roosevelt revelry." In a joking postscript Marvin added, "I want to be Chief Justice," and "send me an invitation to the coming-out party in the White House of fair Alice's successor." Alice Roosevelt Longworth, once the precociously caustic "Princess Alice" of the TR White House, had been married since 1906, at twenty-two, to the powerful, late-thirtyish, compulsively womanizing Ohio congressman Nicholas Longworth. Anna Eleanor Roosevelt ("Sis"), the eldest younger Roosevelt child, was not yet five.

When the 1912 state senate recessed late in April, Franklin, less neglectful than it seemed as a husband and father, left Eleanor to close up their rented house in Albany and move the family back to Manhattan. After all, that was traditionally women's work. He and her younger brother Hall were sailing to Panama on the United Fruit Company's SS *Carillo* to see the nearly completed canal that Uncle Ted had initiated. Eleanor had been invited to join them but had refused to leave Anna, James and Elliott to Gramma Sara and the "help." Hall was about to enter engineering school on graduating from Harvard. Although FDR was interested in any aspect of sea operations, he justified the voyage as educational for his young brother-in-law, and a gesture that Eleanor would appreciate. "I am taking the trip chiefly on Hall's account," Franklin explained to TR in asking for a letter of introduction to the chief engineer, George Washington Goethals, "and feel that it would help his future engineering career if he could see the Isthmus intelligently." To ensure that it would not seem to be a partisan venture he invited along a likeable Republican state senate colleague, J. Mayhew Wainwright.

Goethals gave the group special access, unlike the twelve thousand curious tourists who were hauled across construction sites on the Isthmus in 1912. The FDR party rode behind their special "observation" steam engine "over tracks and switches among the blasts and drills and steam shovels and dump trains," conducted by "the right-hand man of Goethals," Rear Admiral Harry Harwood Rousseau. A "Commission launch" guided by Rousseau took them the next day to see the completed sea-level Pacific side of the Canal, after which they paid a courtesy visit to the American consul.

Returning via New Orleans, Franklin was met by Eleanor for a journey by rail to New Mexico to visit Bob and Isabella Ferguson, who had moved to remote Cat Cañon, near Silver City, in hopes of alleviating Bob Ferguson's tuberculosis. Isabella Selmes Ferguson, a year younger than Eleanor, had been her closest friend in New York, and Bob, now gaunt and failing, had been a Rough Rider under Uncle Ted. A loyal Republican, Ferguson's affection for TR was unreserved, although he realized that "the Colonel" seemed ready to bolt the GOP if Taft were renominated and run for another term under the rival standard of a new Progressive Party. Both men were stirred by the prospect of TR's return to politics, but Franklin diplomatically muted his enthusiasm. The reform-minded New Jersey governor, Woodrow Wilson, a Democrat, was his bet for the White House, and for his own ambitions.

Roosevelt had already met the governor, volunteering support. A Wilson victory would boost FDR's political opportunities, as the governor attacked machine politics, and Tammany stood in the paths of both men. As boss Charles F. Murphy was Democratic power broker in New York, Roosevelt was not offered a delegate seat for the 1912 presidential convention. To see and be seen, he and Eleanor traveled to Baltimore anyway. Sara was happy to supervise, and spoil, her grandchildren.

The GOP on June 22 had ignored TR's defiant primary successes and renominated Taft, his former Cabinet colleague, whose Old Guard sympathies the ex-president had repudiated. That he would run on his own for what amounted to a third term almost guaranteed a Republican split and a Democratic win. Yet Theodore Roosevelt's fighting qualities overwhelmed doubts among his supporters that half of a divided but predominant party could defeat the revitalized minority Democrats. He boasted of being as sturdy as a "bull moose," an image that would quickly identify the new party. It seemed to TR more important to vigorously make his progressive case—to defeat the disappointing Taft even at the gamble of electing the dour Wilson. "It is indeed a marvelous thing," Franklin wrote, employing Uncle Ted's military metaphors, "that, acting with the support of untrained militia, [he] has succeeded in overcoming the well-organized opposition of the trained soldiers of the Republican Party."

Although the austere, academic, Presbyterian Wilson, a former professor, then president, of Princeton, could command an audience beyond the university, he was far from a sure thing at the ballot box. Nevertheless he might share the liberal vote (which had gone Republican with TR) with the Progressives, reducing Taft's chances. Before Franklin left for the Baltimore convention, he had run into Uncle Ted's son Kermit, who confided, "Pop is praying for Clark." House of Representatives Speaker James Beauchamp ("Champ") Clark of Missouri, a committed conservative and weak campaigner, had more promised delegates, but not the two-thirds he needed. Other ballots were largely pledged to Governor Wilson, powerful Alabama senator Oscar Underwood, and feisty, radical William Jennings Bryan, a Nebraskan who at fifty-two had already lost three presidential elections but retained a devoted following.

Eleanor and Franklin had gallery seats at the convention, but Franklin absented himself in the lobbies and corridors encouraging support for Wilson, coyly attracting attention as a Democratic Roosevelt. Josephus Daniels, a Wilson manager and National Committeeman, and editor of the Raleigh, North Carolina, *News & Observer*, watched as Roosevelt, with youthful energy and matinee-idol charm, worked the delegates and the newspapermen in Wilson's behalf. "Roosevelt came to my room with some up-State [New York] editors who wished seats in the press section. . . . I thought," Daniels remembered effusively, "he was as handsome

FDR with Elliott, James, and "Gramma" Sara Delano Roosevelt, Campobello, August, 1913. FDR LIBRARY

a figure of an attractive young man as I have ever seen. At that convention Franklin and I became friends. . . . " On the eleventh ballot, Charles Murphy, who had been backing colorless Ohio governor Judson Harmon, threw New York's 90 votes to Champ Clark. Senator Underwood was stalled at 120 votes. On the fourteenth ballot, realizing he had no chance, Bryan conceded that he could not support a candidate backed by Tammany and offered his votes to Wilson. While Franklin lobbied delegates in the corridors, and no aspirant seemed close to the required two-thirds, Eleanor, weary of noisy and fruitless demonstrations, and the overpowering cigar smoke in the stifling heat, took the train home. Once returned to Hyde Park she left with the children for the family summer compound on Campobello Island in the Bay of Fundy, off the coast of Eastport, Maine. No easy journey, it was six hours by rail from New York City to Boston, then a change of trains and a ferry across the two-mile Narrows. Servants coped with the children and luggage.

The young Roosevelts now owned their own Campobello home, "Fairhaven." First purchase rights had been willed to Sara Roosevelt by

Grace Kuhn, her summer neighbor from Boston who had died in 1910. Mrs. Kuhn had willed that her sprawling red-shingled, green-shuttered 34-room "cottage" could be purchased for $5,000, everything inside included, provided that it go to Franklin and Eleanor. Sara bought the property. It would not be too big. The Roosevelts already had three children and burgeoning household staff.

Eleanor had arrived on Canadian soil—the island was part of the province of New Brunswick—when Franklin wired her on Monday, July 1, after the forty-sixth ballot, "WILSON NOMINATED THIS AFTERNOON ALL MY PLANS VAGUE SPLENDID TRIUMPH." Neither Roosevelt's plans nor his ambitions were vague, but the minimum fee for telegrams limited messages to ten words.

Laid-off political reporter Louis McHenry Howe, who had been close to FDR in Albany, wrote to Roosevelt to congratulate him as if he had been the nominee. "Beloved and Revered Future President," he began, on the make for a job. FDR intended to run again for his Senate seat. As Howe's instincts suggested, if Wilson were elected, Roosevelt expected a political springboard in Washington. Since the last Democratic president had been Grover Cleveland, and the party's chief executive before him was the futile James Buchanan in 1857, Tammany Hall, eager to recover such long-elusive patronage as postmasterships, became conciliatory statewide. The small, reform-minded Empire State Democracy, with Roosevelt as one of its leaders, had urged party progressives to rally to Wilson. Although Boss Murphy despised the elitist New Jersey governor, local political necessities required that he back the party nominee.

Prior to Campobello, Roosevelt hired the familiar Maxwell touring car for a 150-mile, day-long tour of local "henchmen"—FDR's term in a letter to Eleanor—to gather support for his renomination, which, on August 24, proved unanimous. His mother, a tireless traveler visiting her sister in Paris and learning of the convention results, wrote that she was "glad" for him and assumed he would be reelected. Yet Sara also wanted the impossible. She hoped that TR's new party would also endorse him, "to be true to its principles." None of Uncle Ted's extended family nor political operatives among his friends were likely to desert his renegade "Bull Moose" ticket for Franklin.

Early in September the young Roosevelts returned from Campobello, planning a stopover at their house at 47 E. 65th Street in Manhattan. FDR intended to continue on to Hyde Park to initiate his fall campaign. Although they had arranged while in New York to dine with Bob Ferguson's brother, Ronald, on arrival by steamer from Eastport, Franklin was beset by stomach pain and fever. Reluctantly, he went to bed. Eleanor took Ronald to dinner. The next day a physician on a house call could identify no cause. Unable to shake off his fever, FDR remained bedridden. Summoned from Paris, Sara discovered that Eleanor had also fallen ill. Another doctor had recognized typhoid fever. Both Roosevelts had been warned not to drink from the pitcher of water in their steamer's stateroom, yet they had used the worrisome water to brush their teeth. That exposure was enough.

Although the GOP split appeared helpful, FDR's reelection prospects were in jeopardy. Roosevelt had two opponents for his 26th District seat, Jacob Southard, a Republican banker, and the TR Progressive George A. Vossler. Franklin had already engaged "Hawkey" and his red Maxwell but could not campaign. From his narrow bedroom in Manhattan, remote from his constituents, FDR asked Eleanor to send for Louis Howe.

Gnomelike, chronically disheveled Louis McHenry Howe, forty-one but looking older, was an upstate reporter in Albany who had been dropped by the *New York Herald* when he had accepted temporary work for reformist Empire State Democracy. Now without income, he was at his cheap cottage at Horseneck Beach on Buzzards Bay in Massachusetts. Howe's newspaper salary, forty dollars a week, had only been paid during the few months each year when the legislature was in session. His life otherwise was peripatetic and his sources of press support erratic. Earlier, Howe had written anxiously to Roosevelt that he had "jumped into the game" expecting to remain with Wilsonian politics in the state, but his financial backing, after Baltimore, had vanished. "Now I am in a hole," he had appealed, "because there are five long months before Albany [resumes], and the price of living has not gone down any. If you can connect me with a job during the campaign, for heaven's sake help me out, for this mess is bad business for me." While remote in Campobello, Roosevelt had done nothing. Now he was desperate.

Wired now to come to 65th Street, Howe, who had no telephone, picked up Eleanor's telegram at Lulu Hammond's General Store at Horseneck. (Fortunately, Eleanor had only a mild case of typhoid.) Howe took the first train he could get to New York, consulted with the bedridden FDR and was put on the campaign payroll at fifty dollars a week and expenses. Given the rented Maxwell and carte blanche to run the vote-getting, Howe moved his family to a boardinghouse in Poughkeepsie as Roosevelt was assisted back to recover at Hyde Park.

Illness can be politically expedient. Franklin had been extricated from involvement in state party fratricide, and entrapment in Boss Murphy's rigged democracy. FDR's single term, and his anti-Tammany stance, made him acceptable only because he was a Democratic vote in an unstable legislature. Howe's task in part was to keep old-line Democrats from sabotaging Roosevelt's candidacy. Louis's snarky reputation helped. Recognizing early on that TR would be more difficult to beat than Taft in November, and that the ex-president was likely to run, Howe had written a satirical skit for the Legislative Correspondents Dinner in Albany that spring. Its climax had been an invented telegram from the big-game enthusiast Teddy Roosevelt, which Howe leavened with obvious political scorn. The pachyderm was the traditional GOP symbol. "If a crazy man hunting for an elephant sees you, throw him out," the pseudo-TR says. "I was showing [my son] Kermit how I shot the pink rhinoceros one day . . . and got so interested I killed the beast by mistake. . . . Tell the keeper I've got a new job for him taking care of the new beast I've brought back from Africa. Has ears like a [Democratic] donkey, trunk like the [Republican] elephant, whiskers like a [Bull Moose] Populist. . . . "

Although Eleanor and Sara should have been grateful to have the rumpled but efficient Howe rescue the three-county campaign, they were appalled by his lifestyle. The best that could be conceded was that he wore a necktie—always the same stained blue cravat. A cloying Sweet Caporals cigarette dangled from his lips, trailing ash, even as he talked. Leathery, seamed and balding; tough, abrupt and sardonic; adroit, shrewd and incorruptible, he was the living caricature of the contemporary newspaperman made memorable on stage later in the hit *The Front Page*. Eleanor always opened the windows as soon as the chain-smoking Howe departed. "Mr. Howe here a great deal," Sara, fanning away the aftermath of his presence, would note impatiently in her diary. Yet FDR's political future was in effective and opportunistic hands.

Since the ailing candidate could not meet personally with his mostly rural constituents, Howe multigraphed letters over Franklin's alleged signature describing what Senator Roosevelt wanted to do on their behalf, and including stamped, self-addressed envelopes for their comments and advice. Bundles of prepaid mail soon arrived from recipients who had never been asked for anything but their votes, let alone postage-free. Cleverly, Howe placed inexpensive full-page promotions in local newspapers always short on advertising revenue, pledging support for farm prices, votes for women, and empowerment of labor. Proofs went to FDR, who was getting educated politically. "As I have pledged you in it," Howe noted about each mailing, "I thought you might like to know casually what kind of a mess I was getting you into. Please wire o.k. . . . . Your slave and servant, Howe." Hardly visible on the road as he was pencil-thin and only five-feet-two, he motored about energetically in the Maxwell, sometimes accompanied by his wife, Grace. "I'm having more fun than a goat," he bragged to Franklin.

As a Sancho Panza to FDR's Don Quixote, Howe had quickly recognized that he had no future in politics on his own, but that he could create a formidable one out of untiringly furthering the public career of an ambitious novice with immense possibilities for higher office. Roosevelt possessed a glamorous name, an Ivy background, access to old money and landed families and an ebullient personality. The ungainly but adroit Howe had his unexploited political savvy and a crafty persona suited for backrooms.

FDR assisted his campaign while recovering by contacting influential political friends around the state to speak on his behalf, yet anxieties arose as election day neared. The Bishop of Syracuse accused Roosevelt of anti-Catholic bias, as the urban bosses he had attacked all his brief political life were Irish Catholics. Frank Cleary, a prominent Hyde Park Democrat, threatened to urge fellow Romans to desert FDR. Using Franklin's connections, Howe quickly found Cleary a state job and reported to Roosevelt that "everyone is happy and singing the Doxology."*

ON THE NIGHT of November 5, 1912, election Tuesday, Howe telephoned Roosevelt that, without making a single campaign appearance, he had won reelection by a larger margin than in 1910. Howe had even accomplished it on the cheap—$3,420.50, including his salary. And Wilson had been elected overwhelmingly, although the combined votes for Uncle Ted and for Taft were nearly a million and a half more than those for the new president. Wilson secured 435 electoral votes to 88 for TR and a mere 8 for Taft.

Summoning restored energy, Franklin, as chairman of the agriculture committee in the Senate, began pre-session legislative hearings. Yet the state political climate had altered for the worse, as the new governor, Congressman "Plain Bill" Sulzer, although supported cautiously by Boss Murphy, preferred now to attack Tammany corruption, foreshadowing partisan obstruction in Albany. There was, however, another capital—in Washington—and the very visible young Roosevelt was not surprised when Wilson's secretary, Joseph Tumulty, wired him in mid-January to meet in Trenton with the President-elect. (The inauguration date in early March, predicated on primitive post-colonial transport, would not be moved up to January 20 until 1937.) Eager for a post in the Wilson administration, Roosevelt evidenced that by taking rooms for Eleanor and himself at the Ten Eyck Hotel in Albany, near the railway station, rather than, as before, renting a house with space for entertaining and politicking. The children remained happily pampered by Gramma.

---

* "Praise God, from whom all blessings flow. . . ."

Before Franklin and Eleanor took the train to Washington for the inaugural, he had been offered his choice of two appointments by the incoming Secretary of the Treasury, William Gibbs McAdoo—one as an Assistant Secretary of the Treasury (there would be two or three), the other as Collector of Customs for the Port of New York, a position looming rich with political jobs. Chester A. Arthur, the twenty-first president, had gone from Collector to Vice President, very likely to elevate a party hack to Collector, then succeeded to the presidency by gunshot, as had Uncle Ted. However tempted, young Roosevelt turned it down. He knew what he wanted, and that seat was still unfilled.

Wilson's appointment of Josephus Daniels, a paunchy, shrewd North Carolinian newspaper editor in his early fifties, a strict Methodist with pacifist and prohibitionist leanings, as Secretary of the Navy was not as puzzling as it seemed to observers. As a campaign stalwart close to Wilson, Daniels was owed a prestigious post. Although he preferred the postmaster generalship, with its patronage plums, that went to Albert Burleson, a Texas congressman. Burleson had useful political connections. The avuncular, isolationist Daniels, from landlocked Raleigh, knew little about ships or the sea, but that seemed unimportant to the incoming President. Warships were the brief of the careerist caste of Naval Academy–bred admirals. Yet Daniels needed a deputy in the next office with nautical know-how. He went to see Wilson, who acknowledged that he had no one in mind, and asked his formulaic query about prospective appointees, "How well do you know Roosevelt? How well is he equipped?" The job was Franklin's, but he didn't yet know it.

Expectantly, Roosevelt, who had put out feelers for the Navy assignment, came to Washington with Eleanor for the inauguration festivities and for political networking, arriving at the Willard Hotel on Friday, March 1. At Fourteenth Street and Pennsylvania Avenue, the fashionable Willard is only two blocks from the White House. As Franklin remembered it, on the morning of the noon inauguration, Monday, March 4, he was milling about in the crowded lobby of the Willard when he saw Daniels—they had met during the convention in Baltimore—and walked over to congratulate him on his appointment. As they shook hands,

Daniels asked, as he apparently had planned to do more formally, "How would you like to come to Washington as Assistant Secretary of the Navy?"

"How would I like it? I'd like it bully well," said Franklin, employing a favorite adverb of Uncle Ted's and not concealing his enthusiasm. "It would please me better than anything else in the world. All my life I have loved ships and been a student of the Navy, and the Assistant Secretary is the one place, above all others, I would love to hold." Daniels sent the nomination to the White House.

The Secretary's newspaper in Raleigh captioned a portrait of Daniels's youthful new deputy, "He's following in Teddy's footsteps." TR himself wrote a cautious congratulatory note to Franklin, eschewing any symbolism, "I was very much pleased that you were appointed as Assistant Secretary of the Navy. It is interesting that you are in another place which I myself once held. I am sure you will enjoy yourself to the full . . . and that you will do capital work. . . . When I see you and Eleanor I will speak to you more at length about this."

It took a second journey to Washington, on Monday, March 17, for Franklin to secure his keys to the future. Wilson had sent the appointment to the Senate on March 12, but confirmation seems to have been held up by Tammany sachem James Aloysius O'Gorman, who may have been bargaining for patronage perquisites. He had told Daniels without warmth that Roosevelt would be "acceptable." O'Gorman had not been gone long, Daniels noted in his diary, when another "New York gentleman" arrived—Elihu Root, the senior senator from New York, who had held Cabinet posts under McKinley and TR but as a Republican no longer had any patronage clout. Root "warned me against having R as assistant secretary, saying that every person named Roosevelt wished to run everything and would try to be the Secretary. I listened and replied that any man who was afraid his assistant would supplant him thereby confessed that he did not think he was big enough for the job."

"With a queer look" on "his long face," Root added, "You know the Roosevelts, don't you? Whenever a Roosevelt rides, he wishes to ride in front." Daniel lied in a letter to young FDR that he "had a very pleasant talk with Senator Root" about him, and he did not mention O'Gorman.

After Franklin took his oath of office he wrote to Sara in Hyde Park, employing a naval metaphor to fit the occasion, and absent-mindedly using his full name as he was busy signing official papers.

Dearest Mama

I am baptized, confirmed, sworn in, vaccinated—and somewhat at sea! For over an hour I have been signing papers which had to be accepted on faith—but I hope luck will keep me out of jail.

All well, but I will have to work like a new turbine to master this job—but it will be done even if it takes all summer.*

Your affec. son

Franklin D. Roosevelt

---

*Franklin may have assumed wryly that his mother would recall a famous boast from the battlefield in May 1864 by General Grant to General Halleck in Washington— that he "propose[d] to fight it out on this line if it takes me all summer." The attack at Spotsylvania failed.

2

Under the Mansard Roofs

A CARTOON IN the Republican-leaning *Washington Herald* on March 22, 1913, showed young Mr. Roosevelt in a traditional politician's frock coat, which he never wore, holding a toy warship in his right hand. A placard at his left listed his qualifications for Cabinet office: "Knickerbocker Club, Racquet Club, Harvard Club, Fort Orange Club, and Albany Country Club." A childlike rider on a rocking horse in the background carried a banner, "Columbia Law School."

The day after Roosevelt unlocked his door as Assistant Secretary of the Navy, Josephus and Addie Daniels left for Raleigh to arrange for *News & Observer* continuity during his absence, and for Mrs. Daniels "to pack up silver, china, and other things to go to house keeping in a country house we have rented." FDR would sit at the same oversized desk used by Uncle Ted, who, sixteen years before, had extricated the relic from a Navy storeroom. Carved in relief on its side panels were Civil War–era warships. Its original user had been Lincoln's Assistant Secretary of the Navy, Gustavus Vasa Fox. Franklin's $4,500 annual salary, paid in cash every two weeks, would not go very far. Happily, he had family resources.

"Single Oak" on Woodley Lane, beyond the new Connecticut Avenue bridge that crossed Rock Creek, a half-mile away, was the Daniels' "country house"—a long ride from the Navy Department and also from

State, War & Navy Building, Washington, DC, as it appeared in 1913. It was the site of the Department of the Navy until late in 1918. LIBRARY OF CONGRESS

the square brick Mount Vernon Methodist Church which the Secretary had adopted. "Single Oak" had stables, a henhouse with six chickens and a black-and-white cow in the pasture. His deputy preferred to be closer to the action.

"There's another Roosevelt on the job today . . . ," Franklin, grinning broadly, joked to reporters while Daniels was away. "You remember what happened the last time a Roosevelt occupied a similar position?" In blatant insubordination, TR as Acting Secretary in 1898, after the *Maine* episode in Havana harbor, had secretly ordered then-Commodore George Dewey to leave Hong Kong and prepare for "offensive operations" against the Spanish fleet in the Philippines. The brash young Franklin was quoted in the *New York Sun* on the nineteenth, and Eleanor would dismiss the "horrid little remark." (On returning, Daniels prudently ignored it.) To Eleanor, his "Dearest Babbie," FDR claimed that he was already "up to my ears. I must have signed three or four hundred papers today and am *beginning* to catch on." Sara had already advised him, "I just *knew* it was a *very* big job, and everything so new that it will take time to fit into it." His full signature elicited a response. "Try not to write your signature too small, as it gets a cramped look and is not distinct. So many public men have such awful signatures. . . . "

Getting to know significant public men, or renew acquaintance with them, became his primary business outside the office. The peacetime Navy and Marine Corps overseen under the mansard roofs numbered only 6,563 officers worldwide. Aside from aging officeholders of admiral and captain rank, some of them somnolent except when their perquisites seemed at risk, the key occupant in uniform was Charlie McCawley, a Marine lieutenant colonel who was deputy quartermaster chief for that branch of the Navy. According to *Town Topics*, he was "still in the heyday of middle age." His father had been Marine commandant in 1881 when McCawley, at sixteen, entered on the service payroll as a clerk in the general's office. His wealthy, forever ailing wife, a dozen or more years his elder, was a society fixture. FDR had been at the White House at Alice Roosevelt's marriage to Congressman Nicholas Longworth, adjusting the bride's veil for the camera, when "Princess Alice" had wielded McCawley's dress sword to cut the first slice in her tall wedding cake. (Franklin would be the only Democrat in office among the guests at the wedding of TR's younger daughter, Ethel, on April 4, 1913, just after his confirmation as Assistant Secretary.)

On Franklin's first Tuesday evening in Washington, he dined convivially with "Nick and Alice," who resented his unexpected rise, although not yet openly. The three even went to the theater to see Viola Allen in the exotic *Daughter of Heaven*, about a Chinese empress, by Pierre Loti, who was celebrated for his "gentlemanly eroticism." Loti had been a French naval officer who served in East Asia, which made the play almost appropriate for the new bureaucrat. To TR's children, including Alice, a Democratic Roosevelt was an anomaly. Franklin had always been disparaged by them as a lightweight—"Feather Duster" for his initials.

The next afternoon (at the start, work was not nearly so arduous as Franklin's early letters home suggested) he lunched with "Uncle Will" Cowles—a stout, retired rear admiral and husband (she had married him at forty) to Eleanor's Auntie Bye, who lived at 1733 N Street, which Franklin and Eleanor would rent later in the year. The address on narrow, shaded N Street was auspicious. It had become known as the "Little White House" when Anna Roosevelt Cowles's brother Ted stayed there in his first days as President as he waited in 1901 for the newly widowed Ida McKinley to vacate 1600 Pennsylvania Avenue.

That evening Franklin hosted Congressman Lathrop Brown, a Groton and Harvard classmate, and his wife, Helen, for dinner. The Assistant Secretary subsisted at restaurants and clubs. (Once he moved from the expensive Willard to the cheaper Powhatan Hotel, an 11-story block close to his office, where 18th and H Street intersect with Pennsylvania Avenue, Eleanor visited on occasion from Hyde Park.) The next evening he was invited to dinner with blind Oklahoma senator Thomas Gore, a prominent Democrat, to talk about the politics of naval appointments. For diversion, and to develop connections, Franklin joined the exclusive Chevy Chase Club, where he golfed energetically on some weekday afternoons as well as on weekends, and the Metropolitan Club, where he would often lunch or dine. Business did not always take place under the enveloping roofs.

Franklin's social calendar, detailed for Eleanor in his letters, was at odds with the austere lifestyles of his superiors, Wilson and Daniels. President Wilson had vetoed the traditional inaugural balls, the popular openings of past administrations. His friends beyond Princeton were few. Secretary of State William Jennings Bryan, radical in politics but puritanical otherwise, dismayingly prohibited alcoholic beverages at diplomatic functions, and Daniels would soon ban wine messes from navy ships and shore installations. Eschewing alcohol, he claimed, promoted equality between officers and traditionally thirsty (and envious) ranks. Senior admirals grumbled among themselves and hoped for indefinite delay.

In an implicit slap at the elder Roosevelt, President Wilson, at the urging of his wife, Ellen, had immediately banished the dozen hunting trophies from big game safaris which TR had hung in the State Dining Room, and Taft had disliked but retained. Nothing could have been more removed from the new president's style. Yet he let remain the entreaty on the mantel from John Adams, ordered inscribed by TR in 1902: "I pray Heaven to bestow the best blessings on this house and all that shall hereafter inhabit it. May none but honest and wise men ever rule under this roof." It fit Wilson's Presbyterian hopes, but even he, in his first weeks of office, despite the ideals he brought to the White House, would not be wise enough for the admonition.

Young Roosevelt's first priority as Daniels's deputy and Wilson's appointee was to be loyal. In that capacity he took the train from Union Station to the Secretary's hometown, Raleigh, to address students at the land-grant Agricultural and Mechanical College, which would become North Carolina State University. Impeccably tailored and hatted, he arrived by rail with Eleanor to deliver a speech entitled "Stay East, Young Man." It was important, he urged, to give something back to the state that educated them. "I am a hayseed myself," he began, improbably, "and proud of it." Perhaps that meant that he was born and raised upstate in New York, on Roosevelt property tilled by tenant farmers, and took close interest in the land. In 1911 he had bought 194 inexpensive acres adjoining his mother's estate, and in his first year had 8,000 seedlings planted. To the end of his life he would identify himself for voting registration as "tree farmer" and raise and sell Christmas trees.

With Daniels, Franklin paid a courtesy visit to the hero of Manila Bay, Admiral Dewey, who, although seventy-six, remained chairman of the Navy's overseeing General Board, Congress mandating that he remain on active duty for his lifetime. He kept his largely honorific post into his early eighties. Mildred Dewey wrote to her stepson, "The Secretary this morning brought his new assistant to call upon me and see your father's treasures. Mr. Roosevelt is a very handsome young man . . . most charming and enthusiastic. . . . I predict that if this young man lives, he is going far."

Franklin's official duties as deputy were sweeping if routine. He would claim later, "I got my fingers into about everything." Without management experience, but learning quickly, he dealt with procurement, supply, budgets and the thousands of civilian employees at shore installations. Early on, defusing past allegations of bureaucratic neglect, he visited the nearby Washington Navy Yard to assure workers, in a message meant for all yards, "We want [your] cooperation. We want to get down and talk across the table with you, and to right your wrongs." He invited workmen with complaints to visit him or the Secretary and "talk things over . . . anytime they want."

Portrait of the callow young FDR at thirty-one in 1913,
at the time of his appointment as Assistant Secretary
of the Navy, painted by Frank A. Demes years later for
the Navy Memorial in Washington, DC. COURTESY OF
THE NAVY MEMORIAL FOUNDATION.

Other than its officers in upper ranks, promoted by seniority and often
deadwood, the Navy was manned by 59,000 seamen, who maintained,
sometimes inefficiently, a fleet of 259 vessels, including 21 battleships,
many obsolescent and dating from before the war with Spain. The Department budget in 1913 was $143.5 million, 20 percent of total government
expenditure. Care of antiques was costly. FDR learned quickly to employ
implicit and indirect powers beyond his assigned authority. Happily, he inherited a veteran private secretary, Charles H. McCarthy, who knew the
routine work and was a walking history of past administrations and their
tradition-bound personnel. Also under FDR's purview were the Bureau of

Docks, the Bureau of Naval Personnel, and the Bureau of Supplies and Accounts, each with a perquisite-proud captain or admiral in charge. Roosevelt, despite his inexperience, had several things going for him besides a name that conjured up Uncle Ted. Unlike Daniels, he knew nautical terms and naval history, and had an authentic love of the sea which the naval staff recognized. Daniels spoke of *left* and *right* rather than *port* and *starboard*, *floor* rather than *deck*, and *wall* rather than *bulkhead*. The admirals were not amused. Neither was FDR.

To cope with the rebuilding mode he envisioned, Roosevelt intended to recruit Louis Howe as deputy, and Howe was impatient to be drawn into the Washington orbit. The offer to "Dear Ludwig" came quickly, on Wednesday, March 19. "This is real work down here, but I love it. . . . Here is the dope. Secretary—$2,000—expect you April 1, with a new uniform." The *new uniform* witticism implied something bureaucratically unrumpled, but that would not be Howe. His opening salary was not munificent, and was fixed by regulations. A foot in the door, and continuity, were all that Roosevelt could furnish at the start. (Shortly, he slipped in a promotion to Special Assistant, at an additional thousand a year.)

Howe telegraphed that he was "game"—though "it would break me." He knew, as did Roosevelt, that it was big money, given contemporary values, for someone who had lived precariously for years, and that it was the vestibule to national politics, fulfillment of Howe's dream. On a higher level than his, whatever the party in power, political jobs were horse traded like cigarette cards. In the month of Howe's arrival, Daniels noted in his diary that Secretary of State Bryan reported in a Cabinet meeting chaired by the President that he was having "a very hard time" finding "a position paying about $4,000 a year for the brother of the Senator who was also Chairman of the Democratic National Committee." Since the seeker was unqualified for the Consular Service, Bryan's honeypot, the Secretary offered a cynical swap. "I will give a man a position at $4,000 if you will give me [for someone else] a $4,000 job in another Department." Senator Ollie M. James of Kentucky, the bald, booming-voiced chairman of the DNC, was looking for a job for his brother, E. H. James. (Neither was identified in Daniels's diary.) Attorney General James McReynolds, a hidebound Tennessee conservative soon to be appointed, in a gross Wilson blunder, a Supreme Court justice, volunteered, "All right, I will give him a place if you will let me name the Minister to Persia." Bryan said, "speedily," according to Daniels, "send over your man."

Wilson is not recorded as making any comment. Although his new administration had campaigned as the New Freedom, in some ways it became no different in pork-barrel politics from its predecessors, and in other ways much less free. The President had called for the "emancipation" of the generous energies of the American people, but the Virginia-born Presbyterian soon racially and humiliatingly separated the federal workforce, increasing Jim Crow practices in the nation's capital. When Eleanor moved to Washington, Daniels, ostensibly a North Carolinian apostle of reform, complained about her employing, inappropriately, white servants brought from New York. Some elements of Wilson's New Freedom* did not apply below the Mason-Dixon Line. Roosevelt and Howe would have to adjust to the illiberal incongruities under the mansard roofs. The Democratic Party's electoral mandate was dependent upon the solid, standpat, and segregated South.

ONE OF HOWE'S fellow newsmen in Albany, unaware of Roosevelt's joking reference to "new uniform" but realizing what an incongruity Louis Howe would be in proper Washington, proposed that upstate reporters losing the company of their unkempt crony should chip in "a dozen cakes of soap" as a good-bye gift, in hopes that Howe would "finally come clean." When Howe arrived, taking over the anteroom of the Assistant Secretary's office, buttoned-up career officers were dismayed. While young Roosevelt was always shipshape, Howe prided himself on rolled-up shirtsleeves, jacket flung aside, and ashes cascading everywhere from his Sweet Caporals. An exasperated Navy captain vowed to Roosevelt that if Howe ever ventured onto his ship, the crew would "take him up on the foc'sle, strip him and scrub him down with sand and canvas." Howe's home in

---

* Wilson's "New Freedom" failed to extend, also, until under pressure late in his years in the White House, to votes for women.

Washington was close to his chief's, and one of the more curious sights in the capital may have been the pair meeting in the morning to walk to the Navy Department together—Howe short and bent in his informal office garb and the six-foot-one FDR tall and straight and impeccably tailored, even to London-made shoes.

Trim and professional, and more even-tempered than Howe, Charles McCarthy gradually worked out divisions of responsibility that threatened to overlap, leading to misunderstandings which the Assistant Secretary had to adjudicate. As all three needed each other, and the work was increasing with worrisome world events rippling into the building, pragmatism prevailed. Custodian of protocol, McCarthy lost little or nothing in jurisdiction, while Howe shrewdly exploited new areas in which to involve himself as Roosevelt's principal agent—an informal extension of his boss. Assuming authority based on intimacy and contemptuous of naval rank, Howe operated in FDR's interest and always called him "Franklin." McCarthy handled what he had always done efficiently in the Republican administration from which he had survived, and called FDR "Mr. Roosevelt." Howe would become notorious among the bureau chiefs for such memoranda as "The Assistant Secretary desires that the first paragraph of the attached letter to Congressman O'Brien be rewritten in such a way that he will be able to understand what is meant." In a less grandiose action Howe also prepared an order for FDR to sign approving the expenditure of $3.50 for the burial of a dead cow. It had strayed into the Mare Island Naval Shipyard northeast of San Francisco.

Managing the Secretary's spacious anteroom was quiet, industrious Howard A. Banks, whose personality mirrored that of the black-suited, string-tied Daniels, for whom he had worked as a reporter in North Carolina. Like Howe, Banks would make his chief's role his own, leaving the Department only years later to become editor of the *Sunday School Times*.

Soon after Daniels had returned from Raleigh, a photographer from the Philadelphia *Public Ledger* asked the Secretary to pose for a photograph with Roosevelt. Their offices opened, through French doors, onto a balcony. The myopic Franklin removed the pince-nez he usually wore, as a matter of vanity and because his glasses could reflect glare. While the sun threw shadows from the low balustrade, they stood together on the upper portico of the State, War & Navy Building looking across narrow West Executive Avenue toward the White House. FDR was deferentially somewhat to his chief's rear, slim in a double-breasted suit, Daniels short and dowdy in a rumpled single-breasted jacket. When proofs were brought in to examine, Daniels observed, certainly less formally than in his recollection,

> "Franklin, why are you grinning from ear to ear, looking as pleased as if the world were yours, while I, satisfied and happy, have no such smile on my face?"
>
> He said he did not know of any particular reason, only that he was trying to look his best.
>
> "I will tell you. We are both looking down on the White House and you are saying to yourself, being a New Yorker, 'Some day I will be living in that house'—while I, being from the South, know I must be satisfied with no such ambition."
>
> We both laughed as we returned to our desks.

Much later, Franklin (May 25, 1918) recalled the photo to Randolph Marshall as having caught "my chief and myself in the act of casting longing glances at the White House."

DURING THE 1912 campaign, politicians in California had appealed to white voters' anti-Asian prejudices. In the later decades of the nineteenth century the targets were imported Chinese laborers. With the rise of Japan as a power on the Pacific Rim in 1905 after crushing the hapless Czarist fleet, and an influx into the United States of Japanese immigrants who took efficiently to farming on more hospitable soil than they had left, their presence was soon imagined as a "menace." Wilson himself, an inheritor of Virginian racial attitudes, had endorsed when a candidate the exclusion from owning land of Asian immigrants then legally ineligible for citizenship. Yet having it both ways, he now claimed that he wanted "to offend the sensibilities of a friendly nation as little as possible." (It was little different for Western outsiders in Japan, inured to local

FDR with Secretary of the Navy Josephus Daniels, "casting longing glances at the White House." FROM A PHOTO IN THE PHILADELPHIA PUBLIC LEDGER, IN THE FDR LIBRARY

discrimination, but the issue there, with nonexistent pressure from immigration, was far less public.)

When in March 1913 the California legislature banned land ownership by Japanese immigrants, the resentment in the Home Islands, however paralleling—and preceding—American policies, was explosive. A war scare briefly flared, prompting tough talk from Secretary of War Lindley M. Garrison which Wilson and Bryan disowned. Nothing changed.

On May 9, 1913, Japan formally and publicly protested the discriminatory laws against its people in the United States, many long resident and some born on American soil. Thanks to Spain, Americans were now a very visible presence in the central and far Pacific. The Navy had three warships in Chinese waters, as politically and militarily weak China had become an international playground for imperial designs on its rivers and harbors for exclusive trading ports. Secretary Daniels brought to the Cabinet a delicate question posed to him when relations with Japan soured as to whether Navy warships on the Yangtze River were under hazard and should be relocated to the Philippines. Rear Admiral Bradley A. Fiske, his energetic aide for Operations, whose belligerence Daniels deplored and Roosevelt encouraged, had proposed their redeployment to Manila Bay. To Daniels it was "a California question, purely." The Secretary dreaded the plethora of messages almost daily from Fiske, at fifty-nine the most senior of the four admirals on the advisory staff. Compensating for his small stature with a dramatic mustache curled at the ends and emotional but futile memos encouraging action, Fiske was impatient with allegedly ignorant landlubber civilian appointees.

The Assistant Secretary was an exception. He was aware of the fragility of the exposed Philippines, and even Hawaii. Franklin had already received warnings from his Uncle Ted, who realized that the Panama Canal was still more than a year from its opening and worried that the small Atlantic and Pacific fleets were unhelpfully inaccessible to each other. On May 10, 1913, TR had written from New York,

> Dear Franklin
>
> It is not my place to advise, but there is one matter so vital that I want to call your attention to it. I do not anticipate trouble with Japan, but it may come, and if it does it will come suddenly. In that case we shall be in an unpardonable position if we permit ourselves to be caught with our fleet separated. There ought not be a battleship or any formidable fighting craft in the Pacific unless our entire fleet is in the Pacific. Russia's fate ought to be a warning for all time as to the criminal folly of dividing the fleet if there is even the remotest chance of war. . . .

Three days later, Admiral Fiske delivered a wary memo to Daniels which did not escape Franklin. The fertile Philippines, Fiske explained, "would be an extremely desirable possession for Japan as an outlet for their surplus population," also "a strategic position from which to command the coast of China." Further, the Hawaiian islands would be an equally desirable acquisition, for "Japanese people are already on the Islands in great numbers," and Japan had declared before the American war with Spain "that she did not desire the United States to take possession of the Hawaiian Islands." Fiske saw war sometime in the future as an authentic threat, for the Japanese viewed the new American empire in the Pacific as an incubus which Americans deploring a tax burden "would be glad to get rid of. . . . [T]hey would easily come to terms with Japan after an inglorious and expensive war that lasted, say, two years." Fiske's concerns paralleled the hostile vision of an ambitious young Japanese naval officer, Isoroku Yamamoto. Involved in the surprise attack and defeat in 1905 of the hapless Russian fleet off Tsushima, Yamamoto would promote a Pacific war over decades of warship rivalry to come. The planner of the sneak attack on Pearl Harbor, he anticipated in 1941 that Japan would need only a year to disillusion Americans into negotiating peace.

Fiske followed up his memorandum the next day with further warnings, seeing future war with Japan as "possible, and even probable," and that inflammatory discrimination in the United States "hit the Japanese in their tenderest spots—their sense of honor; their pride of race and their patriotism. . . . With the fearlessness of the race, [and] their contempt of death, any of those causes [already mentioned] make war possible. . . . Japan has proved . . . that she can and does make war effectively and without previous warning when she considers that her interests demand it and justify it. . . . " It was his "duty" to recommend that the country should not be found in a "state of unpreparedness."

A prophet decades ahead of his time, Fiske was frustrated by the placid pacifism of Daniels, who, with Wilson and Bryan, considered overt preparedness as warmongering. Without direct power, Roosevelt nevertheless was beginning to find ways to influence policy. In a letter to retired admiral Arthur Thayer Mahan a year later (June 16, 1914), he wrote, "I did all in my power to have [the warships] return nearer their base. . . . Orders were . . . sent against my protest to Admiral Nicholson, telling him not to move out of the Yangtze."

Fourteen months after the surprise attacks on Hawaii and the Philippines in 1941, FDR, then President, held a press conference for the Society of American Newspaper Editors, at which the elderly Daniels, still an editor and member, was present. Reminiscing gently about his "old Chief," Roosevelt recalled,

Back around 1913–14, we had in the Navy a very clever and brilliant Rear Admiral by the name of Bradley Fiske. . . .

Well, old man Fiske, about—oh, five or half-past, when the Secretary was thinking of going home, almost every day would bring him a long twelve- or twenty-page typewritten technical article on armor, or some new form of machine gun, or something like that, which no layman could possibly understand, and tell the Secretary he had to read that because he wanted action on it in the morning.

And I knew what he did with them, but I wasn't always sure.

So he went away one day. And Bradley Fiske came around to see me, and he said, "I have got to have action on about three different documents that I left with the Secretary."

I said, "Where are they?"

"I don't know. I can't find the documents on his desk."

I picked up the telephone. I called up Mrs. Daniels, and I said they were lost, and she said, "Hmm"—thought a minute—"I think I can find them."

I think you know that in those days most of the politicians wore those long, full-tailed cutaway coats. And she said, "I am going to his closet. I think they are in the right-hand rear tail of his spare cutaway coat. (*Loud laughter*)

And they were. We got them back.

No more action was taken on the tailcoated documents than on most of Bradley Fiske's recommendations to Daniels. Like some other prophets in blue, Arthur Mahan on global influence through sea power and Hyman Rickover on nuclear propulsion, both long held back from an admiral's flag, and Albert A. Michelson, who calculated the speed of light and earned a Nobel Prize but found no future in the Navy, Fiske would be regularly frustrated. A nautical technician, he fashioned shipboard fire-control equipment and range finders, and in the dawn of seaborne aircraft developed the mechanics for a torpedo plane that could make sitting ducks of warships. His proposal that an admiral be made Chief of Naval Operations in a modernized administration was shunted aside by the Secretary lest Fiske get the job, but the reorganization was rapidly effected on Fiske's retirement.

Reluctantly, Josephus Daniels took Fiske's memos on Japan to a Cabinet meeting on Friday May 16, 1913, along with a recommendation from the Joint Board of the Army and Navy, echoing FDR, that ships in Chinese waters be ordered to Manila Bay. Daniels disagreed, as did several others, especially Secretary Bryan, an earnest isolationist. Wilson weighed in with his disapproval of anything which suggested a warlike posture. "We must not have war except in an honorable way," he told Daniels afterward, "and I fear the Joint Board made a mistake." Nothing, Daniels conceded, agreeing on continuing passivity, could prevent Japan, should it want to, from seizing the Philippines. He then went to Raleigh for the weekend, to teach his last Sunday School class, on Joseph and his dreams.

FDR's happiest working days were during his chief's absences. He wrote to Eleanor about being "suddenly called upon by the President to make all arrangements for sending surgeons, attendants, supplies, etc. out to the flood district in Ohio—I had a hectic time getting the machinery going, but the force leaves tonight, & I had some interesting work in co-operation with the Secretary of War & [Major] General [Leonard] Wood." The most destructive storm in Ohio history, the March floods overwhelmed Dayton, Miami and Cincinnati, where the Ohio River rose twenty-one feet in twenty-four hours. At least 467 Ohioans died, and more than twenty thousand homes were totally destroyed. It was Roosevelt's first opportunity to work with overwhelmed Ohio governor James Cox, whom he would not get to meet in person until the election year of 1920.

Daniels was away again the first half of May, only reachable by telegraph, and away again in July, when Eleanor and the children were in Campobello for the summer and FDR could find little opportunity to visit.

Steaming on the Department's inelegant but steel-hulled former gunboat *Dolphin*, commissioned in 1885 at John Hanscom's yard in Chester, Pennsylvania, the Secretary, on a learning tour, was going from New England to Key West, then across by rail to San Diego and Seattle, boarding every type of ship the Navy utilized, even going down in a submarine. (The first of the Navy's oceangoing diesel-powered subs, commanded by Lieutenant Chester W. Nimitz, had been commissioned the year before.) Salt water was a new experience for Daniels, who had lived inland and had never handled a tiller, as Franklin did at Campobello, or traveled abroad, while Roosevelt, beginning in childhood, had made twenty Atlantic crossings.

Franklin boasted to Eleanor, who was lonely and unhappy apart from him, that when Daniels returned from his information-gathering tours, they worked "on all the things he should have decided before & as I expected most of them were turned over to me! The trouble is that the Sec'y has expressed half-baked opinions in these matters & I don't agree. . . . However he has given me carte blanche & says he will abide by my decision." In reality Daniels made the major choices himself, sometimes with his uniformed staff, sometimes ignoring them, leaving all of the many minor problems for young Roosevelt, such as coal and fuel oil price bidding. (Much of the Navy was still coal-fired.) FDR was charged with the oversight of Navy yards, supply, outfitting of ships, and training camps. The mandate was broad, and he and Howe, a crack negotiator, claiming strict adherence to guidelines, audaciously stretched them further to break through bureaucratic obstruction. "I beg to report," went one later FDR note to Daniels, "that I have just signed a requisition (with 4 copies attached) calling for the purchase of eight carpet tacks."

"Why this wanton extravagance?" Daniels replied. "I am sure that two would suffice." Inured to red tape, he had once been chief clerk in the Department of the Interior. As he reorganized the bureaucracy he had inherited, he simplified the Assistant Secretary's duties by appointing Samuel McGowan as Paymaster General. Although McGowan got along well with Roosevelt and Howe, he was also a stickler for economies, and he and his assistant, Christian J. Peoples, sometimes held up for examination contracts too hurried in details.

EARLY IN THE Wilson administration, appropriations were authorized for building five battleships to replace coal-burning craft already obsolete at the time of the war with Spain. While Daniels did the lobbying with Congress, supervision of construction would be by Roosevelt, and he and Daniels both worked on pressing suppliers of armor plate and other big-ticket purchases to end their collusive pricing. Opening the bids in the Navy Department Library in the presence of the representatives of Bethlehem, Carnegie and Midvale Steel, Daniels asked for an explanation of the identical estimates of $520 per ton for "Battleship No. 39," which would be christened *Arizona* and, thanks to Isoruku Yamamoto, forever embedded in history. One supplier lied, solemnly, about the prices for armor plate, "Mr. Secretary, it is pure coincidence." Daniels warned them to return the next day, "—and don't have another coincidence."

At noon the next day, the bids again coincided. The Secretary dismissed the three steel men and showed Roosevelt the morning paper. "Do you see who has landed?" he asked. It was still a time when, as Daniels, long an editor, knew, that newspapers published the names of shipboard arrivals and departures. "Sir John Hatfield," said Daniels. Roosevelt had never heard of him. "Why, he is one of the three or four great armor-plate makers in England, and makes a lot of armor plate for the British Navy. Can you take the train right away? Go up to New York, see Sir John Hatfield and ask him if he will take this order for this armor at $460 or less."

Roosevelt met with Hatfield and returned with an offer of $460. Daniels recalled the American agents and showed them the firm bid which Roosevelt had brought back. By no coincidence the revised domestic estimates were identical at $460. Daniels threatened that the government would manufacture the armor plate, but his desk admirals warned that the prospect of success in Congress was low, and that the Navy needed to keep domestic firms in the arms business active. Collusion was reality. Still, Daniels claimed to the press that the threat of foreign competition had reduced the cost of armor plate for merely one warship by $1,110,084.

Not long after, since bids from the same three firms for turbine casings for the *Arizona* were again identical, FDR sought bids abroad, and settled with Cyclops Steel and Iron Works in Sheffield, England, for little more than a third of the extortionate American bids. He was learning. Also, import duty would be charged, he bragged to Wilson—a further profit to the Treasury.

With Louis Howe, Roosevelt had already taken economic issues directly to the White House, explaining to the President that June that the low bid for machinery to be installed in a Navy yard was from a German firm, only marginally better than the bid of an American firm. But if the Germans won the bid, the Treasury would also gain a 15 percent import tariff. "The President took the view," FDR noted, "that the wage earners & capital of this country would gain more by [an] award to the Am firm than w'd be saved to the gov. by award to the Germans." The Assistant Secretary grudgingly gave in, observing that "perhaps some day, pretty far off, we may take a bigger view of economics than the purely nationwide one."

Bids for coal seemed to have political overtones—domestic ones. The Navy's Bureau of Supplies and Accounts maintained an "accepted list" of companies, with specifications so rigid that they appeared to have been drawn up in collusion with friendly bidders, nearly all from West Virginia. Roosevelt and Howe bridled at the overpriced coal, rewriting the specifications, which were re-bid and won by Pennsylvania mines. Outrage arose in Congress, prompted by Navy engineers complaining about allegedly inferior quality—yet they had long supported their favorite firms, with quality not an issue. Daniels claimed innocence. At a hearing, FDR survived unfriendly questioning—and again some measure of competition was restored.

ALSO SIMMERING IN mid-1913 was the question of intervention in the chronic political chaos in Mexico, where rebel groups had driven the eighty-one-year-old dictator, Porfirio Díaz, into exile. With Uncle Ted never out of mind, Franklin had already claimed, in a speech employing an empty bravado at which Daniels may have only smiled, that if the United States became involved in Mexico, he would resign his position, "follow in the steps of T.R. and form a regiment of rough riders." The situation below the border, Franklin warned in a wire to Daniels, who was traveling, was "a very threatening and imminent danger." Unrest in the Caribbean area, political hawks felt, could impact the Panama Canal just as it was nearing completion. President Wilson emptily decreed "watchful waiting."

"Next week," FDR wired Daniels on July 29, "the fleet holds its joint maneuvers with the Army off Block Island, and I am planning to go up for a few days about the time you return and to inspect the Newport station at the same time. . . . You are much missed, and Mr. Banks is wandering around like a lost soul in Israel." Roosevelt was giving the Secretary's secretary nothing to do.

Franklin loved the opportunity for formal inspections, the salutes of seventeen guns and four ruffles to which he was entitled, the honor guard standing at stiff attention, and soon the raising of the Assistant Secretary's white, four-star flag which he would design, as there had never been such a standard. He had already traveled to the Brooklyn Navy Yard, where he was escorted on the commandant's barge by a junior officer, Wilson Brown, who would later be a vice admiral and naval aide to FDR in the White House. Roosevelt, so Brown recalled, "was at home on the water." When the barge "hit the wake of a passing ship and he was doused with spray, he just ducked and laughed and pointed out to his companions how well she rode a wave. Within a few minutes he'd won the hearts of every man of us on board. . . . "

At the Naval War College at Newport, the culture, if not the instruction, would be undergoing change. An ardent prohibitionist like Bryan, Daniels, citing the need for discipline, as promised would soon ban wine from officer messes. Early on he signaled that at the well-appointed War College bar, where, conducted by an admiral, he was asked his choice of drinks. "White Rock," said Daniels. It was a popular brand of upstate New York spring water.

"And you?" the admiral asked the senior officers who had accompanied them. "White Rock," each affirmed, bleakly. "It took nerve to do it," FDR would confide to Howe, "but tho' the Sec'y will be unpopular in a small circle for a while, it will pay in the end." He was demonstrating who was in charge.

After Newport, Daniels spoke in Boston at Bunker Hill along with the show-stealing TR, who confided that he had "good reports" about Daniels from Franklin—a curious approbation coming indirectly from the Secretary's restless underling.

As DANIELS HAD priority to use the *Dolphin*, Franklin could order out, when the ship was unavailable, the smaller, 124-foot, gleaming white *Sylph*. The yacht was intended when necessary for the President, but Wilson rarely requested it, preferring his grander *Mayflower*. First used by William McKinley, the *Sylph* was kept in service by Theodore Roosevelt and William Howard Taft. FDR seldom forgot the junior officers at his call. The *Dolphin* then was skippered by William D. Leahy, much later the crusty naval eminence at the White House. Whatever departmental vessel was at FDR's disposal, it was his opportunity to invite parties of influential politicians and senior Navy personnel largely commanding desks. "White Rock" would not be popular aboard.

In the summer and early fall of 1913, Franklin could rarely make it to Campobello, leaving Eleanor to cope with children, servants and Sara. His local travels were largely by trolley car. His letters to "Dearest Mama" often dealt with his fragile health, which worried her, and his dosing himself with Calomel, Bismuth powder and Pluto water, and breakfasting on rice and hot milk. No one then would have suggested any connection between his compulsive smoking and his frequent respiratory ailments. Regular mentions of golf assured Sara that he was being active. To "Dearest Babs" he wrote of outings on the *Sylph* and his politically connected company, his "quiet [budgetary] work on the Navy Estimates" and the extended Roosevelt and Delano families in the District. Travel to "Campo"—when he could travel there—was far less arduous in logistics than Eleanor's managing with her baggage and entourage. Yet when he could not commandeer a vessel going to Newport or Boston or Portsmouth, it also meant a train to Boston, a stopover during the remainder of the day at the Hotel Touraine, and a wait for the overnight sleeper to northern Maine, where Eastport, in Passamaquoddy Bay, was connected to the mainland by a bridge. A Canada-bound steamer from Boston to St. John in New Bruns-

FDR at the wheel of the *Half Moon II*, Campobello, 1915, with Eleanor and Sara, shielded by headgear from the sun, in the foreground. FDR LIBRARY, GIFT OF LAURA DELANO.

wick was an alternate route, leaving two or three times a week and stopping at Eastport (each adult fare $5.50). Customs officials examined luggage on board, and a local motor launch or the Roosevelts' own 60-foot schooner *Half Moon II* would cross to Campobello.

Once in the summer of 1913 Franklin was able to order a battleship, the 20,000-ton USS *North Dakota*, commissioned in 1908, to anchor offshore at Eastport for Independence Day celebrations. He boarded in straw hat and white summer flannels, accompanied by his family (Sara included), and as Campobello neighbors ferried across to Maine stood by (border legalities were minimal), he received his ceremonial seventeen-gun salute. Eleanor had to organize dinners and teas for the senior staff of the *North Dakota* not only when Franklin was there but after he returned to Washington. When he apologized for burdening her and wrote that he would try to return in August, she hoped the naval visitations would be smaller. "No, no more battleships coming," he promised. "I may come up in a destroyer, but that means only 3 officers."

"I shall welcome you on a destroyer or with a whole fleet," Eleanor wrote back, "if you will just come a little sooner on their account, but of course the destroyer [crew] will be easier to entertain!"

Eleanor remained lonely and melancholy without Franklin nearby, and despite her staff, she was often overwhelmed. On one occasion when she was away shopping in Eastport, Elliott, now three, and often ignored, fell into hot ashes from driftwood burned and abandoned on a Campobello beach. "Nurse says they are only skin burns," she wrote. Fortunately the Canadian summer would end and the family would be relocated to Washington—until the next Campobello season. The oppressive District, once mostly swampland, was too sweltering for year-round living if one could afford an alternative.

Since local ceremonies made local news, Franklin was eager to turn public appearances into references in print to an emerging new Roosevelt. To mark the fiftieth anniversary of the Battle of Chancellorsville that May, memorable for General "Fighting Joe" Hooker's losing his nerve, and the initiative, he boarded a Baltimore & Ohio train and stood on the back platform to gaze at the Virginia scenery, which proved more memorable than the event. It was "very much a one-horse affair," he explained to Eleanor. "I was driven around town interminably—a dirty coal mining town. . . . I spoke in a picnic grove, and went from there to the 3:05 B&O train." He was even guest speaker, in the Capital, at the 62nd anniversary ceremonies of the Daughters of Rebekah, a service offshoot for women of the Independent Order of Odd Fellows. He was learning how to disarm stiff matronly groups, once, later, addressing a Daughters of the American Revolution audience that he was aware disapproved of most newcomers to America. Like them, his ancestors had come, generations before, from abroad. "My fellow immigrants . . . ," he began.

"Funny isn't the word," he told Eleanor about the Rebekahs. "With the Lady Grand Master on my arm, I brought up the rear of a two by two procession which marched five times round an enormous hall. At least a thousand persons engaged in the solemn proceedings." He had tried, without eliciting a smile, "three excruciatingly humorous stories," and, his wit failing, extemporized a "highly pathetic discourse on loyalty, patriotism and the debt of gratitude the human race owes to the female of the species." On that note, as there were hardly any dry eyes in the house, "I am going to take up heavy tragedy when I leave this job." Leaving was not an option. He loved the job. He was finding himself.

3

The Little White House

O<small>N</small> O<small>CTOBER</small> 25, 1913, standing with his binoculars atop the chart house of the *Dolphin*, and wearing a dark blue naval cape that would become his trademark uniform, Franklin reviewed the fleet at Hampton Roads, Virginia. Nine battleships, with auxiliary vessels, steamed into the Atlantic, bound for Mediterranean ports on a goodwill cruise. The venture deliberately evoked—although more modestly—"The Great White Fleet" voyage initiated by his Uncle Ted, which from December 16, 1907, to February 22, 1908, sent sixteen battleships, painted stark white to demonstrate peaceful intentions, and accompanied by escort vessels, around the world. Many of the warships in 1907, like the vessels FDR was sending, were on the edge of obsolescence, but their importance lay in projecting a facade of American sea power.

Roosevelt's guests on the *Dolphin* included a senator, four admirals, several sub-Cabinet appointees like himself and Louis Howe in a nondescript beach hat. They had paid farewell visits to the *Wyoming*, *Arkansas*, and *Connecticut* (the three-stacker flagship for TR's fleet), and also boarded the *Rhode Island*, which, with three other vessels, was leaving for troubled Mexican waters. On returning to the *Dolphin* just after noon, Franklin wrote to Eleanor, they "started ahead of the fleet and anchored just inside the Capes. Soon the nine battleships . . . came along, the three colliers and the supply ship having gone out earlier. The big gray fellows were magnificent as they went past, with all hands at the rail, and I only wish a hundred thousand people could have seen them." Then the Assistant Secretary's party attended war games at the nearby Artillery School.

The seven-week cruise, promoted eagerly by Roosevelt, dramatized the new building program under way and burgeoning American visibility at sea, but was explained to the press as offering real experience in seamanship, and—according to *The New York Times*—enlarging the outlook of crews used to the routine of port duty.

Eleanor and the children had returned from Campobello to Hyde Park, and would be moving to Washington. Auntie Bye's narrow redbrick and still gas-lit "Little White House" on N Street was well known to a generation of Washington elite, and only a five-block walk down Connecticut Avenue to the Navy Department. Its small rooms in four stories were cramped for the Roosevelt family and its staff of live-in servants and nannies. A small lawn in front and a garden with rose trellis in back offered little space for outdoor entertainment, but Eleanor enjoyed breakfast in the garden on fine days. Inevitably her mother-in-law was dissatisfied with the interior arrangements, although she cared little about the lack of electricity. "Dined at 1733 N Street," Sara wrote in her diary after her first visit. "Moved chairs and tables and began to feel at home."

Uncle Ted had alerted Franklin to the overlooked and underpaid middle level of Navy officers' wives, who allegedly needed Eleanor's special attention beyond the protocol and ceremony of Washington officialdom. The spouses of Supreme Court justices received ladies on Mondays; Congressional wives on Tuesdays; Cabinet wives owned Thursdays; the diplomatic corps Fridays. Wednesdays were for socially responsible sub-Cabinet spouses like Mrs. Roosevelt. Suppressing her anxiety, she set out in October with white gloves and card case, often with young Jimmy, to mount the many stairs to deliver her new personal cards with an at-home invitation. If the lady of the house opened the door, she would begin ritually, "I am Mrs. Franklin D. Roosevelt. My husband has just become Assistant Secretary of the Navy. . . ." She hoped only to encounter a maid. "I've paid

60 calls in Washington this week," she wrote to her aunt, Maude Livingston Hall, describing her initiation into the awkward and exhausting social ritual from which there would be no escape,

> and been to a [ladies'] luncheon at the Marine barracks, the kind where the curtains are drawn & candles lit & course after course reduces you to a state of coma which makes it almost impossible to struggle to your feet & leave at 4 P.M. I've received one long afternoon next to Mrs. Daniels until my feet ached and my voice was gone & since then I've done nothing but meet people I saw that day & try to make them think I remember them quite well. We've been out every night, last night a big Navy League affair for Mr. Daniels where there was some really good speaking. Mrs. Daniels is a dear & I'm looking forward to knowing her better.

On Sunday evenings, when the servants were off duty, Eleanor invited Franklin's friends, government officials and junior diplomats, to modest dinners, serving cold meats and scrambled eggs—almost her only culinary feat. (On the hectic Sunday evening of Pearl Harbor, twenty-eight years later, with impromptu guests flooding the White House, Eleanor was still scrambling eggs.)

In the winter season of 1913–1914, overwhelmed by Washington's social ritual, and in the early months of another pregnancy, Eleanor would employ a young woman recommended by Auntie Bye, Lucy Page Mercer, twenty-two, to help organize her life. Tall and elegant, with swept-up light brown hair, Miss Mercer exemplified good breeding and quiet competence. Her once socially prominent mother, marooned by a broken marriage, had fallen on hard times. Lucy needed a salary. For a pittance she was working part-time in the shop of society decorator Elsie Cobb Wilson. Gratefully, Eleanor offered a substantial thirty dollars a week for three days' presence, answering mail, organizing the bills to pay, scheduling and confirming the daily schedule and arranging the future social calendar. With no desk or space for herself in the small house, Miss Mercer used the kitchen table when not in the way of the cook, or sat on the floor amid the paperwork, strewn children's clothes and toys, and scurrying servants.

Lucy Page Mercer, in 1915, when Eleanor first
employed her as social secretary.

Franklin would pass her as he left or returned. Almost invariably his greeting was, "Ah, the lovely Lucy!" Soon he was on closer terms. In an undated letter early in March 1914, when Eleanor was still at Hyde Park
with the children, Franklin wrote to "Dearest Babs" that when he returned home for the fifth Pan-American Conference, Albert, his chauffeur, who had met him that morning at Union Station, "telephoned Miss
Mercer who later came and cleaned up. Then a long day at the office and
dinner alone at 7:30." Lucy was proving more and more valuable.

SARA'S HYDE PARK country house had become increasingly uncomfortable for the young Roosevelts, with three small children and another
on the way, and a retinue of "help." Resisting change, Sara had wired
"Springwood" for electricity and telephone service only in 1908, and it
remained poorly heated. FDR had professional as well as family needs,
from library to nurseries to space for increasing household staff. To pro-

mote the transformation, Franklin sketched out his needs and built a scale model which impressed his mother. Sara showed both to Francis Hoppin, a Campobello-based architect. Although she oversaw the reconstruction in every detail, she felt that it was no longer her house. "For over forty years," she would recall late in life, with considerable exaggeration, "I was only a visitor there." More renovation was to come.

THE NAVY LEAGUE, the influential lobbying organization for a big modern fleet, was run from Washington by retired admirals, politicians with something to gain for their constituencies by naval expansion, and industrial and financial entrepreneurs profiting from naval contracts. Perennial president of the League was Colonel Robert Means Thompson, the broadly mustached chairman of the board of the International Nickel Company. Herbert Livingston Satterlee, son-in-law of J. P. Morgan, was vice president and general counsel. (Thompson, once briefly an ensign, and hardly seafaring owner of a houseboat in Florida, received his honorary colonelcy from a former governor of New Jersey, much as President Wilson's chief political confidant, Colonel Edwin M. House, with no military background whatever, owed his empty title to the governor of Texas.) The League saw a potential ally in a reincarnation of the earlier Roosevelt, and an opponent in Daniels, who noted "Navy League dinner" and "armor plate" side by side in his diary.

With Bryan as well as Daniels at the League banquet, Franklin cautiously put his after-dinner remarks at the service of their pacifism, remarking that "there are as many advocates of arbitration and international peace in the Navy as in any other profession." It was grossly untrue, for the Department needed external threats to gain credence for a buildup beyond replacement of obsolete craft and technology. The fleet's backers saw opportunity in the imminent opening of the Panama Canal, which required security in both oceans into which it would empty. FDR made that known to the Secretary, although each had different views of the Navy's role. Nevertheless, Daniels, who disliked detail, wanted Franklin to be Acting Secretary "even if I have only stepped out to the washroom." Happily for FDR, Daniels was often away, learning his own job by inspecting naval installations around the long American seaboard. While there was little or no nautical connection, he also loved talking to service, civic and religious groups.

The Secretary's pacifist bent remained at odds with that of his deputy. Along with the staunchly unmilitant William Jennings Bryan at State, Daniels was a pillar of the peace movement, encouraging toothless treaties in which nations would pledge to submit disputes to unenforceable international arbitration. The conciliation schemes would test Bryan's faith—and even Wilson's—that the world was "advancing in morals." During the theoretical course of peace commission reviews of controversies, nations would be expected to suspend any increase in armaments, and only when one side rejected presumably reasonable arbitration judgments would it be free to consider solutions by force. A believer in the "big navy" concepts of Admiral Mahan, and in national interest as the ultimate morality, FDR felt that Bryan and his like lacked realism. Like his Uncle Ted, Franklin considered universal peace arrived at by arms limitation agreements and gentlemanly diplomacy as utopian fantasy. Crises required arms adequate to each eventuality.

An example of Bryan's naïveté came in the early months of the Assistant Secretary's tenure when, as Daniels was away, the Secretary of State, whose offices were in the same building, rushed in pleading, "I've got to have a battleship!" Further, it had to arrive in seething Haiti within twenty-four hours, to keep "white people" from "being killed." Learning that the nearest battleship was four days' steaming from Haiti, Bryan proved willing to accept an accessible gunboat. "That's all I wanted," he explained. "Roosevelt, after this, when I talk about battleships, don't think I mean anything technical."* Franklin was always uncomfortable with Bryan, although he would later borrow from his populist domestic platform honed over three losing presidential campaigns. Herbert Hoover would scorn the 1930s FDR New Deal as "Bryanism by another name."

---

*A decade or more later, Robert Benchley allegedly would mistake a uniformed naval officer for a hotel doorman, and demanded a taxi. Learning that the man was a mere admiral, Benchley quipped, "All right, then, get me a battleship."

The intermittent crises with Mexico, like Haiti in constant revolutionary turmoil, would require more than one gunboat, and would soon involve FDR. General Victoriano Huerta had driven reforming president Francisco Madero from office in February 1913, proclaimed himself president, and had Madero murdered. Other revolutionaries in the north, led by General Venustiano Carranza, with Pancho Villa as his deputy, rose against Huerta. For one American administration after another, moral misgivings gave way to massive investments in Mexican oil and minerals which then had to be protected. Americans owned more than half of everything in Mexico that was worth anything. Soon even the Navy Department's *Dolphin* was involved.

By Christmas 1913, when Franklin and family entrained to Hyde Park for the holidays, he had his hands into most Navy matters and confronted the resistance to change. To Daniels, a bloated fleet would become a bullying one. He admonished the Navy League at a dinner that it was time "to have done once and forever with silly boasting . . . that we are able to lick any nation on the face of the earth." The Wilson government's priorities in any case were domestic, as the President dramatized on December 23 by signing the landmark Federal Reserve Act with three golden pens.

As the world seemed increasingly turbulent, from the Pacific Rim to the Rio Grande, pressure for preparedness grew among active and retired officers who bridled at the meager appropriations for the Army and Navy. A vast nation with burgeoning global interests was being safeguarded by a military establishment that would have embarrassed Bulgaria. That December, at the annual dinner of the Order of the Carabao, a Philippines veterans organization, Daniels recognized that his usual "anti-imperialistic" address "found little response." Secretary Bryan was also at the speakers' table, and very likely FDR was present, although unrecorded. Earlier, Bryan had idealized the pacific side of American naval power by imagining warships named *Friendship* and *Fellowship*. Mocking him, Carabao militants carried into the banquet hall models of the USS *Friendship* and USS *Fellowship* for his admiration—along with a third battleship for the Secretary of State's utopian fleet, the USS *Piffle*. When Wilson was informed of press accounts of the taunt, he angrily ordered the service secretaries to issue reprimands to uniformed participants.

Recognizing the rigidity of the former professor and devout Presbyterian now in the White House, FDR knew that building a modern navy up to its likely tasks required deviousness rather than confrontation. He reminded his chief of their broad bicoastal mission, and more, by sending him for Christmas a reproduction of a watercolor from about 1850 of the old battleship *North Carolina*, christened for Daniels's home state. (A newer but venerable *North Carolina* was part of the fleet.) The Assistant Secretary had found that the earlier "line-of-battle" ship had first crossed the Atlantic in 1825, and made its last voyage in 1839. Daniels was delighted. He did not recognize its implicit suggestion that the Navy needed a more modern *North Carolina*. Only in 1937 would that occur—during FDR's second administration.

IN THEIR FIRST Washington winter the Roosevelts became friendly with Oliver Wendell Holmes, Jr. Mr. Justice Holmes, seventy-two, long distinguished for his pithy opinions and familiar to newspaper readers from his broad white handlebar mustache, had been appointed to the Supreme Court by Theodore Roosevelt in 1902. The Roosevelt name assured entry for Eleanor and Franklin, whose Sunday visits with Holmes and his wife, Fanny, were envied by some Washingtonians of lesser cachet.

On January 7, 1914, Franklin wrote to his mother of a "delightful dinner" at the home on Lafayette Square, across from the White House, hosted by another crusty sage even more difficult to access, the historian Henry Adams. Seventy-five, and a widower since his wife, Marian, had died a suicide twenty-nine years earlier, Adams was cranky, difficult, and utterly cynical, believing that one lived in a world of illusions. Henry Adams, Holmes deplored to the Roosevelts, turned everything to "dust and ashes." Yet Adams took a liking to Eleanor, who sometimes stopped in for tea during a respite from her dreary official calls, each of which she tried to limit, realizing their uselessness, to six minutes.

After suffering a stroke in 1912, and recovering only slowly, Adams described himself as a "cave-dweller," but occasionally he would have the

Roosevelts to lunch. As Senator Henry Cabot Lodge, who remained close to TR and was a confidant of Adams, was a severe critic of Woodrow Wilson, Franklin would loyally take the President's side. "Young man," said Adams fiercely, "I have lived in this house many years and have seen the occupants of that White House across the square come and go, and nothing that you minor officials or the occupant of that house can do will affect the history of the world for long!"

FDR intended to try. His closest friends were activists, several of them inherited from Eleanor's Uncle Ted. Sir Cecil Spring-Rice, the British ambassador, at sixty-four had been in the foreign service all his adult life. At the embassy he worried to the younger Roosevelts about increasing instability in Europe. His vicious anti-Semitism, largely kept private, seemed not to alienate any of the Roosevelts. To TR he even attacked Oscar Straus, a friend once in the former President's Cabinet, writing, meanly, "It is no good arguing with these financiers—appealing to their sense of honour is like shooting them in the foreskin." (Ironically, when Spring-Rice was later replaced in Washington, it would be by another despised Jew, Rufus Isaacs, Lord Reading.) Jean Jules Jusserand, sixty-eight, the French ambassador, also a TR connection, was a frequent host, especially pleased that the much-traveled Franklin and the unsophisticated Eleanor spoke fluent French. Although a medieval scholar, Jusserand in 1917 would be awarded the first Pulitzer Prize in History for his *With Americans of Past and Present Days*.

Even closer to them, as one of their own generation, were the French second secretary, the slim, crisply mustached André Lefebvre de Laboulaye, and his wife, Marie. Twenty years later, with FDR in the White House, Laboulaye, because of his earlier friendship with Roosevelt, would be appointed ambassador, explaining that newsmen should ignore his formal title. "I am not an envoy extraordinary. I am a very ordinary ambassador."

Local friends, soon part of a supper group which met every two weeks, were bald, gossipy Franklin K. Lane, Secretary of the Interior, and Anne; the Assistant Secretary, Adolph C. Miller (an economist named to the Federal Reserve Board when it was formed in 1914), and Mary; and Assistant Secretary of State William Phillips, and Caroline. To Phillips, FDR was likeable and energetic "but not a heavyweight." In 1933 Phillips would become undersecretary of state, and then FDR's ambassador to Italy.

Franklin's close associates were sources of information about White House and foreign affairs beyond the circumspect Daniels. With the United States now a colonial power across the Pacific, while, under other flags, Caribbean islands en route to the Panama Canal were in constant crisis, the Wilson administration seemed grudgingly more willing to fund a naval building program than expand a land army. Aware, nevertheless, that critics of military spending attacked "the highly paid idleness" of ships, and their crews, in port, Franklin spent part of January in Washington writing, with the uncredited Louis Howe, "The Problem of Our Navy." In the February 28 issue of *Scientific American* he dealt with the Mahan doctrine seemingly validated by the Japanese victory over the Russians that "naval wars are won when the battleship fleets meet and fight it out to a finish on the high seas." The American navy, however, was scattered across the coastlines and dependencies abroad—and was falling obsolete. In the "unfortunate event of war" it "would amount to little less than murder to send American officers and men out in these old ships to fight against a fleet of modern dreadnoughts."*

The tireless Admiral Fiske abetted Roosevelt's campaign, noting in his diary for March 1, 1914, "I wrote a letter yesterday to Mr. [Lemuel] Padgett, which I asked Mr. Roosevelt to sign, transmitting a copy of information that the German fleet in its autumn cruise will comprise certain numbers of vessels of various kinds—and pointing out its enormous superiority to our fleet and that this superiority was going to increase each year. Mr. Roosevelt signed it and it was mailed." Shrewd Navy bureaucrats often waited for the departure of the Chief to have FDR as Acting Secretary sign

---

*From 1904 into 1907, several nations, including Japan, Germany and the United States, began constructing floating platforms for 12-inch and 14-inch naval guns, displacing 16,000 to 20,000 tons, and more. By the time that the American *Michigan* and *South Carolina* were completed in 1909, the British, in 1906, had activated its heavier entry into the big-gun arms race, HMS *Dreadnought*, and had built nine more. The pioneer *Dreadnought* gave its name to the new class of powerfully armed battleships that could fire punishing salvos at long range.

a memo that Daniels might have brushed aside. Congressman Padgett, a Tennessean and friend of Daniels, was chairman of the House Committee on Naval Affairs. The intelligence about German naval strength was very likely accurate, but its training cruise which Fiske cited was fated for cancellation. The *Kriegsmarine* would have more immediate business.

For *Scientific American*, on a half-page map of North America and its adjacent oceans, the Assistant Secretary noted the locations of every major American warship as of February 12, 1914. Without the complications of war, the understrength Navy was busy "keeping the peace, preventing bloodshed and disorder, governing islands, carrying on scientific work for the benefit of commerce, seeking to rescue castaways, and doing daily a hundred unsung deeds that make it an American institution to be proud of." Yet everything had to be subordinated if necessary to the urgent priorities of national defense. "Just as the police force of a city is of little value in stopping the invasion of a country by a foreign force, so the work of the gunboats and surveying ships and obsolete battleships in time of peace would count for little against the enemy's fleet in time of war."

Time was the immediate enemy. Preparedness took more than a signature or two. A modern battleship took three years to build, and could not be manned by "any kind of a crew." For "preponderant efficiency" the task had to begin without delay. "Would we . . . in time of war be content like the turtle to withdraw into our own shell and see an enemy . . . usurp our commerce and destroy our influence as a nation throughout the world?"

As FDR and others, including John Bernard Walker, the editor of *Scientific American*, struggled to persuade Daniels that modernizing the fleet was neither provocative nor warlike, the Secretary would contribute his own article, as would Walker, the three collected in June and published by Munn & Co. in New York as the eighty-page *The United States Navy, Its Present Standing and Needed Increase*.

Presiding over a symbolic increase in naval power, Assistant Secretary Roosevelt, at eleven on the morning of March 16 at the Brooklyn Navy Yard, ceremonially laid the keel of the *Arizona*. As he arrived, a blue naval cape over his suit, to the boom of seventeen guns from the *North Dakota*, a tall traveling crane moved over the great cradle in which the new warship would be built and lowered the first steel plate. Captain Albert Greaves, the yard commandant, handed Roosevelt a hammer and a silver-plated bolt. While the yard's band played "The Star-Spangled Banner" and the gathering of officers, bluejackets, bureaucrats, service families and local dignitaries stood with bared heads, FDR nailed into place the keel plate of "No. 39," classified as a "superdreadnaught" and twin to the *Pennsylvania*, already under construction at Newport News. As he finished, four little boys stepped forward, each the son of a yard officer or workman, and in turn drove in additional spikes. Then on cue the boys ran to the wooden support of the cradle in the position of the future bow, and, completing an old naval tradition, nailed to it an old horseshoe for good luck. Neither of the sister ships, to be the most formidable in the burgeoning fleet, would have much luck in their declining years. On the morning of Pearl Harbor in December 1941 the *Pennsylvania*, in drydock for renovations, was hit by Japanese dive bombers and disabled. The *Arizona*, in harbor, was blasted to the bottom. Below decks, 1,102 trapped seamen drowned.

Admiral Fiske was increasingly certain that war was coming, more likely now across the Atlantic rather than with Japan. On March 19 he took to Daniels the finding of the Navy's General Board "showing that the Dept. had no plans or system for getting prepared for war." After arguing fruitlessly for half an hour, Fiske went to see "Asst. Sec. Roosevelt. Of course, he understood the principles at stake." The admiral was persistent. On the twenty-fifth he and FDR (according to Fiske's diary) "concluded our (tentative) plans for the combined fleet & Army maneuvers next August." He then took their proposals to the War Department, where three generals and the Assistant Secretary of War were "delighted," recommending a joint conference to work out details. Daniels was still busy with inspection tours and with preparing his long-anticipated ban of the Navy "wine mess," to which he appended the Navy surgeon-general's invited opinion of the iniquitous effects of alcohol. Fiske, among other admirals, considered the ban at best "unwise & that the effect will be to influence officers to smuggle whiskey & cocaine on board, & take meals on shore, where they can drink whiskey—instead of wine & beer on board." Daniels's order abolished only

FDR at the Brooklyn Navy Yard, March 16, 1914, to
ceremonially lay the keel of Battleship #39, the USS *Arizona*.
FDR LIBRARY

the use of wine and beer, as other "spirituous liquors" had been banned
aboard fifty years earlier. (In the Royal Navy the rum ration for all hands
was almost a sacred mandate; and in the British Army during the war now
imminent the rum ration would be required for all ranks in active theaters
on every day that it rained, an interpretation that would be imaginatively
stretched.)

America's small military establishment was becoming increasingly
drawn into small conflicts in its backyards, especially the Caribbean. Still,
Daniels felt, with FDR's backing, that there were naval installations poorly
located for such emergencies, prompted originally by someone's political

clout in Congress. One of the Secretary's goals in his relentless inspection jaunts was to identify, to painful protests, some bases for closure. In April 1914 he sent Franklin to the Pacific coast to survey real needs, and in San Diego the Assistant Secretary increased the staff at the recently activated naval radio station. Since the sinking of the *Titanic* in 1912, and frantic rescue attempts, wireless devices had escalated in importance for shipping, and FDR was actively promoting the burgeoning utility of radio.

While he was in California, the Mexican problem worsened. The *Dolphin*, sometimes employed by Roosevelt for Campobello visits, had been offshore in the Gulf of Mexico to watch over American interests during the continuing unrest. Among White House concerns was that on April 14 a German freighter loaded with arms and ammunition for Huerta's forces had arrived in Veracruz. The cargo and its source seemed a gross violation of the sacred Monroe Doctrine abjuring European military involvement in the hemisphere.

Much farther north, when the *Dolphin* lowered a small boat to fetch supplies at Tampico, and three of its crewmen were arrested ashore on orders from a zealous colonel in Huerta's army, the local Mexican commander intervened. The sailors were released with profuse regrets, which should have closed the incident—but not for Rear Admiral Henry Mayo, overseeing the Caribbean region. Without authority from Washington, Mayo hot-headedly demanded apologies, including an extreme twenty-one-gun salute and the raising of the American flag on Mexican soil. Huerta refused. To Daniels's consternation, as he saw the episode as trivial, the usually pacific Wilson, who despised Huerta, had the Secretary order warships to compensate for the affront. "Seize custom house," read the message from the usually placid Daniels to Rear Admiral Frank Friday Fletcher, off Veracruz. "Do not permit war supplies to be delivered to Huerta government or any other party."

American forces landed and seized the German freighter, the customs house, and the offloaded arms, but at an unanticipated cost. Mexican troops resisted. Nineteen sailors and Marines were killed, and seventy-one wounded. Abashed admirals handed out fifty-five Medals of Honor for the Veracruz affair, a dubious gesture diluting the ultimate award to nothingness. One of the wounded was a young naval officer, Husband E. Kimmel, whom FDR would soon acquire as an aide—and, much later, sack. Vice Admiral Kimmel's fleet failed to be on the alert at Pearl Harbor.

Huerta's forces sustained 126 dead and 195 wounded, and the misguided affair became a press sensation. Anti-American riots erupted across Latin America. "We're not looking for trouble, but we're ready for anything," Roosevelt, who had been in San Francisco, and then at the Bremerton Navy Yard below Seattle, excitedly told a newspaperman. He had no idea how sloppy the operation had been and how unready Americans were for anything.

With the Panama Canal to be operable in August, as FDR pointed out, the split two-ocean navy had to be expanded and strengthened forthwith. ("You can't fight Germany's and England's dreadnoughts . . . with gunboats.") He would cajole both his Uncle Ted (July 17, 1914) and Admiral Mahan into writing articles deploring the weaknesses of an unmodernized and divided navy. "Halve the fleet," Mahan would argue, "and it is inferior in both oceans."

Concerned about what the Assistant Secretary might do, and was doing, Daniels ordered Roosevelt to entrain home. "Secretary says," Howe wired gently, "that as most of the vessels on the west coast will be down in Mexico and in view of the great help you will be to him in Washington, he thinks the wise course is for you to return as originally planned."

At each rail stop eastward, Roosevelt's inexperience emerged. He predicted to awaiting reporters that war below the Rio Grande might be imminent, yet offers of mediation by Argentina, Brazil and Chile would soon defuse whatever emergency existed. Asked in Minneapolis what the crisis meant, FDR answered fervidly, "War! And we're ready!" In Milwaukee on April 26, the next day, he told newspapermen, "I do not want war, but I do not see how we can avoid it. Sooner or later, it seems, the United States must go down there and clean up the Mexican political mess." In Chicago he imagined a "war spirit . . . sweeping the West."

Back in Washington and better informed, he was prudently more guarded. "Of course things at the moment look quiet and not as warlike as last week," he wrote to a friend in May, "but I am not convinced the worst is over." The German ambassador had pointed out that a state of war with Mexico did not exist, and as a sovereign nation it was entitled to import arms for itself. Admiral Fletcher* was ordered to apologize to the ship's captain and the legal cargo of 200 machine guns and fifteen million cartridges was restored and delivered into Mexican hands.

Although Frank Fletcher's reputation was damaged at no fault of his own, Henry Mayo's insistence upon vindication of national honor pleased Wilson, who saw to it in June 1915 that Mayo would be promoted to Vice Admiral and appointed commander of the Atlantic fleet. When further crises in Mexico, Haiti and Santo Domingo suggested the possibility of European intervention in what were becoming very troubled waters, Roosevelt as Acting Secretary in Daniels's absence conferred with the President and Secretary Bryan on July 14 and ordered seven hundred Marines to Guantanamo Bay, Cuba, for "watchful waiting"—a favorite Wilson term.

For the politically impetuous FDR, watchful waiting seemed insufficient inducement to remain in subordinate office once more attractive opportunities surfaced. In New York in 1914 the governorship and a senate seat were at stake. From Campobello he surveyed his chances, and back in Washington played golf as usual with his moneyed and leisured Harvard classmate Livingston Davis, a Boston stockbroker often absent from his office. The Roosevelt family had traveled north for the summer as the District was already awash in marshland humidity. Franklin planned short stays at Campobello with Eleanor and the children between departmental duties. Anna was now seven; Elliott and James were younger, and Eleanor was again expectant. One excuse for a visit to the island (with Daniels accompanying on the *Dolphin* to Quincy, Massachusetts, and the Fore River shipyard) was the launching of the battleship *Nevada*. (Still on the active rolls on December 7, 1941, the *Nevada* was at Pearl Harbor, where, although disabled by an air-launched torpedo, it was skillfully beached, upright.)

---

*His nephew, Frank Jack Fletcher, then a lieutenant, would be a much-decorated carrier admiral in the Pacific in World War II.

In Washington in sultry mid-July, Franklin wrote happily to Eleanor, and then "Mama," that in Mexico, Huerta "had climbed down" (into exile). FDR was "working on a thousand things." One now completed was the sale to Greece of two undersized battleships, *Idaho* and *Mississippi*, commissioned in 1908 but now useless against the new class of warships. Greece recently had fought two wars against Turkey and, as a third Balkan conflict loomed, had immediate need of deterrents. The sale had been approved by Congress on June 30, 1914, embarrassing the American ambassador to the Ottoman Empire, Henry Morgenthau, whose Hudson Valley son and namesake was Franklin's friend, and would become his Treasury Secretary in the 1930s.

Delivery of the undersized battleships was accomplished under Turkish protests while further war anxieties emanated from the Balkans following unexpected violence in Sarajevo. Late in June, Archduke Franz Ferdinand, the heir to the Austrian throne, had been assassinated by a Serbian nationalist, leading to impossible demands upon the Serb government from Vienna, and warnings of intervention from opposing powers. Returning from Campobello later in the month on a Navy destroyer, Franklin learned on July 28 that Austria-Hungary had declared war on hapless Serbia, with further consequences inevitable. Webs of treaties by associated nations promised armed resistance to aggression, actual or alleged.

Aloof behind the Atlantic, the United States was not a party to such interlocking pacts. Although alarmed, the Assistant Secretary saw no need to rush back to the Department. In Massachusetts the next day, Franklin represented the Navy from the deck of the lead destroyer (of six) at the ceremonial opening of the Cape Cod Canal. Flanked by two submarines at the entrance, the flotilla steamed slowly through. Since, in the strong currents, his destroyer, the *McDougal*, could not anchor, he went ashore at Buzzard's Bay by motor launch, amid the cheering of thousands and the honking of auto horns, to deliver his address, knowing all the while via an anxious telegram from the Department received en route that he would not be returning to Campobello.

Leaving for Washington overnight by boat, automobile and train, he intended when back to push naval preparedness, now seemingly more urgent than before the shooting at Sarajevo. From the Department he wrote to Eleanor, "Nobody seemed the least bit excited about the European crisis—Mr. Daniels feeling chiefly very sad that his faith in human nature and civilization, and similar idealistic nonsense was receiving such a rude shock. So I started in alone to get things ready and prepare plans for what ought to be done by the Navy end of things."

As war loomed in Europe, seemingly unstoppable worldwide were the industrial races for new weapons technology, greed for colonies and for trade, the faltering of decadent monarchies and the risings of suppressed nationalisms. In anxious foreign capitals, control of events was being lost—but not in placid Washington. Roosevelt had anticipated the faint response at home, he recalled to a press conference late in 1940, by his experience in returning to the Department by rail. "The smoking room of the express was filled with gentlemen from banking and brokerage offices in New York, most of whom were old friends of mine; and they began giving me their opinion about impending war in Europe." They assured Franklin "that there wasn't enough money in all the world to carry on a European war for more than three months—bets at even money . . . that the [overseas] bankers would stop the war within six months." Further, that it was "humanly impossible—physically impossible—for a European war to last for six months. . . . Well, you know what happened."

Daniels considered it unnecessary for Roosevelt to cancel a public appearance the next day at Reading, Pennsylvania. Campaigning for reelection in the district was a congressman who had promoted his alleged influence in Washington by extracting from the Navy Department for local display an anchor from the ill-fated *Maine*, the ostensible precipitant of the war with Spain. His primary opponent called the anchor a fake, one of a proliferation of dubious souvenirs from the wreck in Havana harbor—including the captain's alleged bathtub, salvaged and acquired by a town in Ohio. The unveiling of the relic for Reading was preceded by a parade, and Franklin wrote to Eleanor, "an impassioned oration by hubby to 5,000 people in the park!" The *Reading Eagle* published FDR's address in full, explaining in detail how two of the cruiser's anchors were recovered and returned to the United States in April 1913. The gift was,

Roosevelt conceded, entirely a political gesture, with no deceit involved, but history is likely to remember a more numerical aspect of his address:

> There have been two kinds of successful politics devised in our system of government. . . . The first is the kind which seeks to build up party strength by obtaining . . . power based on the personal domination of a few men and the perpetuation in places of authority of those few men and their own appointed successors. That has been in the past, we must admit to our shame, a successful kind of politics, but the day of its success has just about come to an end. The administration in Washington believes in a very different kind of successful politics. It goes back to the fundamental theory that the success of a government depends upon the freely expressed consent of the governed. It is seeking so to handle the affairs of the nation that no man, no group and no class shall have privilege to the exclusion of any other man or group or class to the end that there may be equal opportunity for all. The administration believes that the national government should be conducted for the benefit of the 99 per cent, and not, as has sometimes been the case in the past, for the benefit of the 1 per cent. . . .

In a political life that would span many more years, Franklin would seldom deliver a closing metaphor that has had such a continuing resonance.* Yet it had little impact then in Representative John H. Rothermel's district. He would lose the primary to Arthur Granville Dewalt, who would serve three undistinguished terms. The *Maine* anchor, and the metaphor, survive.

"I am on the train returning to Washington . . . ," Franklin wrote to Eleanor the next morning, a Saturday. "The latest news is that Germany has declared war against Russia. A complete smash up is inevitable, and

---

* In 1942, FDR proposed a wartime marginal tax rate of 100 percent on high incomes that would bookend the minimum wage he had signed into law during the early years of the Depression. He was targeting dramatic inequality of income. Although he knew Congress would object, he wanted to contend that the nation was run by the moneyed, for the moneyed. Nothing would change but the names of the presidents, for congressional campaigns became increasingly costly.

there are a great many problems for us to consider. Mr. D. totally fails to grasp this situation and I am to see the President Monday a.m. [August 3] to go over our own situation. . . . These are history-making days. It will be the greatest war in the world's history."

Although France was already at war with Germany, as Britain would be on Tuesday, Wilson at Monday's meeting with Franklin evoked the deliberative professor, preferring to watch and wait. Wilson also had a personal crisis. His wife, Ellen, long ill with cancer, was dying, and would succumb on August 6.

Daniels, the cautious country editor at heart, condoned the tepid responses of Congress, which saw a broad ocean between the United States and belligerent Europe. Ranking admirals would hold emergency requisitions for signature until Daniels was away and then take them to the Acting Secretary. At State, William Jennings Bryan was unmoved by the war, which to him had no compelling American interest. "Some fine day," Franklin carped to Eleanor, "the State Department will want the *moral* backing of a 'fleet in being' and it *won't be there.*"

Britain's declaration of war, which seemed imminent as Germany was certain to continue its invasion of Belgium, came on August 4. Making war a day earlier seemed too hasty. Monday, August 3, had been a bank holiday, which the government quickly extended to prevent a panicky run on withdrawals. The next morning, reservists received the anticipated British mobilization telegram: MOBILIZE STOP ACKNOWLEDGE.

In Berlin, Count Harry Kessler, half-British and once a schoolboy at Ascot, faced the events with tangled emotions, but his priorities were obvious. In his forties, he was a Prussian officer. Reporting to his regiment, *Graf* Kessler found "a calm, cheerful confidence. One knows that the war will be frightful, that we will suffer perhaps occasional setbacks, but . . . the qualities of the German character—dutifulness, seriousness, and stubbornness—will in the end bring us victory. Everyone is clear that this war must result in Germany's world domination or its ruin."

Americans abroad worried about imminent ruin. Stranded overseas, unable to obtain cash at banks for steamship tickets home, or even for day-to-day needs, citizens besieged European embassies, especially in

London. Ambassador Walter Hines Page cabled Washington for emergency assistance to relieve "acute temporary destitution. . . . Thousands of perfectly solvent Americans possess letters of credit but cannot cash them. No banking transactions have taken place since the closing of banking hours [on August 1]." A committee of volunteers then in London, led by Fred I. Kent, vice president of Bankers Trust Company in New York; Oscar Straus, former Secretary of Commerce and Labor under TR; Theodore Hetzler, president of the Fifth Avenue Bank; and wealthy mining engineer Herbert Hoover set up a Citizens' Relief Committee in a ballroom of the Savoy Hotel to accommodate thousands eager to escape the war zone. Even Americans long resident in Britain were urged by Hoover to leave for home in order to conserve local food supplies.

To furnish American currency and credit, an emergency meeting convened under the mansard roofs with State, Army and Navy officials, Roosevelt representing the Navy. At first he misunderstood what the Navy could accomplish. "Tourists (female) couldn't sleep in hammocks, and . . . battleships haven't got passenger accommodations," he wrote to Eleanor, assuming that warships would be sent to convey stranded American nationals home. Rather, to purchase commercial passage, the cruiser *Tennessee* would be dispatched from the Brooklyn Navy Yard with a $2,500,000 cargo of gold coins, authorized by Congress, and packed in oaken casks. For reasons Franklin did not divulge, but would become clear, he opted not to lead the mission, which could mean a month or more abroad; however he did arrange for the cruiser's departure. His friend, Assistant Secretary of the Army Henry Breckinridge, was assigned instead, taking with him twenty-four army officers to watch over the coin cache, and also a cadre of clerks—an enormous personnel boondoggle.

In the interim, Fred Kent in London borrowed $20,000 in gold to distribute up to forty dollars to holders of American Bankers Association traveler's checks, and with Hetzler borrowed an additional $300,000 as an advance on the *Tennessee*'s arrival. While the cruiser was still at sea, Hoover's agents required those seeking loans to divulge their own resources as security, and those with insufficient funds were furnished chits for cheap passages by steerage. An Associated Press dispatch would headline, "AMERICANS ARE HURRYING HOME. Thousands Leaving English Ports Weekly for Home, Sweet Home." Having done its temporary duty the emergency committee, its apparatus replaced by Washington official-dom, would disband on August 19, 1914, having unexpectedly launched Herbert Hoover's public career.

When a more pathetic wave of Americans poured in from Germany and central Europe through early September, some penniless and hungry, the emergency committee reorganized at the Savoy, which again provided the space, fed—in Hoover's description—the "busted Yankees" on railway station platforms, and arranged for lodgings and steamship tickets. Among the unhappy travelers was elderly Henry Adams, on a rare trip abroad, and stranded at first in Paris. "To me," he claimed ruefully, "the crumbling of worlds is always fun." Of the hundred thousand who evacuated Europe through Britain, 42,000 were assisted by the volunteer American Com-mittee. The overwhelmed Breckinridge conceded that a "paid organiza-tion" (his own swollen staff) could not have accomplished more.

Echoing the blinkered neutrality of the ambassador's superiors in Washington, Walter Hines Page would write to Wilson, "Again and again I thank Heaven for the Atlantic Ocean."

The timid responses at levels higher than Roosevelt's own to a war likely to sweep the world and engulf the United States left FDR disgusted, and confirmed to him an impetuous decision he had made just before his last visit to Campobello—to contest the Democratic nomination for the Senate in New York. Winning the seat would make him his own boss, and propel his increasingly visible career forward. He had consulted neither Eleanor, nor Mama, nor Howe. Before the news was out in Washington, Louis Howe, in Massachusetts vacationing at Horseneck Beach on the eastern end of Buzzard's Bay, opened a letter from Charles McCarthy, who was minding the Assistant Secretary's shop, "The Boss has been the whole cheese in this European business and he is going along great." Franklin was working into the night and leaving the useless Livy Davis without a golfing partner. Once the Senate bid became public, however, Howe received a telegram from his unwise chief: "MY SENSES HAVE NOT YET LEFT ME."

4

War across the Sea

HOWEVER REALISTIC AMERICAN neutrality seemed as the war across the Atlantic began, Franklin wrote to Bob Ferguson, a former Rough Rider with Uncle Ted, that he understood his invalid friend's frustration at being out of the fight. "Even I long to go over into the thick of it & do something to help right the wrong. England's course has been magnificent—Oh, if only that German fleet would come out and fight!" There seemed no chance of a North Sea encounter, nor of Franklin's getting into the action—not even the likelihood of his pushing a hidebound American Navy into preparedness.

Nor could the German merchant marine emerge safely, if at all. In the United States, the Wilson government interned at Hoboken, New Jersey, along with twenty-five other German-flag vessels, two of the most capacious passenger liners afloat, the Bremen-based North German Lloyd 37,000-ton *George Washington* and the 54,282-ton *Vaterland*, which eclipsed in size the English White Star Line *Britannic* and *Olympic* and their lost sister ship, *Titanic*. The trapped German vessels, remaining under control of their crews, were considered as belonging to a belligerent nation, and at hazard. Had any ventured to sea they would have been cheap British targets.* (As nearly

---

* To circumvent the blockade, the Krupp munitions firm would build a large prototype "merchant submarine," *Deutschland*, which made two voyages to the United States to

landlocked Austria, with only ports on the Adriatic, was allied with Germany, four of its ships were also interned at Hoboken, then the major harbor for New York City.)

Two weeks after the European war crowded newspaper columns, Roosevelt's surprising announcement that he would enter the New York senatorial primary reached the press. On August 14, 1914, in the *Poughkeepsie Eagle* he was quoted as declaring that his campaign was for "intelligent progress and honest administration of government" and against "reactionary politics and politicians." He would be, the Republican-leaning *Eagle* sneered, an easy candidate to beat. Franklin was more concerned about the primary. Keeping to Department affairs, however, he wrote to Daniels from Campobello on August 24 to ask for a nearby destroyer to fetch him from Eastport, Maine, so that he could inspect the Boston and Portsmouth, New Hampshire, navy yards on his return trip to Washington. Commanding the destroyer was a young lieutenant, William F. Halsey, Jr. (Thirty years later on FDR's watch Halsey would be an admiral familiar on the front pages.) Reaching Passamaquoddy Bay below Campobello Island, at the mouth of the St. Croix River, known for its strong tidal flow, Roosevelt suggested that since he was familiar with the channel, he should guide the destroyer between Deer Island and Campobello. Aware of the differences in skill required to "sail a catboat out to a buoy" and "to handle a high-speed destroyer in narrow waters," Halsey feared a career-ending mishap, but he yielded to his civilian superior, a "white-flanneled yachtsman." To the lieutenant's relief, Roosevelt "knew his business" and "took the ship through easily."

"I hear very little political news, but certainly hope the report that [William Randolph] Hearst is to run against me [in the primary] is true," FDR wrote cockily to Daniels before leaving Campobello. "It raises my fighting and sporting blood. . . ." Arrogantly ambitious for office (despite

---

pick up war materiel before it appeared in danger of confiscation. By 1916 seven were in use or under construction, to fetch scarce commodities like rubber or nickel from South America. They would be converted to attack use. At least one was lost at sea. In World War II several such submarines plied between Germany and Japan.

spending a lot of his own money he had already lost an election for governor), the publisher would overplay his hand, suggesting that if Boss Murphy did not make Hearst the Democratic candidate, he might run as a TR Progressive. Murphy did not take the bait.

"Tammany will doubtless put up a respectable rubber stamp against me," Franklin wrote to Bob Ferguson's wife, Isabella. "I am going to keep trying to clean out that old gang if it takes twenty years." Although he was acquiring a visibility that should have been helpful in a war climate, his opponent backed by Murphy and Old Guard Democrats was Wilson's ambassador to Germany. James W. Gerard assured no real contest by using the war as excuse not to return to campaign. Roosevelt would have Gerard's reputation rather than Gerard himself to battle, and also the implication that Wilson's envoy was the President's choice.

Secretary Bryan had queried Wilson, "Asst. Sec. Roosevelt is as you know a candidate [for the Senate] & has, as I understand, the endorsement of Secs. [William Gibbs] McAdoo & [William] Redfield. I have also felt that Roosevelt would be the best man. Gerard, of course, could not leave Berlin in the near future. What do you wish to say to Gerard? He will do as you wish." Wilson declined to intervene. To Tammany's ire, Roosevelt had been quietly successful, through connections Louis Howe had cultivated in the Post Office Department, in obtaining postmaster appointments and other patronage posts for his anti-Tammany backers in New York, but Wilson needed his party's votes in Congress, whatever their origin.

On August 17, somewhat early, the Roosevelts' fifth child and third son to survive infancy was born at Campobello. Busy in Washington, Franklin had crossed the Narrows from Eastport too late for the onset of Eleanor's labor, and Albert Ely, her gynecologist in New York, supposedly on call, failed altogether to arrive. Roosevelt boated across to fetch Dr. E. H. Bennett, of Lubec, Maine, in general practice in the village. Delivering the children of the wives of fishermen and sardine cannery workers was his routine. By the time Franklin returned, with Bennett, the housekeeper, by the light of an oil lamp, had delivered the baby, and in the shadows Bennett at first mistook the newborn's gender.

"Future admiral arrived last night," FDR telegraphed Daniels. "Congratulations to the young Senator and his mother," the Secretary wired back. (Franklin D. Roosevelt, Jr., was the second child to bear the name. The first Franklin, Jr., born in March 1909, had died that November of endocarditis, an inflammation of the wall of the heart.) Roosevelt could spend little time in fatherhood duties at Campobello. He was dividing his schedule between the "grindstone" in Washington and a failing primary campaign which took in the entire state of New York rather than the limited 26th District, his former seat. Away from Washington, he dealt with Daniels by post about construction matters at the navy yard in New Orleans, for Daniels wanted warehouses remodeled into barracks for Marines soon to be returned from Mexico. (There were, then, only 15,500 Marines, mostly in the Caribbean.) Franklin dealt with labor issues at the many yards, most now gearing up for additional work.

Early in October, despite Roosevelt's boasting to Eleanor of "successful" engagements upstate, and useful connections in New York City, the invisible Gerard would win the primary easily, but lose to a Republican in the general election. Stumping upstate for the Progressive candidate for governor and attacking Wilson at every opportunity, TR had been invited, as family, by Sara to overnight at Springwood when he planned to be in the area. "If it were not for the campaign," he wrote to her, "there is no place I would rather go"—but he added that his appearance at Hyde Park would only do political harm to Franklin. FDR was soon beyond primary harm. Daniels noted in his diary that although Franklin had been "hurt" by his rejection, he did what was expected of losers. Before returning to Washington, he cabled his congratulations to the ambassador in Berlin. Roosevelt would write to a friend that he "carried a majority of the counties of the State and was beaten only through the solid lineup of [Tammany] New York City." The boast was false. He carried only twenty-two of the sixty-one counties, losing even his own.

After summering at Campobello, Eleanor went to Hyde Park with the children, remaining until late in October. Taking additional time away from the Department and his family, Franklin, unsubdued, campaigned for candidates on the Democratic ticket until Election Day early in November. He was deliberately acquiring political indebtednesses. There would be another day.

Nationally, the Democrats would lose seats in the Senate in 1914 but gain in the House. Beset by the distractions of the war and the disappointing midterm results, Wilson recognized that his domestic agenda could no longer include legislation on the scale of the Federal Reserve Act and the Underwood-Simmons Tariff Act. (Wilson had signed the tariff-lowering bill on October 3, 1913. Roosevelt was invited to watch as one of the fifty leading Democrats.) "Every reform we have won," Wilson worried to Daniels, "will be lost if we go into this war." Even without intervention, long-ignored deficiencies in defense had to be addressed, and militants had already begun the attack during the election cycle. Who would go to a Harvard-Yale football game, Uncle Ted asked, if either school had fielded a team that had not practiced? Influential Republican Congressman Augustus Peabody ("Gussie") Gardner, son-in-law of Senator Henry Cabot Lodge—both had been marooned briefly in France— was back in October to condemn sluggish military preparedness. As allies of TR, neither politician threw any blame at Franklin, who had quietly kept them aware of inside doings at Navy. Gardner had even written to Franklin the year before, "You are the promptest and most efficient Assistant Secretary in any Department with whom we have dealt in our eleven years of service here."

Franklin had received another, and unexpected, vote of confidence when Admiral Mahan, who had never met young Roosevelt, had written to him while FDR was at Campobello, recommending that because of the war in Europe, the Navy should recall its ships from Mexican waters. "I write to you," advised the ailing proponent of sea power, "because I know of no one in the Administration [otherwise] to whom I should care to write." Mahan would even call at the Navy Department late in November, hoping to talk to Franklin, who unfortunately was away. A week later, Mahan, seventy-four, was dead.

An admirer of German militarism ("a stern[,] virile and masterful people") yet also an unashamed Anglophile, Theodore Roosevelt was conflicted in his sympathies. Amidst an outpouring of sympathy for the violated Belgians, he could not appear as steadfastly neutral as Wilson, who had mandated that all government officials refrain from publicly taking sides. In *The Outlook*, for which TR wrote regularly and where he maintained a New York City office, he wrote on September 23, shifting his tone toward Belgium, "We can maintain our neutrality only by our refusal to do anything to aid unoffending weak powers which are dragged into the gulf of bloodshed and misery through no fault of their own."

Franklin loyally said little about the war, but was called by the House Naval Committee to testify on preparedness in mid-December. Uncle Ted declined to appear, declaring, "I do not see what I can add, other than what I have again and again written." By then, TR (still "the Colonel" to those on his side) had ended his relationship with *The Outlook* and began publishing articles through the Wheeler Syndicate, including two for *The New York Times* criticizing Wilson's "infirmity of purpose." The Colonel sought a larger audience for his burgeoning pro-British truculence, and Franklin, encouraged by the more militant admirals on the Department staff in Washington, conceded that passive neutrality was shortsighted, and that intervention, however deferred by distance, was inevitable. "The difference, I think," TR explained to Rudyard Kipling, "is to be found in the comparative widths of the [English] Channel and the Atlantic Ocean."

Late in October, again while Daniels was away, Franklin as Acting Secretary released a memorandum to the press declaring that the Navy needed 18,000 more men to keep thirteen second-class battleships on active status. Perhaps the key words were the strong hint in "second-class." When the press picked up his charge, he wrote to Eleanor, then at Hyde Park, that it was "the truth, and even if it gets me into trouble I am perfectly ready to stand by it. The country needs the truth about the Army and Navy instead of the soft mush about everlasting peace which so many statesmen are handing out to a gullible public." Congress evidenced interest, and with his impetuous Senate bid now only a humiliating memory, Franklin described, to "Dearest Mama," his appearance at the Capitol as "great fun."

In his diary for December 15, the bellicose Admiral Fiske wrote, "Asst. Sec. Roosevelt goes [testifying] today. He was in my office two hours yesterday, getting data, etc." It was FDR's introduction to the fencing match of parrying hostile questions "with thrusts that went home." To isolationist Congressmen, any naval buildup violated neutrality. "I was able to get in my own views," he claimed, "without particular embarrassment to the Secretary."

Despite Wilson's assertion that his administration had "not been negligent of national defense," Franklin testified that aging, coal-burning warships requiring excessive maintenance and coaling stations abroad belonged to yesterday. He recalled that when a review of President Taft's fleet took place in New York harbor in 1912, some vessels had to be towed to their stations and others were kept afloat by continuous pumping. The Navy needed rapid upgrading by modern ships with modern technology. A trained naval reserve of 50,000 was also urgently needed to man vessels under way and projected. The *New York Sun* reported that Roosevelt had "exhibited a grasp of naval affairs that seemed to astonish members of the [naval affairs] committee who had been studying the question for years."

"War is in all our thoughts & the horror of it grows," Eleanor wrote to Isabella Ferguson. "We are most distinctly 'not ready,' & F. tried to make his testimony . . . very plain & I think brought out his facts clearly without saying anything about the administration policy which would, of course, be [disloyal]."

Recognizing Wilson's cautious minimalism, Daniels proposed construction of two new battleships. Each would take three years, after authorization and construction bids, to put into service. Despite Franklin's testimony, he recommended no increase in manpower. The Secretary was accompanied by two admirals chosen for their willingness to agree with his positions. The Navy, they claimed, "ship for ship," was "as good as the navy of any other nation." As for Roosevelt's obvious disloyalty in reaching out to critics, yet his effectiveness in running the Department, Daniels later conceded, "I did not require that his friends be my friends."

Wilson had worried to Edwin House late in August that if Germany won, "it would change the course of our civilization and make the United States a military nation." Still, the President stubbornly advocated total neutrality in his State of the Union address on December 8. Preparedness for someone else's war was not on his agenda. "We have never had," he declared, "and while we retain our present principles and ideals we never shall have, a large standing Army." As for the Navy, "We shall take leave to be strong upon the seas, for the future as in the past, and there will be no thought of offense or of provocation in that."

Without appearing hawkish, Roosevelt made certain in his testimony a week later that Congress understood that the fleet Wilson inherited was obsolete, and that as Assistant Secretary he was edging within his limits toward its modernization. "More than this [upgrading by Daniels], proposed at this time," the President had insisted, "would mean merely that we had lost our self-possession, that we had been thrown off balance by a war with which we have nothing to do, whose causes cannot touch us." Rather, Wilson proposed with a detachment ignoring the likely consequences of delayed preparedness that America's "very existence affords us opportunities of friendship and disinterested service which should make us ashamed of any thought of hostility or fearful preparation for trouble." In response, Colonel Roosevelt contended in the kind of homely metaphor that FDR would often adopt later that preparedness did not avert war any more than a fire department averted a fire. It was nevertheless "the only insurance against overwhelming disgrace and disaster in war."

Privately, the Assistant Secretary made no secret of his pro-Ally sentiments, but he would not publicly cross Daniels by overtly taking sides. Privately he complained to Eleanor about the pacifist "nonsense" of "dear good people like W.J.B. and J.D.," who had "as much conception of what a general European war means as Elliott"—then four—"has of higher mathematics." Cautiously, FDR was seeing little, but for occasional (and arranged) social opportunities, of "Springy" Rice, the British ambassador, whom he admired, as Rice, on formal occasions, was above Franklin's bracket in rank. Even so, together at a lunch at the Metropolitan Club, they suspected that the German ambassador, Count Johann von Bernstorff, at the next table perhaps by coincidence, was trying to overhear their conversation, which then became more cautious. Bernstorff had been trying to sway American opinion from the one-sided trade that banking favored toward an embargo on all arms exports. "I just *know*," Franklin wrote to Eleanor after the episode, "I shall do some awful un-neutral thing before I get through."

One of his new friends, eight years younger, and soon a lively golf and boating partner, was Nigel Law, Third Secretary at the British embassy, who arrived on the posh liner *Lusitania* in December and was soon dining with the Roosevelts and sharing confidences. (He lived nearby on H Street in bachelor digs with other Britons.) "I found him the most attrac-tive man whom it was my good fortune to meet during my four years in America," Law would recall to Jonathan Daniels, the Secretary's son. Nigel Law's father was a senior official in the Foreign Office. The younger Law—very likely it was part of his covert embassy charge—quickly became a companion of Roosevelt's at the Chevy Chase Club and the Lock Tavern Club on the Potomac. When Law became Lucy Mercer's ostensible com-panion for weekend sailings on the *Sylph*, no one could have guessed that it was Franklin's deft strategy to see more of Lucy away from N Street.

IN THE DARK December of 1914 in Washington, snow fell at Christmas. At his fireplace looking out on Lafayette Square and the White House, frail Henry Adams, glum as usual, wrote to his dearest friend, Elizabeth Cameron, in embattled France, "I am St. Augustine of Hippo, writing the *Civitas*"—The City of God—"in a corrective sense, before the Germans come." Augustine's treatise dealt with predestination. "Life cannot produce anything; let the Germans come," Adams repeated on the twenty-ninth. In the slush and rain he had his "old crowd" over, and "Franklin Roosevelt and his wife—who promises to be a favorite." Also "Springy [Rice], seem-ing quite bright, &c., &c., with Cabot [Lodge] himself who does not strike me as developing into a century-plant."* The Roosevelts were uncon-cerned about having been seen with far-from-neutral Wilson adversaries.

_____

*Senator Cabot Lodge would die in 1924 at seventy-four.

One way that Daniels was able to distance FDR for a time from conspiring with the Department's more militant admirals and pro-Ally Washingtonians was to arrange his dispatch as Navy commissioner to the Panama-Pacific International Exposition in San Francisco early in 1915. Some of FDR's friends were also going, as a holiday, and William Philips as a State Department commissioner, with his wife, Caroline. It would be, Franklin promised Livy Davis in Uncle Ted's terms, "a splendid party, perfectly bully." Sara was left with the children and household staff at N Street.

The Exposition opening on February 20 along the northern shore of San Francisco Bay was to celebrate the completion of the Panama Canal, but it was seen also as an opportunity for San Franciscans to showcase their recovery from the disastrous earthquake and fire of 1906. The FDR party traveled across the continent leisurely by train, as did, in its own special carriage, the venerable and fragile Liberty Bell, on what would be its last removal from Philadelphia. (A further appearance on its return was scheduled at the Panama-California Exposition in San Diego in the autumn. Then the bell was placed on a railway car on November 15 on a ten-day homeward journey, for whistle-stop display across the southwest, then Missouri, Illinois, Indiana, Ohio and Pennsylvania.)

Roosevelt had planned the inaugural spectacle, with fifty or more warships from many nations assembling off the Atlantic coast and Hampton Roads. The flotilla was to steam through the new canal and arrive to open the fair. Sarajevo and its consequences had foreclosed Franklin's gala opening, and events abroad had even eclipsed, in the press, the first ocean-to-ocean voyage through the Canal, which took place on August 15, 1914. With war abroad as excuse, Woodrow Wilson canceled his own appearance. He was to have been on the lead vessel, the venerable and symbolic battleship *Oregon*, which in 1898 had steamed 12,000 miles around South America in sixty-seven days to Santiago Bay in Cuba.

Other cancellations included a round-the-world airplane race, which might have been a folly of mishaps; an international yacht race; and a celebration, by then an irony, of "One Hundred Years of Peace among English-Speaking Peoples." Nevertheless, a five-acre model of the Panama

Canal, traversed by specially built spectator vehicles, drew crowds on prerecorded guided tours, which learned about the engineering success through "telephonic communication with a phonograph." Featured on the Avenue of Progress was a floodlit 453-foot "Tower of Jewels"—fifty thousand hanging glass prisms which shifted and sparkled in the Pacific breezes.

Along with Franklin's party-prone friends the train from Washington included the dour Thomas Marshall, a former governor of Indiana and Wilson's vice president, remembered since for his reflection, "What this country needs is a really good five-cent cigar." A gray-mustached little man with a big cigar, a large wife and a gift for silence, he was to represent the absent Wilson. Marshall's role was beyond his job description. According to the Constitution, he once remarked, "the duties of the Vice President are, first, to preside over the Senate when it is in session, second, to loaf the rest of the time."

Despite the lower-key circumstances, Franklin arranged a review of the Pacific Fleet, which was to proceed through the Golden Gate, still without (until 1937) its iconic bridge. The Assistant Secretary boarded the flagship *Oregon* with full honors, and "my flag was hoisted." The other commissioners followed aboard, then the Marshalls. In a colorful memorandum FDR dictated in 1941 he recalled, almost as a vaudeville act,

> We were lined up thirty feet from the gangway. . . . The Vice President's barge came alongside, the band and the side boys [waiting sailors] were all set, and in a minute the Vice President's silk hat and frock coat appeared at the top of the gangway. He had a cigar in his mouth, yellow gloves in his left hand and a cane in his right.
>
> The Vice President . . . stood there while the four ruffles were given on the drum. But when the Star-Spangled Banner was started, confusion followed. The poor man had an awful time shifting his cane to his left hand with the gloves. He reached for his hat, got it half way off, remembered the cigar, put his hat on again, got the cigar out of his mouth, fumbled it in with the gloves and the cane, and got his hat off again just before the National Anthem finished. Then came the reverse process—back went his hat, back went the cigar, and back went the cane into his right hand.

At that awful moment the first gun of the salute was fired almost over his head. He jumped two feet in the air and stayed there during the whole of the nineteen guns. . . .

Formal lunches and dinners abounded at the Fair, and a ball, at which, according to press accounts, Eleanor, in a white satin gown with train, and "magnificent jewels of diamonds and pearls," rare attire for her, towered above the Vice President. Afterward, as a token of thanks for Roosevelt's presiding, and his guidance through the dizzying events, the Marshalls sent FDR a gift box from Gorham's, with Mrs. Marshall's card enclosed. Franklin wrote to Eleanor, then at Campobello, that they were now the possessors of twenty-four "silver corn-handlers or whatever the name is."

He failed to acquire the memento he really wanted. Although the attractions of San Francisco included, for Franklin, the lavishly endowed and gowned ladies at the balls and banquets, the principal memory he took back with him was of a small nude in bronze. His press assistant William Hassett recalled twenty-seven years later, "Something set the President talking about a bronze statue he saw at the San Francisco exhibition . . . , a young girl, beautiful in form and feature, petite and posed most impressively in a kneeling attitude, the hands of great delicacy, the curve of the neck and shoulders being exceedingly graceful. It was, the President said, a conception of youthful feminine beauty and spirituality which had always lingered in his mind."

Worship, a Rodinesque miniature by young California sculptor Ralph Stackpole, was not then for sale, but Roosevelt never forgot it. In 1938, when he contacted Stackpole, then fifty-three, to track it down, the artist offered to create a copy. To the President's disappointment, the "copy" was a blunt modernist echo in travertine limestone. (Much larger than the bronze, the statue is now on the FDR Library grounds.) In January 1944 the nubile nine-inch original was located by Jesse Lilienthal, a writer and friend of the sculptor, who presented it to the President. Inexplicably sold at auction after FDR's death, its whereabouts are unknown. His library has only a photograph.

Worship, a Rodinesque bronze miniature by Ralph Stackpole, admired by FDR at the San Francisco Exposition in early 1915 and never forgotten. It was located in 1944 by Jesse Lilienthal and presented to the President. Whereabouts now unknown. FDR LIBRARY

Worship II, created in travertine limestone by Ralph Stackpole for FDR in 1938 when the original, much smaller and different original could not be located. It remains on the grounds of the Roosevelt library. FDR LIBRARY

Bored by the endless social schedule, and anxious about the children at home with Sara, Eleanor was increasingly eager to leave the festivities. Louis Howe, FDR's earnest promoter, was peeved because the rank-conscious press emphasized Vice President Marshall and largely ignored the director-in-chief of the Washington contingent. "Mr. Daniels," Howe wrote, " . . . called my attention to the fact that no published account in the East of the various fetes and functions for the Vice President has mentioned that you were there, or thereabouts. You had better tell Phillips to fire whoever is acting as press agent for your blooming commission and try to get at least a line in amongst the patent medicine advertisers."

In Los Angeles, as the Washingtonians were preparing to return, Roosevelt was handed a telegram from Howe. The Navy's submarine *F-4* had failed to surface after a dive off Pearl Harbor, with all hands lost. The Assistant Secretary earned his missing line in print, and more, acknowledging to newspapermen that however "sad" the sinking was, it was something "that must be expected in any great navy." Then he hurried to the Navy Shipyard at Long Beach to locate an operational submarine and ordered it down. "Come on boys," he challenged the curious sailors along the wharf. "Don't you want to go along? Plenty of room. Glad to have you."

A few die-hards followed him below. The water was choppy and the sky lowering, but the sub captain performed as ordered, and proceeded out to submerge as spectators ashore cheered. One seaman aboard told a reporter after they resurfaced and docked that Roosevelt had "taken off his coat and dug into everything." In TR terms, the Assistant Secretary told the press, "It was fine, and for the first time since we left Washington we felt perfectly at home." Soon after, he boarded a destroyer for San Diego. He was to meet Eleanor there for the leisurely rail journey eastward. They stopped in New Mexico for a visit with Isabella and Bob Ferguson in desert country. As they rumbled on toward Washington the war situation worsened.

From late March into May, as Roosevelt was returning to the Department, reports came of German submarine attacks on British liners in the Atlantic which killed or injured American citizens aboard. Then on May 1 the American tanker *Gulflight*, out of Texas, was torpedoed in the Irish Sea, with three lives lost. On the same day the German embassy in

Washington issued a warning through the press to "travellers intending to embark on the Atlantic voyage." A war zone around the British Isles was declared in effect and vessels flying the British flag were liable "to destruction in those waters." That Sunday the 30,396-ton Cunard liner *Lusitania* steamed out of New York harbor for Liverpool with 1,257 travelers aboard. Few had canceled passage.

Whether the Navy Department should respond in any way to German threats, considered in Berlin a "trade war" to curtail British imports, provoked friction between Roosevelt and Daniels. Nevertheless, Franklin wrote to Eleanor in Hyde Park that his chief "seems cheerful and still glad to see me!" The Secretary's good cheer may have come from his ousting, in FDR's absence, the combative Operations aide, Rear Admiral Bradley Fiske. Although Daniels had wired Franklin, still traveling back to Washington, that he would take "no action" on administrative changes until he consulted the Assistant Secretary, on April 28, Daniels had elevated Captain William S. Benson, the mild commandant of the Philadelphia Navy Yard, to a new post as Chief of Naval Operations, jumping him over five more senior captains and twenty-six admirals. However irate, Roosevelt kept silent.

Of all flag officers in the Department, Fiske seemed to FDR overwhelmingly the best for the job. Although it was a reorganization which the efficient but difficult Fiske had long proposed, Daniels had excluded him. In his diary the admiral had written earlier, curiously in the third person, "Roosevelt and I agree that opinion of all [in the Department] is that Fiske ought to be Ch.Nav.Op." However one key opinion had differed—that of the Secretary. An elderly Georgian with a white mustache, Benson was Daniels's type—"a dignified gentleman," according to Fiske, "of thoroughly correct habits, very religious and conscientious, . . . but I never heard that he had even shown the slightest interest in strategy." From London, Walter Hume Long, a Conservative member of H. H. Asquith's coalition cabinet and later First Lord of the Admiralty, derided Benson as "not very quick to grasp any ideas other than his own."

A brief break in the Assistant Secretary's Washington schedule came when Uncle Ted asked for assistance in a trial for libel in Syracuse. TR was the defendant in a lawsuit by William J. Barnes, Jr., Republican state chairman and local boss of Albany, who the Colonel had claimed had identical interests to Tammany Hall. Franklin knew of alliances between the opposing party machines, and was willing to risk further enmity from Tammany Democrats.

Before the trial opened on May 4, a press photographer snapped the two Roosevelts walking to the courthouse with TR's attorney. For the moment the tall young Roosevelt overshadowed his stocky Uncle Ted. In his opening remarks TR found it useful to refer to "my cousin, Franklin Roosevelt." On the stand, FDR identified himself as "fifth cousin by blood and a nephew by law." He recalled the collusion between party bosses in the 1914 senatorial campaign, and attorneys for Barnes could not shake his testimony or convince the jury that he was merely doing TR a favor or getting even with party rivals.

Franklin, TR wrote to his wife in Oyster Bay, "made the best witness we have had yet." After forty-three hours of deliberation, the jurors on May 22 exonerated the former president. Back in Washington, Franklin sent a warm message to the Colonel. In response on May 29, TR wrote, "You have a right to congratulate me on the verdict, because you were part of it. I shall never forget the capital way in which you gave your testimony and the impression upon the jury."

Not long after, Uncle Ted began using his family ties to lobby Franklin to have Roger Williams, Jr., son of a friend, accepted at the Naval Academy ("first rate family and of the best fitting stock"); to furnish information for a Preparedness article in Collier's to Finley Peter Dunne (who wrote as "Mr. Dooley"); to listen to "certain schemes" for the Army and Navy proposed by artist and printmaker Ernest Haskell ("a man of character and repute"); and to secure the reinstatement in the Navy of James L. McSweeney, once a seaman on the presidential Mayflower, who had been "discharged for breaking his liberty in Vera Cruz." The two Roosevelts also shared experiences of moose hunting, Uncle Ted having shot two with "good antlers," FDR failing to find a moose in New Brunswick because "the weather was too hot and they refused to come out of the swamps."

Franklin (center) with Theodore Roosevelt (left) and Uncle
Ted's lawyer, W. R. Van Benschoten (right), during the William
Barnes libel trial, Syracuse, NY, May 4, 1915. FDR LIBRARY

The trial of the Colonel had been big news when it began, but on the
afternoon of May 7 a messenger brought to the courtroom a shocking
telegram for TR. The *Lusitania* had been torpedoed in the Irish Sea within
sight of the shore. The liner sank within eighteen minutes with the loss of
1,201 lives, 124 of them American. Press and public indignation surged at
the atrocity. German authorities reminded governments of prior warnings,
and charged (yet the British denied) that the *Lusitania* was carrying contraband munitions. New York Custom House authorities would confirm that
in the *Lusitania*'s cargo were 4,200 cases of rifle ammunition, 1,250 cases

of 3.3-inch shrapnel shells and 18 cases of percussion fuses. Wartime British regulations forbade mention of munitions shipments, and in one of the government's more feeble responses to the sinking, Kaiser Wilhelm's Order of the Garter, bestowed on him thirty-four years earlier by Queen Victoria, was revoked. (On their return the crew of the U-20 would be feted.)

Although the *Lusitania* was visibly British, and the liner did not conceal that, British vessels sometimes ran up an illegal American flag when a sub was sighted or feared, and a cartoon in the *New York American* would imagine a sailor on a surfaced sub asking a ship's captain, "Who iss it—vat boat?" Pointing to the American flag run up on the ship identified as *Lusitania,* the Cockney captain shouts from the bridge, "Cawnt you see I'm a blooming Yankee?"

Possibly putting his libel defense in jeopardy because two jurors were of German origin, Colonel Roosevelt in Syracuse had called the sinking "piracy on a vaster scale of murder than the old-time pirates ever practiced." Franklin believed that American national character required some form of intervention on the Allied side other than being blind to contraband cargo, but he continued to keep his feelings private, writing now to "Dearest Babs" that he was "disgusted clear through" at the continued professions of neutrality by Bryan, Daniels and Wilson.

An emotional post-*Lusitania* telegram from Ambassador Page in London had warned Wilson and Bryan, "THE UNITED STATES MUST DECLARE WAR OR FORFEIT EUROPEAN RESPECT." More realistically in the face of persistent pacifism, especially in middle America, Sir Cecil Spring-Rice cabled the Foreign Office, "AS OUR MAIN INTEREST IS TO PRESERVE U.S. AS A BASE OF SUPPLIES, I HOPE LANGUAGE OF OUR PRESS WILL BE VERY GUARDED." He had reason for concern. On May 10, the next day, Wilson declared from his utopian summit to an audience of 15,000 in Philadelphia that "the example of America must be . . . not merely of peace because it will not fight but because peace is the healing and elevating influence of the world and strife is not. There is such a thing as a man being too proud to fight. There is such a thing as a nation being so right that it does not need to convince others by force that it is right." *The New York Herald* headlined in response, "WHAT A PITY THEODORE ROOSEVELT IS NOT PRESIDENT!"

FDR, far right, chatting with President Woodrow Wilson, smiling broadly for the cameraman, on the White House lawn, summer, 1915. FDR LIBRARY. (48–22–4262)

Some of Wilson's advisers recommended a stern if toothless protest over the sinking, which the President drafted and had the reluctant Bryan sign. "You are all pro-Ally," conceded the unhappy Secretary of State. The note virtually demanded that Germany cease submarine warfare against unarmed merchant vessels; yet the *Lusitania*, however unarmed, was carrying not only innocent passengers but war materiel ignored in an examination by the official U.S. Neutrality Squad. "England has been using our citizens to protect her ammunition," Bryan objected, refusing to sign a second, stronger, note after the German government dismissed the first. On June 8, with a "heavy heart," Bryan resigned. "I go out into the dark," he mourned. His Counselor and successor, Robert Lansing, an FDR friend, would sign yet a third note to Germany drafted by Wilson—that further violence to shipping of any kind would be considered as "deliberately unfriendly" acts that could lead to a break in diplomatic relations.

"J.D. will *not* resign!" a disappointed FDR wrote to Eleanor. Rather than departing with Bryan, Daniels still hoped that war could be avoided, while Wilson was only buying time for his reelection prospects in 1916. Bryan, the President may have worried, might try once again for the presidency, competing with him for the pacifist vote.

Roosevelt now realized that he would never succeed Daniels, who would be with Wilson to the end. As Assistant Secretary he could only manipulate his subordinate position to push readiness as best he could. Still, circumstances were turning Wilson into a reluctant convert to preparedness. War seemed inevitable. Franklin had to wait, or go; and leaving office on whatever pretext would almost surely mean leaving politics. Further, if Daniels departed in sympathy with Bryan and was replaced by an appointee other than Franklin himself, he might lose his own job.

With the General Board behind him, FDR exploited Wilson's fading pacifism, accepted still by isolationist Americans who appeared to be the majority of those Democrats likely to vote in the election looming in 1916. Writing in longhand to evade a typist, he sent a letter to the White House reeking of unctuous and self-serving hypocrisy. "I want to tell you simply," he wrote, "that you have been in my thoughts during these days and that I realize to the full all that you have had to go through. . . . I feel most strongly that the Nation approves and sustains your course and that it is *American* in the highest sense." Wilson replied on June 14, 1915, also in the privacy of longhand, that Roosevelt's sentiments "touch me very much. . . . Such messages make the performance of duty worth while, because, after all, the people who are nearest are those whose judgment we most value."

Soon after, Daniels invited Franklin to lunch at a hotel where they were to meet the Secretary of Commerce, William C. Redfield. As they walked together, Daniels, mindful of Bryan's dilemma, worried to Franklin about the dire possibility of the German government's making no concessions on submarine warfare. The day before, Franklin had discussed preparing for the inevitable with the Secretary of War, Lindley M. Garrison, who quoted Daniels at a Cabinet meeting, decrying hawkish solutions, "I hope I shall never live to see the day when the schools of this country are used to give any form of military training. If that happens it will be proof positive that the American form of government is a failure."

Aware of that reluctance about readiness, Roosevelt, suggesting a strategy to inhibit German attacks on neutral shipping by some concrete and dramatic step, asked Daniels, "Do you think the people would stand for [our] raising an army?"

"It would create terrible divisions of opinion," the Secretary insisted. "You know, it was just that which made Bryan resign—this fear of the next step if Germany does not give in. It is a mistake to look too far ahead, to cross the bridges before we get to them; it is sufficient to take each step as it comes up." Mobilizing an army from little more than a constabulary was a process rather than a "step."

In a penciled note he kept to himself mocking his chief's timidity, FDR recalled Daniels also responding to the dilemma about what might be done if the submarine campaign continued, "Why, as a matter of fact we couldn't do anything . . . except withdraw [Ambassador] Gerard, and what good would that do?"

Franklin thought—but to himself—that "military and economic steps short of war could be employed to demonstrate American determination." Preparedness could not be accomplished overnight. To Daniels he observed that it would be useless to continue "negotiating by notes & more notes. . . . Of this there is a limit—witness the War of 1812."

Roosevelt would have his own tough choices to make when he sat in Wilson's seat and another war encroached on the near shore.

OFF NEW YORK harbor soon after, the ageing Atlantic Fleet passed in review before the President, who applauded from a VIP barge near the *Dolphin*. There, eager gawkers had their first public view of the fifty-nine-year-old Wilson's distraction from events, Edith Bolling Galt, a buxom widow of forty-three whom he would soon marry. Retired admiral George Dewey was absent from the Navy League banquet celebrating the fleet review, but his letter, read on the occasion, claimed absurdly that the Navy was "not excelled, except in size, by the fleets of any nation in the world." He had been president of the General Board of the Navy for fifteen years, Dewey added, and he was confident that the efficiency of the service had "never been as high as it is today." In his address Wilson agreed, and expressed his admiration for the keen oversight and splendid example of Secretary Daniels. The Navy, the President averred, was "a body specially entrusted with the ideals of America."

It was May 17, the eve of the Secretary's fifty-third birthday. In his dinner remarks he championed, as would the General Board, a powerful fleet, and, almost certainly referring to Roosevelt and to the Navy League hawks at the high table, warned against "the depressing pessimists, who are resolved not to see anything but the hole in the doughnut." The Assistant Secretary followed, and without naming names, chanced being blunt. "Most of our citizens," he said, "don't know what national defense means. Our extraordinary good fortune in our earlier wars has blinded us to facts. Let us learn to trust to the judgment of the real experts, the naval officers. Let us insist that Congress shall carry out their recommendations."

Although Franklin had carefully chosen his words, which could have referred to the Secretary's toadyish retinue of admirals rather than the hawks, he was surprised when, back in Washington, Adelaide and Josephus Daniels invited him to dinner and, he wrote to Eleanor afterward, "no reference was made to the New York episodes."

Inspection tours and backlogs of paperwork occupied Franklin in June 1915. He could do nothing about the unsatisfactory German responses to the White House about what Wilson called crimes against humanity. Yet again, Ambassador Bernstorff in Washington anxiously warned the Chancellor and the *Kriegsmarine* command that unrestricted submarine attacks might lead to war, but Berlin saw few signs of a bellicose mood rising in an irresolute America.

Franklin was also preoccupied by a domestic issue that would create increasing discord. Eleanor was again expecting a child—her sixth pregnancy. She wanted no more. Eleanor had long suppressed her aversion to what were considered marital duties; yet, as she realized in San Francisco, her husband, in his virile early thirties, was a magnet to attractive women, and made little effort to conceal his interest in them. Insisting upon abstinence as her birth-control solution, she began denying Franklin what she considered her unappealing self. In spacious Campobello they could divide into separate bedrooms; in Washington they would need another

Flag Day ceremonies at the State War and Navy Building, June 14, 1915. William Jennings Bryan and Woodrow Wilson are on the far left, FDR on the far right. FDR LIBRARY

domicile, especially after John was born on March 13, 1916. They never again slept together as husband and wife. There would be a price.

EARLY ON THE morning of July 1, 1915, Louis Howe was roused from sleep by his insistent telephone. Since Eleanor was away for the summer at Campobello, Franklin was calling his adviser of closer resort. The Chief had intense pain in his right side and did not know what to do. "Oh, take a pill," said Howe. "It's nothing but that cherry pie and glass of milk you had for lunch [yesterday]. I told you not to eat it."

Roosevelt soon called back. The pain pill proved useless. Howe telephoned for a doctor and hurried over to N Street himself. It was acute appendicitis. The Assistant Secretary was out of action.

5

Rattling the Sword

FRANKLIN UNDERWENT SURGERY for appendicitis at Washington Naval Hospital. In a Pennsylvania Railroad car clattering from New York to Washington, Eleanor heard a trainman walking through the carriages calling her name. He handed her a telegram: FRANKLIN DOING WELL YOUR MOTHER-IN-LAW WITH HIM—LOUIS HOWE. Sara had been at FDR's bedside with a silk kimono for him. She returned to Hyde Park when Eleanor arrived from Campobello. When he could sit up again Franklin wrote to his mother that "at last I have something respectable and not bulky to wear to take on visits to the country houses of my rich friends!" Yet he was hardly among the underprivileged.

From the first day, Secretary Daniels was unfailingly avuncular and accommodating, writing, late on the day that FDR was hospitalized,

> The doctor has just telephoned that your temperature is normal, that you came out from the operation in fine shape. . . . You know my plan was to get three days at the seashore with my family, but [I] had decided to postpone the trip. . . . But now that your mother is here and you are getting on so well I will run down to North Carolina and stay till Tuesday morning. My plans are made then to remain in Washington during the month of July. You can, therefore, make your arrangements to go to [Eastport,]

Maine as soon as the doctor will let you travel, . . . and it will be a pleasure to me to remain on deck. You will need the salt air and bracing
climate. . . .

Recuperating, Franklin would be absent from the Department for
nearly two months. While Howe remained in Washington, he sent Department papers to Roosevelt, received responses, and shared news and
gossip. Daniels would report that the Department staff was "working har-
moniously" and that the President would be recommending "a constructive program" in which "the hard nut to crack will be navy yards. . . . I
hope you will put your mind on the things we ought to do." It was clear
from Wilson's call for "an adequate defense" that, under pressure, the administration's tone was shifting from doctrinaire neutrality. FDR replied
that "national preparedness" would only be defused as a party issue in 1916
by Wilson's "coming forward with a definite program." Despite earlier cost-
cutting ideas to eradicate waste, Roosevelt now felt that "abolishing" some
navy yards was no longer practical, for "in event of war" each yard would
have to be "readily expanded to the utmost capacity." Still, they had to be
reined in from traditionally running themselves on their "own lines" and
turning out "any kind of work."

"You must not fail to telegraph me if I can be of any help," he wrote to
Daniels early in August, "because I am really quite able to come to Washington from now on at any time." Yet Franklin would remain at Campobello for five weeks. Running his share of the Department from a distance,
he had Charles McCarthy come north on the *Dolphin* with Navy papers,
and his former Groton master and now friend, George Marvin, visited,
with preparedness ideas. Marvin was Washington editor for *The World's
Work*, where Franklin's articles on the Navy were widening his visibility.

During his absence at Campobello he apparently wrote "The Future of
the Submarine," which appeared in the rival *North American Review* on
October 15, 1915, and "The Cost of the Navy," in the September issue of
The Economic World. The submarine, FDR began, was a "mechanical
whale," in that it operated submerged but had to come to the surface at
intervals to breathe. Invisibility was the source of its menace, yet the sub

had to raise its periscope "eyes" above the surface to locate a target. "For every new weapon an antidote is found," and the submarine remained vulnerable to fast, armed patrol vessels, to the new airplane and dirigible, to radio signals "now in the infancy of development" that would detect a sub's presence, and to underwater deterrents becoming practicable, such as mines and nets. However dangerous to merchant vessels, he wrote, still accepting the Mahan view, "I would say without hesitation that the submarine has not replaced the battleship as the principal factor in war at sea," but it has "come to stay." Seaborne conflict was "a very complicated science." The characteristics of the battleship "may greatly change," and "step by step the submarine will take its place as one, but only one, of the many instruments of offense and defense on the seas; that it will fit into its well-appointed place."

Wearying of "making toy boats for children," Franklin began planning to return, and late in August the *Sylph* retrieved him. "It is a curious coincidence that as soon as I go away, we seem to land Marines somewhere," he remarked to Daniels. Seven Haitian presidents were assassinated between 1911 and 1915. Amid the unrest on the island shared with Santo Domingo, concern had arisen in Washington that Germany might exploit the instability to covertly set up submarine bases near the Canal Zone.

Expecting him back imminently, Daniels ordered Marines to Haiti, then left the steamy capital for a belated vacation. FDR exchanged greetings on August 21 when Daniels, traveling down the Potomac on the *Dolphin*, encountered Franklin sailing upriver on the *Sylph*. "This means things will hum," Roosevelt, again Acting Secretary, claimed to Howe. Humming had already arisen on the preparedness issue. TR was attacking Wilson's "*half*-preparedness" and "supine inaction." At Plattsburg in northern New York, the Colonel's hawkish Rough Rider colleague Leonard Wood, a former army chief of staff, had organized an elite summer training camp as well as a student facility with funds contributed by millionaire investor Bernard Baruch and like-minded businessmen associates. General Wood had derided the army that he had been unable, politically, to modernize as "just about equal to the police forces of Boston, New York and Philadelphia." Press coverage of Plattsburg was intense, for among those indulging in strenuous drilling and weapons training under Wood during the summer of 1915 were former war correspondent Richard Harding Davis and New York City mayor John Purroy Mitchel; and in the student section were TR's sons. Other "Plattsburg camps" were soon springing up across the country. Wilson was being left behind.

On the neutrality side, Henry Ford, who had rattled rival industrialists in 1914 by establishing a minimum wage of five dollars a day to build his automobiles, exasperated FDR by adopting Bryanesque pacifism and deploring naval expansion. "Henry Ford," said Franklin, " . . . until he saw a chance for publicity free of charge, thought a submarine was something to eat." A peace crank, Ford had set aside a million dollars—then far more in buying power than since—to undermine "preparedness," and described such organizations as the Navy League as warmongers and agents of munitions manufacturers. He intended to send a "Peace Ship," packed with ardent pacifists, to Europe. Effective at advertising slogans, Ford publicized the venture as "Out of the trenches by Christmas, never to go back."

The *New York Tribune* on November 25, 1915, headlined, sardonically, "Great War Ends Christmas Day; Ford to Stop It!" Ridiculed in the press as a ship of fools, and unwelcome in belligerent ports, the chartered *Oscar II* would sail anyway, to neutral Norway, Sweden, Denmark and the Netherlands. Bryan rejected an invitation to join the protest. Arriving overseas and now dreading a fiasco, Ford claimed a bad cold and escaped the ship in Oslo, returning on the next liner available to New York. Having achieved nothing, the "Peace Ship" returned quietly in January 1916.

Promoting preparedness rather than peace in a scarifying novel, Cleveland Langston Moffett published, the month after, *The Conquest of America*, with a preface symbolically dated Washington's Birthday 1916. Sowing fear, it echoed prewar invasion prophecies published in London in which unready England was attacked by *Kaiserliche* Germany. Set in 1920–1921 after the Germans have—fictionally—won the European war, it purported to be extracts from the diary of James E. Langston, correspondent of *The Times* of London. The novel's invented Langston quotes Theodore Roosevelt as warning, "What befell Antwerp and Brussels surely some day will befall New York and San Francisco." In a sneak attack the Germans destroy the antiquated American fleet, which lacks personnel even to crew its obsolete "pre-dreadnaught" warships. Long Island is invaded and the Brooklyn Bridge destroyed. A bloody Christmas Eve battle takes place near Boston, and led by Field Marshal Paul von Hindenburg, the Germans move south through New England. Echoing the 1770s, a Battle of Trenton takes place. After a naval encounter in the Caribbean, the massive Gatun Locks of the Panama Canal are blown up.

Still President, the novel's Woodrow Wilson orders a reluctant General Wood, whose army is smaller than that of Bulgaria (and who in reality Wilson would refuse a fighting command), to launch a disastrous frontal assault. When the counter-attack fails, the President tries to buy peace by offering the Germans a huge indemnity, but the Kaiser insists on keeping the occupied East Coast. A decisive battle finally occurs between the *Kriegsmarine* and innovative American torpedo planes—which in fact the hidebound Navy hierarchy had resisted—and on land 113,000 German troops are incinerated by flame-throwers* igniting gasoline. The United States survives.

In a discussion in the Department later with Democratic Party chairman and newspaper publisher Vance C. McCormick and Roosevelt, Daniels decried "the spectacle of Gen. Wood & [General George] Goethals . . . saying America could be taken, had no army and navy to defend itself." FDR, Daniels objected in his diary, "defended Wood's propaganda." The general "ought to retire from the army and take the stump, or observe military orders." It was evident that they were arguing over the controversial Moffett fantasy.

Pressed by political operatives sensitive to the shifting popular mood, Wilson had already realized that with his reelection at risk, he had to balance the fading desire to maintain peace with the need to prepare for war. Yet rearmament could only be promoted as defense, for pacifists questioned

---

*The novel's implication is that the use of *Flammenwerfer* surprised the invaders. Yet the Germans, who invented the liquid fire weapon in 1901, first employed it in battle at Melancourt, near Verdun, in February 1915. Allied armies adopted the flamethrower in 1916.

what threat existed to a nation walled off from trouble by two broad oceans. Despite rising anxieties for the faltering Western Front, Wilson, who knew his history, could not buy into TR's absurd contention that failing to aid like-minded nations was turning American backs on the "courageous purposes of Washington and Lincoln." Nevertheless, Secretary of War Lindley Garrison threatened to resign if the army were not expanded, and published his un-Wilsonian ideas in a magazine article. Colonel House, who did the President's thinking on such matters, advised Wilson to let Garrison go. Independently, however, the Army War College produced a plan for increasing the standing army by a third, to 141,000 officers and men, with a reserve force of 400,000 independent of the politics-ridden state National Guard divisions. Wilson had little choice but to approve, while forcing the resignation of the irksome Garrison. Egged on by Howe, some newspapers suggested that young Roosevelt was in the running as replacement.

Recuperating in Atlantic City, Franklin read about the unlikely speculation. A recurrent throat infection had taken him there for ten days of boredom, therapeutically walking the boardwalk in the winter sun. "This 'health resort' is purgatory," he complained to Eleanor on February 21, as the press reported the appointment of a new Secretary of War. Defying logic, Newton D. Baker, the mild mayor of Cleveland, despite accepting his militant new title, was a spokesman for the League to Enforce Peace. To Baker, war was "an anachronism . . . from the barbaric past."

While Acting Secretary earlier, Franklin had exploited news of the torpedoing, without warning, of the British liner *Arabic*, sailing for New York, in which two Americans were among the forty-four dead, to see Secretary of State Lansing and press Wilson for a strong protest to Germany. The President determined to wait for more facts, Franklin explained to Eleanor. "But it seems very hard to wait until Germany tells us her version and I personally doubt if I should be quite so polite." Since then, there had been further sinkings, but American casualties remained few, and the German high command felt complacently that its government's response had been "dignified and clever."

Eleanor called the continued attacks "an outrage." So did Sara, who chastised Franklin, "I feel as TR feels, in fact, a good deal." While again Acting Secretary, FDR crossed Executive Avenue to the White House to propose a Council of National Defense to coordinate sluggish industrial mobilization, but with his reelection doubtful, Wilson was not ready. He had only won the presidency in 1912 because of a divided Republican party. "It seems that I can accomplish little just now," Franklin told Eleanor, "as the President does not want to 'rattle the sword' while Germany seems anxious to meet us more than half way, but he was interested and will I think really take it up soon." Cynically, however, Germany considered Wilson's protests as signaling no change in policy, and exploited its ambiguous "half way" responses to slow American readiness.

Despite its submarine successes, in the first months of 1916, Germany was gaining moral ground across the Atlantic, where a politically active Irish urban population bolstered the Democratic Party. Chronic unrest in Ireland, long under the British boot, was about to culminate in a popular rising. Bloody suppression of the Easter Rebellion in Dublin in April, and arrest and execution of Irish nationalists, created more appalling headlines in the American press than German U-boat depredations. Laboring to identify Britain with peace, Foreign Secretary Sir Edward Grey proposed a League of Nations to enforce "rules of warfare on land and sea," but President Wilson in his neutrality mode opposed a mass meeting in Washington on May 27 of a lobbying organization, the League to Enforce Peace. FDR, nevertheless, was among the two thousand at the New Willard Hotel to hear Uncle Ted's ally, Senator Lodge, declare that the "limit of voluntary arbitration" had been breached, and that governments had to "put force behind international peace."

Wilson then found it politic to change course, and declared that the United States was "willing to become a partner in any feasible association of nations." Since the President now accepted an enforcement policy, Lodge would soon find reason to change his mind. Anything Wilsonian became, quickly, objectionable. The explanation for the Republican reversal would appear in print via Theodore Roosevelt's article for *Metropolitan*

Magazine, written later in the year for the January 1917 issue. TR opposed any participation with other nations that could dilute American sovereignty. George Washington, he claimed, had warned of "entangling alliances"* and James Monroe, whose "doctrine" seemed to have the force of law, claimed American hegemony in the Western Hemisphere. The utopian concept of association for peace had become a political plaything.

PEACE WAS NOT in the minds of the Navy's General Board, its planning arm, when it presented a reluctant Wilson, through Daniels, with a massive bill for warship construction, certain to be denounced by Bryanites as a gift to the steel trusts. Armed neutrality magnified, the draft recommended building 156 ships at a cost of $500 million, perhaps a twentieth of its twenty-first century equivalent. The proposal included funds for ten battleships, six battle cruisers, fifty destroyers, and sixty-seven submarines. As Wilson's reelection politicking approached, he took his new preparedness case to the people with studied caution, describing the Brobdingnagian naval program as entirely defensive. "The world is on fire," he said, "and there is tinder everywhere." It had become "absolutely necessary that this country should prepare herself, not for war, not for anything that smacks in the least of aggression, but for adequate national defense." From New York to St. Louis and Kansas City, he argued from the rear platform of his campaign train, "Have you ever let your imagination dwell upon the enormous stretch of coast from the Canal to Alaska—from the Canal to the northern coast of Maine? There is no other navy in the world that has to cover so great an area of defense as the American navy, and it ought, in my judgment, to be incomparably the greatest navy in the world."

The Naval Affairs Committee in the House, dominated by Majority Leader Claude Kitchin, a tight-fisted North Carolinian, whittled the appropriation down. The Navy will rush for bids, Kitchin charged in Bryan mode, "not that the country is in any danger of a foreign foe, but that the shipbuilders and munition-makers will be in danger of losing their high

---

* Actually it was Thomas Jefferson, at his first inaugural in 1801, but it has long been attributed erroneously to Washington's "Farewell Address."

war prices if the Secretary should delay until the end of the European War gets in sight."

News from across the Atlantic had suggested urgency for even the most unrealistic aspects of the bill. Admiral Alfred von Tirpitz, creator of the German High Seas Fleet, had resigned in March after failing to effect a restoration of unrestricted submarine warfare. The regime worried that it might prompt American intervention. In a parallel decision, Ferdinand, Count von Zeppelin, father of the German airship fleet, when asked why the London docks were not bombed, whatever the hazards, confided that Supreme Headquarters had argued against such strikes "because neutral ships, perhaps even American ships, would be destroyed." It was crucial to keep the United States out of the war as long as possible, to wreck the economies, and support for the armies, of France and Britain.

In parallel came what seemed to be a great German success at sea. Although readers of newspapers across the *Reich* on June 3, 1915, celebrated a hard-fought victory with flags and banners, the reality was a costly standoff. Four days earlier, off Jutland in the North Sea west of Denmark, in the greatest naval encounter of the war, both the Grand Fleet and the *Kriegsflotte* had suffered crippling casualties. The Admiralty lost fifteen ships and 6,094 men, and the Germans eleven ships and 2,551 men— despite the numbers, mutual destruction rather than one-sided success. Afterward the *Kriegsflotte* seldom ventured out, and most of its assaults at sea would be conducted by submarines. Censorship on both sides kept the massive losses in the Skagerrak dimly known, yet Congress got the message. Battle fleets had engaged in battle.

As the Naval Appropriations Act was being debated, and what was known of Jutland absorbed, a symbolic achievement in naval upgrading made American newspapers. On June 19, the battleship *Arizona*, its keel laid the year before by FDR, was launched at the Brooklyn Navy Yard. At eleven that morning, powerful hammers began knocking loose the giant supports holding back the hull. The booming keyed up the crowd, which included Daniels and Roosevelt, Admirals Fletcher and Mayo, and General Wood. In sunny weather and in high tide at one in the afternoon, seventy thousand spectators applauded as the *Arizona* slid down the ways to join the new *Pennsylvania*. But both had much further pre-commissioning work to be done. Battleships were slow to make ready, and, although not apparent to the admirals, were already floating anachronisms at the peak of their firepower.

Two months later, on August 29, 1916, Wilson would sign the Navy appropriation bill. Lobbying reluctant legislators had not been "cheerful work," Franklin noted. He wrote to Eleanor that he was trying "to eliminate a number of fool features in it." To assure the support of one senator, he agreed to spend a "dreary" weekend with Colonel Henry A. du Pont,* father of FDR's Harvard classmate, Harry, at his vast Winterthur estate in upper Delaware. In his late seventies, the senator was a West Pointer who had earned a Medal of Honor in the Civil War. Although they were not alone—Mrs. William du Pont, a "charming widow," arrived in her auto to take them to lunch with the Russian naval attaché and his wife— Franklin endured two lengthy walks, before and after, in the spry senator's beloved and seemingly endless gardens. After the second stroll, Franklin wrote wearily to Eleanor, "I begin to feel much the same age."

Earlier, in mid-June, Franklin, with Nigel Law, had embarked from New York City at dawn on Torpedo Boat No. 59, en route to the Hyde Park wedding of Ruth Wales, niece of Elihu Root, to Harry du Pont. FDR, Law recalled, "took charge and we proceeded up the Hudson at such speed that our wash nearly sank some barges moored to the bank." On Flag Day, June 14, Franklin was back in Washington. He was one of the prominent dignitaries in a Preparedness parade in Washington—prominent because most Democrats of higher rank were attending their national convention in St. Louis, a formality to renominate President Wilson. Roosevelt's role would be to campaign for Wilson as proponent of "a Navy second to none."

Suspicious of Wilson's intentions, as he campaigned with the party slogan, "He kept us out of war," Theodore Roosevelt, on the political trail, denounced the President's "incapable leadership." Americans, he charged, had become, under Wilson, "sordid, soft, and spineless." Nell Wilson remembered her father's reaction. "Father did not deny Roosevelt's popular-

---

*Now usually spelled DuPont.

FDR boarding a warship on an inspection visit, 1916. FDR Library

ity and influence, but he said, 'Are people interested in personalities rather than in principles? If that is true, they will not vote for me.'"

Congress was usually efficient at obstruction. The projected five-year shipbuilding program as passed was pared by a joint committee to three years. Yet given the bureaucratic minutiae of bidding and contracting for every screw and bolt, and inevitable shortages and delays, it was questionable that all the ships authorized would ever reach salt water. Many ships were not even necessary, except to create jobs and promote votes. Bids from private firms would often be so steep that the Department turned over much of the work to its own yards, even creating new ones. TR charged in an entirely partisan fiction, blaming Daniels, that "the dominant idea in the Navy is to get possession of and break down all private yards, not with a view to preparation [for war] but in order to advance on the road to socialism." The former president knew that there were not enough private, and reliable, facilities for the Navy's needs.

On Hog Island, on the Delaware River below Philadelphia, the Navy would contract for a huge shipyard—overseeing yards was one of FDR's primary roles in the Department—to be built on marshland where pigs once roamed. Landfill now connected the island to the riverbank. The labor force gradually expanded to 34,000 to construct fifty standardized cargo ships. Many months passed before the first freighter was fitted out. Almost too late to be useful, the *Quistconck* was christened on August 5, 1918, by Edith Galt Wilson.* Preparedness had depended upon politics. Mobilization plans became mammoth, but realization remained agonizingly slow.

While Daniels was again away, Franklin announced the establishment of a Naval Reserve to enlist fifty thousand men, and the formation of small regional squadrons of private power boats for coastal defense—in reality, a submarine patrol. Exploiting the example of Leonard Wood's preparedness camps, he also began planning what he would describe in an article in *The Outlook* (June 28, 1916) as "The Naval Plattsburg." "I trust J.D. will like it!" he wrote to Eleanor at Campobello. "It is of the utmost importance and I have failed for a year to get him to take any action, though he has never objected to it. I suppose the bullet may bounce back on me, but it is . . . not alarmist and is just common sense." On returning from vacation Daniels accepted the seagoing training venture for civilian enthusiasts, but added a word of caution. Since the Plattsburg encampment largely recruited future officers from well-to-do backgrounds, he warned FDR that the seagoing program should not be limited to Harvard and Yale alumni, society types and well-to-do yachtsmen.

The Secretary's suspicions were justified. Franklin already had Livingston Davis and like-minded friends recruiting potential candidates and offering their pleasure craft for armed patrols—an apparently amateurish concept at which senior naval officers bridled. To the pragmatic Roosevelt, boats that existed, and their experienced handlers, were better than bottoms in theory, and their nonexistent officers—hostages to votes

---

*Eventually, most too late for the war, 122 "Hog Islanders" were launched. The site is now part of Philadelphia International Airport.

in Congress. He enlisted his millionaire (and lifelong) friend Vincent Astor, still in his middle twenties, and the even wealthier J. P. Morgan among those who promised to donate their yachts in time of war. Defending his proposal in the article he was writing for *The Outlook*, he suggested that war at sea comprised "two fairly distinct fields of action"—the "great fighting aggregation" of the battle fleet and the "secondary defense" of shore patrols by reservists trained in "naval discipline and naval requirements." He saw "no reason . . . why a graduate of the Naval Academy should be taken away from more important duties to be placed in command of a patrol-boat along the coast."

Yachtsmen proved to be only a minority of the applicants for the twenty-five-day civilian training regimen, which, Franklin wrote to Howe, then on seaside vacation, had been "baptized" by the public relations-minded Daniels as the "John Paul Jones Cruise." Nineteen hundred applicants would participate during the summer of 1916, trained in navigation, gunnery and seamanship. A year later, most would be awarded wartime commissions.

The Roosevelt family was at Campobello while Franklin, but for a weeklong visit late in July, remained at work in Washington, anxious that the children stay away until a polio epidemic in the Northeast, with at least seven thousand deaths already reported, subsided. While on the island briefly he spent hours swatting at flies, believed then to be carriers of the disease. "*Please* kill all the flies I left," he wrote to Eleanor on his return. "I think it is really important." Anxious about contagion, he did not want the family to travel by rail to Hyde Park, and he tried to cadge the *Dolphin*, but Daniels, ever the politician, was concerned, with early elections as usual in Maine, that Republicans might make private use of a government vessel a campaign issue. "He is scared blue," Franklin wrote "Babs" on August 18. "and *Dolphin* won't be allowed within 1000 miles of Maine till after September 11." Although it seemed politic, at first, for Daniels to offer Representative Lemuel P. Padgett of Tennessee, Chairman of the House Naval Affairs Committee, the *Dolphin* for a few days that August, the Secretary soon had second thoughts. Padgett mustered votes in Congress, but Daniels worried about criticism at the ballot box. The *Dolphin* remained in port.

Franklin's letters to "Campo" often concluded with his litany of affection and details of a crowded schedule that kept him in Washington or on official travel. "Kiss the chicks and take very good care of yourself, dearest," he wrote on July 10. "I so long to be with you and this bachelor life isn't what it's cracked up to be even though I dine with . . . "—and he listed lunch and dinner engagements, golfing dates, and sailing weekends. On occasion he mentioned Miss Mercer, described cautiously as accompanying Nigel Law. In cooler weather when back in Washington, Eleanor would accompany Franklin to dinner parties, but found herself bored as always by social and political talk, uninterested in drinking at the level of most others, and eager to return to the "chicks." Her catty cousin Alice Roosevelt Longworth, describing Eleanor's finding "so little amusement" and "being so insecure about so many things," remembered

an evening once when Eleanor had returned early from a party, leaving Franklin to enjoy himself alone. After she had been dropped off [by taxi] at her house, she found she hadn't got her key with her. So what did she do? Raise the servants? No, she lay down on the mat in the vestibule so that when Franklin came back in the small hours of the morning, all flushed with wine and good cheer, he was greeted by this wan apparition, looking like a string bean that had been raised in a cellar. "Why didn't you phone someone for help?" asked Franklin. "I've always understood one should try and be considerate of other people," she replied. . . . She could be quite maddening that way and she always seemed to manage to hold Franklin back from having a good time.

In September, Maine as usual went Republican, and Franklin was again at Campobello (by rail and post boat) on October 1 when, in "tick* and dirty weather," the *Dolphin*, to the delight of the children, arrived to fetch them, steaming down the Atlantic coast and up the Hudson to Hyde Park. The family, minus Franklin, remained until mid-November, when anxieties about polio had passed.

---

* "tick": nautically unpleasant

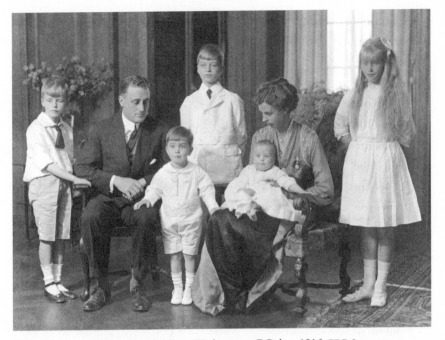

FDR, Eleanor, and their five children, Washington, DC, late 1916. FDR LIBRARY

During election week in early November, with his political future at stake, he experienced what he described as "the most extraordinary day of my life." Bookmakers had been laying odds of ten to six in favor of Charles Evans Hughes, who had resigned from the Supreme Court to run against Wilson. Despite being characterized as "the bearded lady" for his luxuriant whiskers and flaccid campaign style, Hughes charged that the Democratic administration was dangerously slow on preparedness, pointing to the Navy's attempts under Daniels to train illiterate seamen in spelling as well as in shelling. The Secretary had FDR note to the press that the "hollow shell" of a Navy inherited in 1913 from the Republicans was becoming "an organization that now would not break down in case of war." It was using its appropriations "wisely and honestly," and needed "boosting and not knocking."

Busy boosting Wilson, however, Franklin's enthusiasm for the reviving service led him to knock Uncle Ted's allegedly undermanned navy, inherited from Taft by the Democrats. TR, the Assistant Secretary claimed, had sent his "Great White Fleet" abroad in 1907 with sixteen battleships for which crews had to be found by "strip[ping] many other vessels of their officers." The fleet had been a facade. Returning from a Caribbean cruise, the elder Roosevelt reprimanded his relative gently—that his own memory "was not in accord with the statement as you made it." TR claimed he had checked with ranking veterans of the voyage—and if the Navy had been depleted, it was not on his watch. Franklin contended that he was trying "to give only correct facts." Their cordial relations frayed but survived.

Franklin was often on his own as the campaign wound down. Wilson's austere, cerebral style needed the Secretary's compensatory folksy touch, prompting him often to be away speechmaking. To his activist delight, Franklin was Acting Secretary, happy not to be on the hustings. The weekly *Life* editorialized, "There probably never was a presidential election in this country in which so many voters voted for a man they didn't want. Thousands of votes were cast for Wilson not from any pleasure in Wilson but because the alternative was to vote for Hughes." Yet the dour Hughes seemed likely to secure enough states to go Republican, and reach the 266 electoral votes needed to win. Colonel Roosevelt might have stumped more vigorously for the ticket, but Republican regulars opposed his involvement and he had found excuses to absent himself. His apostasy in 1912 had elected Wilson. Even so, politician and editor Ludwig Stein in Berlin predicted gloomily that if Hughes won the White House, "He would make [Theodore] Roosevelt his war minister and declare war on us."

In Manhattan on the evening of Election Day, November 7, FDR was among the guests at a dinner in the Biltmore given, in a show of optimism, by the elder Henry Morgenthau, the gray-bearded former Wilson ambassador to Ottoman Turkey, now the Democratic National Committee finance chairman. As midnight neared and ticker-tape tallies kept revising the statistics, hope mingled with despair. Most eastern states had gone Republican. *The New York Times* had already conceded Wilson's defeat. Discounting the Pacific coast, three time zones distant and still to report, other newspapers also bannered Hughes's sweeping victory. Resignedly, Franklin boarded a Pullman to sleep his way back to the Capital.

No one seemed interested in work at the Department on Wednesday. The *Washington Star* continued to post the returns for crowds on the streets via lantern slides, which Eleanor and Franklin could see as becoming increasingly indecisive that evening when they went to dinner with Anne and Franklin Lane. (The amiable Lane hoped to be elevated from Interior to the Supreme Court if Wilson were reelected, as the Hughes seat was vacant, but he would be disappointed.*) Thursday's results added to the uncertainty. By early Friday, November 10, the remaining tallies from California had trickled in. Wilson was ahead by 3,806 votes, and its thirteen electoral votes made the difference. Forgetting "uncle" for the moment, Franklin would quip jubilantly that rumor had it that "a certain distinguished cousin of mine is now engaged in revising an edition of his most noted historical work, *The Winning of the West*."

In the post-election hiatus, confident now about his immediate future, the Assistant Secretary cajoled a winter holiday mission for himself from Daniels, who had weathered fierce campaign attacks and, loyal to Wilson, showed no signs of retiring. For Franklin it was a respite from covertly ramping up preparedness, and he would be doing what Vice President John Garner would advise him in the early 1930s after a flurry of activity, "You know you have to let the cattle graze." As Marines were in occupation in Haiti and Santo Domingo, Roosevelt lobbied for an inspection tour. Haiti remained chaotic, while disorder on the Dominican side was less dramatic; yet both parts of the island of Hispaniola, which FDR called "the Darkest Africa of the West Indies," were effectively American protectorates. Franklin argued that further instability might be an excuse for warring European powers to intervene.

As he assembled his touring party ("inspection" would have exaggerated its intent), Franklin on New Year's Day 1917 addressed a letter with an enclosure to President Wilson. In FDR's historical collections—he seemed to collect everything—was a memorandum written by James

---

*To the surprise of many, Wilson would appoint Louis Brandeis of Massachusetts, who would weather a storm of pre-confirmation attacks in the Senate as a radical and as a Jew.

Monroe when in the Cabinet of James Madison in 1814. "A war in Europe, to which Great Britain with her floating thunder, and other maritime powers, are always parties," the Secretary of State wrote, "has long been found to spread its calamities into the remotest regions." Obviously intended to promote preparedness in an earlier day, the manuscript could not be misunderstood. Wilson replied on January 3 that it was a "most generous" gift. "It is unusually interesting and I shall value it highly." Yet on January 16, with FDR away, Ambassador Cecil Spring-Rice informed the British Foreign Office that a "high official" told him that "neither President nor Secretary of the Navy would consent to any naval agreement with the Allies in anticipation of joint defensive measures." Wilson and Daniels intended to risk limited readiness for inevitable war as long as they could. The Army would be even less prepared.

The commandant of Marines, Major General George Barnett, ostensibly headed the official party to Haiti. Roosevelt also brought along John H. McIlhenny, a golf partner and head of the Civil Service Commission; Livy Davis, a good-times friend bored with brokerage; and George Marvin of *The World's Work*. They sailed via Cuba, downing countless daiquiris in Havana; however, Franklin's official excuse for a stopover was to call on the corrupt Cuban president, Mario Garcia Menocal, recent victor in a fraudulent election, but to the Assistant Secretary, looking the other way, "distinctly the gentleman-business man." A few days after FDR left for Haiti an uprising nearly overthrew Menocal's regime. Wilson blamed German agents and sent in American troops, who would remain for five years. In a sense it validated Roosevelt's claims about the Caribbean, but he had no role in the colonialist intervention.

The destroyer *Wainwright* took FDR's party to the harbor of Port-au-Prince, where seventy-two ships, much of the Atlantic Fleet, were lined up in two rows, each saluting the Assistant Secretary as his warship passed. In formal dress despite the heat, the American entourage debarked, greeted at the pier by Haitians in cutaways and silk hats. Assuming they were his welcoming committee, Franklin bowed and delivered the speech he had prepared in halting French. Automobiles took them up the long pier, "where we were met by another delegation. This time it was the Mayor, and as I had but one speech, I redelivered it." Then the party was taken to the presidential palace, where in a sweltering red plush and gold drawing room they "met the President and the Cabinet, and I made the same speech for the third time."

Haiti, ostensibly independent, was run by a tough Marine major, Smedley Butler, only a year older than Franklin, who had braved fire in China during the Boxer Rebellion, where he earned a Medal of Honor, and later landed with occupation forces in the Philippines, Honduras, Santo Domingo, Nicaragua and Mexico. Butler had handpicked the current president, the tall, black Sure Dartiguenave. The delegation's pièce de résistance was a four-day horseback tour of the interior, accompanied by Major Butler, fifty Marines and one hundred and fifty Haitian gendarmes. FDR wore a Marine uniform and sat on a saddle made for him in London and shipped from Hyde Park. They forded rivers, climbed hills, slept in the open, and evaded fire from dissidents, all of which Franklin, decades later, embroidered, as he did the near-slavery by which Butler had roads constructed by press gangs. Seeing the wreckage of French-built Fort Rivière, where Butler had led an assault in 1915, FDR, suitably impressed, recommended him on return for a second Medal of Honor. When the continued brutality of Butler's gendarmerie provoked a rebellion in 1918, Roosevelt condoned—although Daniels did not—its even more brutal yearlong suppression on Wilson's order.

In a bitter postwar reversal after Butler was passed over as Marine commandant, he unhappily retired as a major general and described his colonialist former self as "a racketeer for capitalism," confessing that his troops in Haiti "hunted the *Cacos*"—the rebels—"like pigs." In 1934 he would claim to a Congressional committee that in an alleged "Business Plot" a group of wealthy industrialists (who denied everything) had approached him to lead a military coup to unseat Roosevelt, then President.

By destroyer the party continued on to Santo Domingo. On February 3, 1917, they were dining in the lush courtyard of Santiago de los Caballeros, the Spanish colonial house in which Marine colonel T. P. Kane resided with his wife. "My orderly," Franklin recalled, "brought me a code message just received over the field radio set. I went out to decode it." (He had to consult a marked pocket dictionary, copies of which both he and Daniels carried.) The message was "BECAUSE OF POLITICAL SITUATION PLEASE RETURN WASHINGTON AT ONCE. AM SENDING SHIP TO MEET YOU AND PARTY AT PUERTO PLATA TOMORROW MORNING."

Roosevelt was being recalled because of political considerations. He explained that vaguely to Mrs. Kane. "What can 'political considerations' mean?" she asked. "It must be that Charles E. Hughes has led a revolution against President Wilson."

"My dear lady," Franklin said, "you have been in the tropics too long."

Hoping to force the British into negotiations, on February 1, 1917, the Germans had openly returned to unrestricted submarine warfare. In Switzerland on Foreign Office business, Count Kessler shared concerns about the decision with Hans von Haeften, a confidant of General Erich von Ludendorff, who had become the de facto military dictator of Germany the previous August. "There was no other way of ending the war," Ludendorff had explained to von Haeften. "Otherwise it would become a long siege, and we could not survive that." The winter of 1916–1917 was already described in Germany as the "turnip winter." After the collapse of the fertilizer-deprived potato harvest, turnips had become the disheartening staple. "The Navy believes," *Graf* Kessler wrote in his diary, "that they can defeat England in four months; the Supreme Command reckons on six months. . . . If things don't work out this way, however, at least England would be brought down with us, and out of this deep abyss we would recover faster. . . . "

On February 3 a U-boat now cleared for action sank the American freighter *Housatonic*. Further American ships, and lives, were at immediate risk. In Washington, Ambassador von Bernstorff, who had protested the policy to Berlin, was politely handed his passports—a step just short of entirely breaking relations. The pro-TR magazine *Life* crowed, "Much obliged to Germany for once! Nobody else could have put us where we belong."

Franklin's party embarked for home aboard the slow collier *Neptune*, as unmilitary a vessel as sailed the seas. It was available. They approached Hampton Roads before dawn on February 8. "Late that afternoon," Franklin remembered, "we were back in Washington. I dashed to the Navy Department and found . . . no diplomatic relations with Germany broken off, no excitement, no preparations, no orders to the fleet at Guantanamo [Bay] to return to their home yards on the East Coast." Bernstorff's banishment to Berlin seemed to have closed the crisis.

Dissatisfied, Franklin wrote an article for *The World's Work*, possibly, given all the statistics included, with an assist from Howe: "How Can I Serve My Country?" It began, "What can I do in case of war?" That was a commonly asked question, he contended, from February 1st on: "Well, what would you do?" The orientation piece was obviously intended for male readers, and referred to German submarine attacks and the inevitability of war. Preparedness, FDR advised, began for men of military age with getting into, or maintaining, good health. Service, he noted, was not only uniformed. "Ten months will turn almost any healthy, sound man into a soldier, but three times ten months won't evolve a skilled rifle maker out of a farm hand or a dry goods clerk." He went on to describe in detail, almost sufficing as a handbook, opportunities in the Reserves, promoting among them his own "Naval Plattsburg." And he closed with an unveiled swipe at the sluggish leadership he represented. "The whole question of how a man can best serve the United States in a war is difficult to answer, because the Government has made no comprehensive plan for the utilization of the country's various kinds of abilities." He had been pushing preparedness since accepting office, but given the stubborn isolationist mood, especially in middle America, Wilson had been sensitive to accusations of shifting away from neutrality—a charge which a high German official in Berlin had inadvertently helped reverse.

Attempting to keep American interests close to home, the German foreign minister, Arthur Zimmermann, had, in January, 1917, secretly— so he thought—promised to the Mexican government, in exchange for a diversionary border war against the United States, restoration which he could not realistically effect of territories lost in the 1840s, from Texas westward. British intelligence ("Room 40") intercepted the message, delivered it via the American envoy in London to Wilson in February, and made it public.

Without referring to the outrage over the provocative "Zimmermann Telegram," although recognizing the return of unrestricted submarine warfare, Franklin prepared still another article to spur anti-German feeling, this time for *Scribner's Magazine*. "On Your Own Heads" took its title from a line in a Rudyard Kipling poem, "The Islanders," about giving up prewar delusions. "Do we wait for the spattered shrapnel," Kipling—a TR favorite—asked, "ere ye learn how a gun is laid?" FDR had been trying, he wrote in *Scribner's*, "to put my finger on . . . the causes of the Great Inertia." He saw widespread geographical ignorance resulting in "smug satisfaction" about the supposedly "impregnable" barriers of the Atlantic and Pacific Oceans"—an illusory "comfort" zone for Americans. That was living a "lie."

As war neared, Roosevelt's charge that Americans were not immunized from the outside world (the point of the Monroe document he gave to Wilson) would be confirmed. Further, he warned, although he knew it was already too late, "If some seer could assure us that in case of a great war we should have a year or so to prepare for it, we could continue on our happy-go-lucky course. That has not been the history of the way wars commence."

Unwilling to prepare for war, Wilson was eager to broker the peace, and conceded to a delegation at the White House from the Emergency Peace Federation that on behalf of a neutral nation he would be a powerless outsider. He would only be able to "call through a crack in the door." For the world-betterer that he grandly saw in his mirror, that was hardly enough, but to crack open the door meant participating in the war. He seemed to imagine himself as a *deus ex machina* figure entering at the last moment in the ongoing Greek tragedy.

Preparing to arm merchant ships, as "an intolerable situation is beginning to arise," FDR on February 10, newly back from Haiti, proposed to Daniels that under existing law "guns may be *loaned* provided a suitable bond be given. . . . I would suggest that we can properly loan these guns with their mounts and ammunition. . . . I believe it points a way out of the difficulty of asking the authority of Congress." He began, deviously, to explore extralegal contractual means to do so, saying extravagantly, in a

March 1919 interview, that he and Departmental activists had, between February 6 and March 4, 1917, "committed acts for which we could be, and may yet be sent to jail for 999 years." Possibly Roosevelt recalled his scheme twenty-four years later when effecting his "Lend-Lease" program to supply embattled Britain as war again loomed for the United States.

Although the Administration was in a delicate preparedness pause as it awaited Wilson's second inauguration on March 5, 1917—March 4 was a Sunday, and inappropriate—sinkings had continued and the Department finally—and quietly—began arming merchant ships. It was not what Wilson wanted, but under pressure from Daniels after long goading by Roosevelt, the President would request such authority. Wilson had told Congress in January that his goal as a neutral was "a peace without victory," and not "a balance of power" to follow but "a community of power." Neutrals lacked clout, and both warring sides had spurned his unrealism.

Franklin crossed Executive Avenue to the White House to ask for permission to bring the fleet back from Cuba to be readied for inevitable hostilities. TR had written, privately, about Wilson's apparent timidity, "As for shame, he has none." Franklin found Wilson still reluctant to approve any preliminary action. "I am going to tell you something I cannot tell the public," he recalled the President as saying. "I owe you an explanation. I don't want to do anything in a military way. . . . I want history to show not only that we have tried every diplomatic means to keep out of the war, to show that war has been forced upon us deliberately by Germany, but also that we have come into the court of history with clean hands." He wanted no allegations of "an unfriendly act against the Central Powers."

As preparedness advocates, liberally quoted in the press, could not force Wilson out, they clamored for the ousting of Daniels. The *Chicago Post* editorialized that the Secretary's "virile-minded, hardheaded civilian assistant" should take his place, noting that his name, "uncuriously enough, is Roosevelt." Impatient as Franklin was for action, he knew that Wilson was stalling until Inauguration Day, and the further coalescing of public opinion toward war. When the day came, grey and blustery, Wilson and his new wife, Edith, rode down Pennsylvania Avenue to the Capitol in a carriage almost unseen within columns of cavalry, Navy units and mounted police, and he spoke from behind a wind screen. "Too far away to hear address," Franklin wrote. "Little enthusiasm in crowd. . . . Awful mistake to review troops from glass cage."

At six he had an appointment with Edwin House. While a crowd watched a fireworks display, FDR slipped across the street from his office to meet with the honorary colonel on "the condition of the Navy," noting in a seldom-kept diary that he "opposed strongly sending fleet through the Canal [to the Pacific] in event of war. Looks like running away. Bad for morale of fleet and country and too far to bring home if Canal [were] blocked or German submarines [were] in Caribbean." That might have been Wilson's intent, but Daniels wanted to bring the Atlantic fleet into Chesapeake Bay.

Anticipating the mobilization that the President still refused to order, Franklin went to Boston and New York to check on readiness at the Charlestown and Brooklyn navy yards, and on "plans and enrollment of boats and men for reserve." Frustrated by inaction, he wrote in a rare diary entry on March 9, a Friday, "White House statement that W has power to arm & *inference* that he will use it. J.D. says that he will use it by Monday. Why doesn't President say so without equivocation[?]." At Colonel House's residence in Manhattan on Sunday, March 11, however disloyal to Daniels, FDR prodded Wilson indirectly:

> Outlined principal weaknesses of Navy—J.D.'s procrastination—[Admiral] Benson's dislike of England—failure to make plans with France and England and study their methods—necessity if war comes of going into it with all force—money, troops, etc. He was sympathetic and agreed to main point.

"Had call from F.D.R. in New York," Daniels noted in his diary that busy Sunday, "and asked him to see newspapermen about [not] publishing news of sailings—to get their advice." It was easy for U-boats to be radioed when surfaced about ships embarking to become potential targets. "Also to see Usher about fixing merchant ships with guns." Rear Admiral

Nathaniel R. Usher was commandant of the New York Navy Yard. Clearly, events—or Roosevelt's pressure—were finally having some impact.

Later that Sunday, Franklin attended a dinner at the Metropolitan Club with his acerbic Uncle Ted, Leonard Wood, Elihu Root, J. P. Morgan, Mayor John Purroy Mitchel and Governor Walter Edge of New Jersey—all opposed to Wilson's foot-dragging. Franklin's diary noted the discussion about making Wilson "steer [a] clear course" and "how to get action [to] increase Army and Navy." Colonel Roosevelt, he added, "wanted more vigorous demand about future course—less endorsement of past. I backed T.R.'s theory."

Echoing his chief's exasperation with the sluggish preparedness that had left the nation unready, Louis Howe, a theater buff involved with the Drama League Players, put the message, implicitly, on the boards. He became stage manager for Bernard Shaw's one-act satire about incompetent home-front bureaucracy, *Augustus Does His Bit*. Almost as if written for him, Howe was Colonel the Lord Augustus Highcastle's slovenly clerk, Horatio Beamish. The production at Poli's Theater was its American premiere. "This country is going to the dogs, if you ask me," says the overage Beamish. "I will not allow you to say such things in my presence," Lord Highcastle expostulates. "Our statesmen are the greatest known to history. Our generals are invincible. Our army is the admiration of the world. How dare you tell me that this country is going to the dogs!"

Again in Washington, with Congressional sanction still lacking, Roosevelt discussed with Daniels and Benson instructions for gun crews who would be placed on merchant ships. On Inauguration Day an anti-interventionist bloc of senators led by Robert M. LaFollette of Wisconsin and James Aloysius O'Gorman of New York, long unfriendly to Franklin, had filibustered the arming bill to death. However ambivalent, and calling the doves a "little group of willful men," Wilson signed an executive order on March 12, permitting what he had long resisted. Still stubbornly pacifist, Daniels, in his diary, deplored, "I felt I might be signing what would be the death warrant of young Americans and the arming of ships may bring us into war." On March 15, four days later, the despotic and incompetent regime of Czar Nicholas of Russia, failing in its war with Germany, was

overthrown and replaced by an unstable coalition in which the most influential leader was the moderate socialist Alexander Kerensky. For Wilson
the event seemed "glorious." No longer did the Allies include an abso-
lutism he despised. Still, the President remained reluctant to go "the final
step." On March 18 three American freighters were torpedoed. Two days
later, Theodore Roosevelt declared to the press that there was no longer
any question about going to war, as Germany was "already at war with us."
Would we make war "nobly or ignobly"?

Although on March 20 Daniels recorded the President as confiding in
his stubborn, supposedly even-handed, neutrality mode that he "opposed
German militarism on land and England's militarism on sea," Wilson
called his Cabinet into session, asking unhappily for their opinions. He
saw the Eastern, mostly Republican, establishment as indignant and eager for war but the rest of the country as "apathetic." Eight of the ten
spoke out for war. "Burleson," said the President, "you and Daniels have
not spoken." Albert Burleson, the Postmaster General, echoing TR, observed that the nation was already at war. If not, popular will would
"force action." Unlike FDR, when in the White House in 1941, however
menacing Germany was in the Atlantic, and elsewhere, Wilson would
not wage defensive war before Congress declared it.

"I don't care for popular demand," Wilson insisted. "I want to do right
whether popular or not." Then he turned to the Navy Secretary with
"Well, Daniels?"

Agonized, Daniels gave in. "Having tried patience," he said, "there
was no course open to us except to protect our rights on the seas." If,
without American intervention,, Germany won, he now felt, the United
States would have to become what he most feared—"a military nation."
He had resisted until then, he wrote later, "every influence that was at
work to carry the United States into the war." And those influences included his deputy, FDR.

Prominent among the militarists were Wilson's leading political ene-
mies among the "outs," who gathered in the club's grill room at New York's
Union League to hear belligerent speeches from Elihu Root, Charles Evans
Hughes and Theodore Roosevelt, who—banking on increasing public dis-

affection with the Democrats—was considering making another run for the presidency in 1920. The Colonel spoke of leading a division of volunteers to the front lines, if Wilson permitted a role for him. If he made it to the front, he said, he did not expect to return and would be buried in France. "Do you really mean that?" asked Root. Yes, he did, said Roosevelt. "Theodore," Root quipped, "if you can convince Wilson of that I am sure he will give you a commission."

Late in the afternoon on March 27, Colonel House arrived from New York to see Wilson and discuss the inevitable declaration of war. Wilson, he said with unusual realism, was "not well fitted" to be a war president. He was "too refined, too civilized, too intellectual." House argued that the pacifist military secretaries, Baker and Daniels, should be replaced as unsuited for war, and Lansing at State was "unsatisfactory"—Bryan's successor "was good for a second place but unfitted for the first." Wilson listened without responding. Removing key appointees would be an implicit confession of his own misjudgment. He would go to war with them.

With war now certain, the Navy had to send, as its ambassador to London had urged, a senior officer to liaison with the British navy. Rear Admiral William B. Sims, president of the War College and a Canadian by birth, was tapped. He was to leave quietly on a merchant liner in civilian clothes. Although once a TR favorite, and tactless and rigid, he had close connections to the Admiralty. The next step for Wilson was to convene Congress on April 2 for a war message.

From their new and more roomy residence at 2131 R Street, replacing the rental from Auntie Bye, Franklin and Eleanor left for Capitol Hill. The four-story tree-shaded townhouse, between Sheridan and Dupont Circles, was close to other invitees—senators, presidential appointees, and even Wilson's predecessor, William Howard Taft. Many, including the diplomatic corps, would arrive in full evening dress. At 8:30 in the evening, with a spring rain failing to scatter curious crowds, including die-hard pacifists kept remote and under surveillance by District police, Wilson spoke to a joint session of Congress. Neither gesturing to, nor glancing at, his audience, he read stolidly from his typescript. The Germans, he charged, had violated "all scruples of humanity." The nation "will not choose the path of submission. . . . The world must be made safe for democracy." He asked for a national draft for military service of a million men and "the immediate full equipment of the navy in all respects."

Returning home through the throngs, Franklin prepared a statement he hoped the press would print about the President's "high purpose." More significantly he took Wilson's call for "full equipment" for the Navy as implicit backing for the Rooseveltian shoreline flotilla of fifty-foot submarine-patrol boats as well as more formidable 110-foot sub chasers. Daniels and the admirals scorned fifty-foot motorcraft as "junk" only fit for "smooth water."* Yet as early as January 16, British ambassador Spring-Rice, through his naval attaché, anticipating joint defensive measures, suggested such sub patrols, certainly something about which Roosevelt was aware. Now he sent a memorandum to the Secretary that he was "entirely dissatisfied" with Department negativism and that as a small craft sailor he knew their value. That he was charmed by Arthur Patch Homer, a shady, glad-handing lobbyist for Sterling Motors of Boston, whose engines would power the 50-footers, is unquestionable. (Later, at Navy expense, Roosevelt would send him twice to Europe to inquire about aircraft engines.) On April 6, Daniels would give in, reluctantly. "Contrary to my belief in their worth I told F.D.R. to go ahead and buy a number." Many years later Roosevelt would finally repudiate the devious Homer.

The patrol boat controversy was ongoing as Congress debated the war resolution. Before dawn on April 6, Good Friday, after a hundred Representatives had spoken, the tally at 3:12 AM was 373–50. Congressman Kitchin voted *no*, as did the only woman in the House, Jeannette Rankin of Montana. (Again in Congress in 1941, she was the only *no* vote after Pearl Harbor that December.) With the Senate in concurrence, the United States was formally at war.

---

*Nevertheless, because of the shortage of patrol craft, Daniels had ordered his own *Dolphin* that very day to the Caribbean to take possession of the Virgin Islands, newly purchased from Denmark. The *Dolphin* would remain to patrol Caribbean waters and the Gulf of Mexico.

FDR at his desk, April 4, 1917, just after President Wilson delivered his war message to Congress. A map of Europe as it then was is behind him.
FDR LIBRARY

6

Limits of an Assistant Secretary

ALTHOUGH TOO YOUNG to remember the occasion on their own, and very likely assisted later by their mother, the two youngest Roosevelt children, Franklin, Jr., nearly three, and John, only one, were awakened on Monday evening, April 9, 1917, when a burly stranger with a broad mustache charged through the door of the fourth-floor nursery as Eleanor turned on the lights. "Boys," she said, "this is Uncle Theodore."

"I don't care what *anybody* says," the Colonel bellowed, pulling back their blankets, "You don't belong in bed yet." He tucked the boys, now wide-eyed, under each arm, and bumped down the stairs, shouting, "*These* two piggies are going to market!"

Awakened by the clamor along the hallway, James, now nine, came down on his own and watched his great-uncle pace back and forth in front of the fireplace, roaring something and waving his arms. Eleanor poured coffee for Uncle Ted while Franklin watched in awe. He was the one for whom the Colonel, now without clout, had really come. The nation was finally at war, and TR wanted to be in the midst of the action. With Easter weekend over, during which he had written a piece for *Metropolitan Magazine* praising the President's war message, perhaps the only time he had ever had a good word for Wilson, he was staying with the

Longworths on Massachusetts Avenue, near Dupont Circle, and needed someone in office to press his case with the White House.

Although fifty-eight, overweight, intermittently ill from tropical diseases after adventures in Africa and the Amazon, and his left eye blind since 1904, the Colonel wanted to raise a division of volunteers and lead them to France while a military draft not yet adopted would be slowly gearing up. He also had a message directly for Franklin. "You must resign. You must go into uniform at once!"

For FDR the advice had romantic if not realistic appeal. It suggested the career trajectory that had carried Uncle Ted to the White House. Yet disconcerting drawbacks existed—a protective Mama Roosevelt, an increasingly difficult Eleanor, a brood of small children, and Franklin's awareness that he would be an unremarkable figure in a burgeoning military bureaucracy. The "Splendid Little War," despite its mostly concealed disorganization, had boomed TR in 1898. Donning a uniform now would not lead inevitably to nautical or front-line heroics with political promise. Yet Franklin would consider it—again and again and again.

The next morning, he left the Department corridor to speak with Secretary of War Baker, who made no promises but agreed to talk to the Colonel. Franklin then pursued Senator Claude Swanson of the Naval Affairs Committee (FDR's Secretary of the Navy in 1933). Swanson, who had Congressional clout, telephoned Daniels about interceding with the President. Without asking, Daniels understood who was responsible. TR had also gone ahead on his own. Learning of the Colonel's arrival in Washington, Wilson's secretary Joe Tumulty had telephoned to the Longworth residence to invite TR to the White House. It would be only an empty courtesy, but TR tried to cajole Tumulty by slapping him on the back and suggesting, "You get me across and I will put you on my staff. Tell Mrs. Tumulty I will not allow them to place you at any point of danger."

A crowd of newsmen waited for the Colonel's exit after a visit of nearly an hour with Wilson. With the war ongoing, and uncharacteristically humbling himself, TR had conceded to the President that their past differences were now "all dust in a windy street." He wanted a chance at "an early moment" to "make good" Wilson's war message by leading experienced volunteers to France. It would be a concrete gesture anticipating the vast numbers of recruits still to be drafted and then trained, a process which would take many months, very likely into the next year. TR offered to serve under the commander of any expeditionary force the President would select. "I am aware," he would concede to Secretary Baker, "that I have not had enough experience to lead a division myself."

All TR would tell reporters was that he had raised his request about recruiting volunteers, and that the President would come to a decision "in his own good time." Baker would furnish no encouragement, and on April 15 the Colonel learned from the Secretary of War that the Army's General Staff (probably leaned upon by Wilson) had denied the request on "purely military" grounds, considering TR's gesture only of "sentimental value." In effect he was a former amateur warrior of limited experience from a minor conflict now antique.

The President soon telegraphed TR to explain lamely "that my conclusions were based entirely upon imperative considerations of public policy and not upon personal or private choice." Privately—and meanly—he confided to an aide, "I really think that the best way to treat Mr. Roosevelt is to take no notice of him. That breaks his heart and is the best punishment that can be administered." Yet a token overseas appointment, suggesting nonpartisan prosecution of the war, would have silenced domestic critics and been a tonic to the faltering English and French.

Wilson's belated mobilization would elevate unseasoned and often incompetent careerists to command a mushrooming conscript army and navy. That looming problem failed to concern administration planners. Neither did an amendment to the draft bill, with TR obviously in mind, empowering the President to create as many as four volunteer divisions outside conscription. The legislation, maneuvered by Henry Cabot Lodge, an obstinate Wilson enemy, but going forward under the name of an obscure senator from Ohio, Warren G. Harding, would not move the President. Nor would cabled appeals to Wilson from Marshal Joseph Joffre and Premier Georges Clemenceau. Stemming the flow of thousands of enlistment applications, the Colonel had to concede bitterly on May 21 that despite vast enthusiasm for his proposed volunteer division, he was left with no alternative but to "disband and abandon all further effort . . . thereby leaving each man free to get into military service in some other way, if that is possible." TR's four sons would enlist separately and serve honorably. The youngest, Quentin, would not return.

Wilson's alleged mastery in creating public support for intervention during more than two years of insistent unpreparedness falsifies the facts. Blindness to realities, reluctant leadership and sluggish mobilization would exact a heavy cost. Until war came, newspapers were full of shipping details—arrivals and departures—and in many cities with navy yards, a column, "Navy Yard News," had proudly reported the ins and outs of every warship until FDR under new powers ordered the unintended advice to German U-boats stopped. In a memorandum to Daniels that furnished an example of bureaucratic sloppiness, FDR charged, "Again I want to prophesy that we are going to fall down very sadly in the actual delivery of these [340 patrol] boats . . . ostensibly ordered. . . . Today is April 18th, nearly three months after the definite need became evident and, except in the case of one or two navy yards, practically not a timber that will go into their construction has been sawed." Although the desk admirals saw no practical use for small anti-sub craft, the Department would be embarrassed time and again by U-boat activity close to American shores, especially off the New Jersey, Delaware and Virginia coastlines, where mines laid by subs cut telegraphic cables and sunk small freighters and schooners well into 1918. When newspapers raised concern, and critics in Congress began echoing it, some shipping began to be convoyed.

Construction of larger vessels was also unhurried and bureaucratically delayed. Although marginally trained and effectively useless conscripts would be ferried to France by the hundreds of thousands before the close of 1917, most would sail in the former German liners long interned at Eastern piers. Under Vice Admiral Albert Greaves the Navy possessed only one barely seaworthy troop transport, with another nearly ready for commission. The Navy Department under Executive Order 2651 confiscated sixteen stranded enemy liners, including the huge *Vaterland*, now renamed *Leviathan* by order of President Wilson. In anticipation, their crews had disabled whatever machinery they could on February 1, when news of unrestricted submarine warfare made it certain that the ships would be seized. Including smaller freighters and fishing craft, eighty-seven German-flag vessels fell into American hands. The government also took over neutral liners, giving Gleaves forty-two transports in addition to his two, to be refitted over the months for taking conscripts yet to be inducted and trained across the Atlantic. Further, four times as much tonnage was required for equipment and supplies as for the soldiers themselves.

Delayed preparedness meant that production of almost every sort of weaponry had to be legislated, contracted for, and facilities constructed after formal declaration of war. American artillery, tanks and planes in action would largely be of French and British manufacture, although by war's end, vast arsenals of American war materiel would be piled up in French ports, still unavailable on the front lines. Officer ranks, especially the inexperienced and seniority-ridden (but well-connected) upper echelons, would earn early contempt from their blooded allies. More than a year would pass before American troops could be committed to battle.

From his subordinate position, FDR in word and deed had done his utmost, his audacity hobbled by politics and procrastination. Like TR he failed to secure a uniform. "Neither you nor I nor Franklin Roosevelt has the right to select the place of service . . . ," Wilson told Daniels. "Tell the young man . . . to stay where he is." However Franklin's brashness often grated upon the President and the Secretary, FDR had become an efficient executive with irreplaceable earned experience, while as a uniformed middling naval officer he would only be of symbolic value. No admirer of Wilson, General Leonard Wood, who would be kept from overseas assignment as an alleged "agitator and not amenable to discipline," speculated that Franklin's talked-of resignation would be "a public calamity." It would have been that—at least to Daniels, despite their differences in style and purpose. "Within the Department," he claimed, naming no names, "it was said that inasmuch as his cousin Theodore left the position of Assistant Secretary to become a Rough Rider, later Governor of New York and then [Vice] President, and both had served in the Legislature of New York, Franklin actually thought fighting in the war was that necessary step toward reaching the White House."

While other departments, with the war buildup accelerating, were adding assistant secretaries and other administrative echelons, often unnecessary except to feed the egos of upper executives, Daniels was content to keep FDR as his only titled civilian deputy. His effectiveness in procurement, abetted by Howe, was confirmed, Roosevelt claimed long after the war, when, that April, he was summoned to the White House and told by Wilson, as Brigadier General Hugh Scott, then the Army Chief of Staff, stood by, that FDR had "cornered the market for [military] supplies," and would have to "divide up with the Army." The Navy would have two public relations staffers, already aboard—John Wilber Jenkins, who had worked on Daniels's *News & Observer* in Raleigh, and Marvin McIntyre, a Tennessee newspaperman. (McIntrye would later be in Roosevelt's White House.)

As Franklin felt that he needed a senior naval assistant to operate where the openly aggrandizing Louis Howe could not, he wanted someone of flag rank who could go around Daniels's lackluster Chief of Naval Operations, Admiral Benson. Typical of his tunnel vision, Benson, wagging a finger, had warned Admiral Sims, when he was leaving for liaison in London, "Don't let the British pull the wool over your eyes. It's not our business, pulling their chestnuts out of the fire. We would as soon fight the British as the Germans." In his diary Daniels wrote about FDR's request, "Declined. Should not have a retired admiral for such service." Benson saw Roosevelt's proposal as aimed at him.

Eager to get close to the war, Franklin also wanted to head a consultative mission to London for which Daniels recommended a Wilson favorite, Admiral Henry Mayo. Sims was already there. The Assistant Secretary urged Daniels, "We would get nothing from the Naval officers. . . . Need a civilian commission." The Secretary refused. Roosevelt apparently leaned on a British newspaperman in Washington, Arthur Willert, who contacted Sir William Wiseman, head of the British intelligence mission in New York. In a message to Lord Balfour, Wiseman referred to Roosevelt as "the best man here . . . to arrange for effective joint policy. . . . Prompt action is necessary as President will make his decision next week." Balfour failed to respond. As Benson foresaw, but for far different reasons than his prejudices, Sims indeed had to battle the hide-bound British, much as Roosevelt was confronting lethargy in Washington. Wartime price rises were a conspicuous exception. Although Senator Lodge charged that "we cannot carry on a war against American business and against Germany at the same time," Daniels and Wilson were at one with FDR on resisting inevitable war profiteering. Examples were plentiful. Franklin would send a message on May 2, four weeks into the war, to the House Naval Affairs Committee that "when an emergency arose that required the purchase of vessels suitable for mine-sweeping," the Navy Department was forced to obtain thirty-four "at prices away beyond reason. Owners of most of the tugs and fishing-boats suitable for this work absolutely refused to consider either lease or purchase; others asked outrageous prices, . . . more than the cost of the vessel." He wanted authority to seize them at appraised value.

Franklin's messages, often feisty, were usually taken down by Renah H. Camalier as the Assistant Secretary, leaning back in his chair, examined sheet after sheet on his desk each morning. (The veteran Charles McCarthy had moved to the Emergency Fleet Corporation.) The heavy-set "Camy," sometimes called, affectionately, "Roly Poly," recalled his boss's "clear enunciation, perfect English and everything that goes with it." Often Roosevelt would pause, jaw thrust upward, to puff jauntily on a cigarette in the ubiquitous long holder that would later become his most recognizable visual prop.

Some messages must have amused Camalier. Daniels had recruited a reforming Sing Sing warden, Thomas Mott Osborne, to rehabilitate the Portsmouth Naval Prison. Osborne asked for an Army draftee with requisite experience for his staff. FDR wrote to Camp Upton at Yaphank on Long Island, a basic training site famed later for producing a soldier show featuring Sergeant Irving Berlin singing his "Oh! How I Hate to Get Up in the Morning."* Identifying the draftee Osborne wanted, Roosevelt explained disarmingly to the commanding general, "Here is a man whom

---

*Camp Upton during World War II became the site of the Brookhaven National Laboratory, a nuclear research facility.

you will probably shoot if he doesn't turn up at Yaphank this afternoon. On the other hand, as he is [now] in the Navy, we will shoot him if he does turn up at Yaphank. Please prevent this by leaving him in the Navy. He is web-footed." After about fifteen minutes of dictation, another assistant would enter and retrieve the notebook for typing, handing the stenographer a fresh one. Before Camalier exited, the first batch of letters was ready for signature, or for cable or telegraph dispatch.

Negotiating with London as to how much to allocate for transporting American troops to Europe while confiscated liners were being refitted, the Department rejected an arrogant demand for $150 per person (excluding food). Exacting profits for being rescued seemed outrageous to Daniels and Roosevelt. The two governments settled on $81.75, based on war risk loss—which would prove minimal. Early in July the first—only token—soldiers arrived in France, and on that news the long cracked Liberty Bell in Philadelphia was rung—in reality, merely tapped. The problem of troopships returning from France empty was partially solved by Hollywood. Agents for blossoming film studios began buying out, for eagerly accepted American dollars, the interiors of French chateaus and other properties, to acquire antique, or seemingly antique, mantels, sideboards, sofas, tables, chairs, bureaus and bedsteads of any style, any period, which then languished in warehouses, notably in Clichy, north of Montmartre, until packed by the carriage load for the port of Brest.

Arriving in England and discovering how catastrophic the losses of merchant ships to U-boats were—they averaged 600,000 tons a month— Admiral Sims found the Admiralty, nevertheless, stubbornly unwilling to employ convoy tactics. Merchant ships were too slow, the British argued; escort vessels could not keep them together. Further, detaching seventy-nine destroyers from empty duty guarding useless battleships holed up in port against attack by German *Kriegschiffen* unlikely to venture out seemed dangerous to deskbound, risk-averse admirals. Token drills, and dinners aboard, appeared preferable to sea duty hurling dynamite. Further, the Admiralty insisted on building useless additional capital ships rather than replacing lost freighters. Commerce protection was not nearly as important as the postwar maintenance of British imperial strategy.

The straitlaced U.S. Navy operated under similar astigmatism. The Naval Act of 1916, promoted by senior admirals, had authorized a huge program to construct expensive and unneeded battleships and battle cruisers. Finally, on July 20, 1917, American priorities would be revised, belatedly but realistically, in favor of building "tin can" destroyers. Bearing out FDR's prophecies, by war's end only 44 four stackers had come down the ways; 223 more destroyers were commissioned after the Armistice. Many rusted into the next war.

When, after Wilson's new militancy, British and French missions hurried to Washington, urgently seeking aid of every kind, FDR met with them and proposed the convoying solution he had already shared with Sims, who had reported Admiralty disinterest. As a courtesy, Roosevelt offered to meet the commissioners, with accompanying Department admirals, on their arrival in the Chesapeake at Old Point Comfort in Hampton Roads. "R wished to go down to meet them as [an] honor," Daniels noted in his diary on April 9. "I said no. He did not like it, but—" Daniels left the intemperate line unfinished.

Putting down his impetuous deputy was something the Secretary seemed to relish. It was pulling rank to keep Franklin in his place. Later in 1917, FDR proposed christening the plethora of new destroyers under construction with Indian names, as a link with history. "No," Daniels said. "Hold for heroes. We may lose many before this war ends." Then the unreconstructed Southerner named a new destroyer for a Confederate naval officer he admired, Matthew Maury.

On such token matters, the Secretary got his quirky way, yet on more substantive issues he often lost on their merits. Franklin was learning on the job that power did not necessarily derive from the ballot box, but from exploiting the sense in others, even political or bureaucratic superiors, of effectiveness in their interest. Without consulting Daniels or Wilson, Roosevelt offered to lend the Admiralty thirty destroyers to assist in convoying merchantmen—a precursor of the 1941 fifty-destroyers deal with Britain that he engineered months before the United States entered the next war. (On April 30, Daniels and Wilson met after the fact and, assuming that they were upstaging the Assistant Secretary, agreed "to send 36." With remarkable efficiency, all the destroyers arrived in England by May 16.) Shipping unescorted war materiel, FDR kept insisting, made no sense. Before long, London grudgingly accepted the convoy system, keeping desperately needed supplies, and the freighters carrying them, from the ocean bottom.

Since 1914 the British and French had maintained some warships in the Western Atlantic to inhibit the chances of interned German vessels from escaping, and for ineffective submarine searches. Now the Americans would take over the sub patrol mission, from Canada into South American waters, including the Caribbean and the Gulf of Mexico. The Navy would also "look after" the west coasts of North America from Canada to Columbia. "In pursuance of the policy of the United States adopted at this conference," the joint document noted, "the American Navy continued"—since the move had already begun—"to send destroyers, submarine chasers, yachts and other craft overseas until their number in Europe reached 373." That line in the agreement was an FDR triumph.

Roosevelt also faced resistance on both sides of the Atlantic to an ambitious plan to mine escape routes into the English Channel and from the North Sea by which German subs entered the Atlantic. He proposed the strategy of a "mine barrage" which he had picked up from his friend William Redfield, the mutton-chop-whiskered Commerce Secretary, to French and British delegations in Washington, which did not take it seriously. He had first taken it to Wilson in a prewar memorandum, "Prepared Measures to Close English Channel and North Sea against Submarines by Mine Barrage." In October 1916, the President, keeping to strict neutrality, answered in a cryptic note, "I am interesting myself in the matter." That shelved any prospect of carrying the mine barrage further, to future allies, but Franklin recalled, in a letter to Daniels in 1921, reviving the far-out idea during

the first week we were in the war[.] I had been studying a map of European waters, had measured the distances across the English Channel, across the North Sea from Scotland to Norway and across the Strait of

Otranto at the mouth of the Adriatic. I had examined the depths of the waters in those places, and had come to the conclusion that some kind of barrier, if it could be worked out on the technical side, offered the proper strategical solution of keeping German submarines out of the Atlantic and out of the Mediterranean.

He consulted officers in Operations and in Ordnance, and all were skeptical with the exception of Commander S. P. Fullenweider in Ordnance's Mine Section, who envisioned a deeper sea mine than currently in use. Alerted to the concept, a colonel in the Coast and Geodetic Survey and an admiral in Yards and Docks encouraged Roosevelt to follow up its feasibility.

At a Navy League dinner for the British Mission headed by former prime minister Arthur Balfour, FDR argued for congressional "action *at once*" on the barrage that went beyond militant language: "action that will give something—definite ships, definite men—on a definite day." British admiral Dudley S. DeChair "did not enthuse over the subject," and Balfour, wary of blocking sea access to Scandinavian neutrals like Norway by mining, "pointed out the [negative] diplomatic effect." Admiral Benson, the Secretary's Operations chief, "also showed little enthusiasm," FDR reminded Daniels, until Fullenweider "had worked out a new type of mine."

Eleanor wrote to Sara on May 17, 1917, that Franklin had asked to discuss the mine barrage with Wilson after senior admirals, citing technological difficulties and excessive costs, deplored its impracticality. The President suggested a study commission—often a political burial mechanism. Franklin pushed the scheme further with a former naval personage visiting from London late in July. The new Minister of Munitions, Winston Spencer Churchill, was to see Wilson. Churchill had been First Lord of the Admiralty when the Dardanelles adventure he promoted went sour, and he was sacked. Rescuing his reputation by commanding a battalion of the 6th Royal Scots Fusiliers in Flanders, he wrote with nautical ebullience to his wife, "It is a good thing to fly the flag at the main." Now he was back in Cabinet office—a rehabilitation which Franklin, who had been denied a uniform to brave the shellfire, must have envied.*

Since the depredations by U-boats, costing millions of tons of shipping and thousands of seamen, were continuing, on October 29 FDR chanced a "stinging" (as he described it to Eleanor) "Memorandum for the Secretary." In his diary, Daniels had downplayed the "stupendous undertaking" as of "doubtful practicability." Reluctantly, under continuing prodding, both the Admiralty and the Navy Department finally approved the mine barrage—but only on paper—after a visit to London by Admiral Mayo. Sims had rejected it, too, as "considered and abandoned." Franklin had crossed to the White House "several times" on the issue, as he reminded the Secretary, for prior to American entrance into the war Wilson had asked, rather innocently, "Daniels, why don't the British shut up the hornets in their nests?" Yet neither he nor Daniels had offered any alternatives. Since the proposal remained toothless, Franklin brazenly sent a copy of the memo to Wilson, with an exasperated forwarding letter. "It is my duty to tell you that if the plan is put into execution with the same speed and method employed in the past[,] other priceless months will be wasted and the success of the plan will be jeopardized. . . . I dislike exaggeration, but it is really true that the elimination of all submarines from the waters between the United States and Europe must of necessity be a vital factor in winning the war."

Eight months later the barrage was under construction, directed by Rear Admiral Joseph Strauss, chief of the Bureau of Ordnance until 1916 and then commander of the *Nevada*. Proximity antennae for the mines conceived by a Massachusetts inventor, Ralph C. Browne, who was recommended to FDR, became crucial to the scheme. Despite the sensitive triggering mechanism which reduced the number of explosives to be laid,

---

* FDR was in closer touch with another Winston Churchill, an Annapolis graduate, historical novelist, and friend of President Wilson. As war began, Churchill, from his home in New Hampshire, offered to assist Roosevelt by writing about the Navy for popular magazines and, inferentially, by lobbying Wilson. Churchill published his first article in the August 1917 *Atlantic Monthly* and visited the President to promote naval interests—and Daniels and Roosevelt.

the cost of the cumbersome operation would be enormous in terms of the time: $80,000,000. The auto industry would produce more than fifty thousand mines, each to be loaded with 300 pounds of explosives. A fleet of cargo ships transported 22,000,000 pounds of TNT, 50,000,000 feet of wire cable and the casings for a hundred thousand devices. Factories in Britain assembled thousands more.

Although the mining began far less urgently than FDR wanted, combined with the effective use of convoys and of sub chasers, the barrage had some impact, both real and psychological. Late in October 1918, after more than 70,000 mines had been laid, the likelihood that the war was ending suspended further operations. Although only seven sinkings of subs had been confirmed, others had been damaged and put out of action. After the war a German U-boat commander claimed that the barrage was "irrational as well as completely impracticable," as it could be evaded by diving below the barrier. Such successes are unproven. The threat of the barrage's existence was also a factor in keeping much of the surface *Kriegs-flotte* close to harbor. Desperate orders early that November to venture out to sea helped to precipitate mutinies by German sailors which spread as far inland as Berlin.

In the White House in 1941 as conflict again loomed, Roosevelt may have remembered his role in abetting the vast weapons enterprise across three thousand miles of ocean when he authorized the ultra-secret $2 billion Manhattan Project situated across three thousand miles of the American landscape. The first two bombs from the atomic research laboratories (after a test device worked) made unnecessary a massive invasion of Japan, with enormous likely casualties, and abruptly ended the war.

IN MID-JUNE, AS a break from the Department, Franklin requisitioned the *Sylph* for a weekend Potomac cruise, toward the Virginia shores of Chesapeake Bay, inviting along John McIlhenny and his wife, Nigel Law and Lucy Mercer, and two Marine officers from the Department. It was obviously an attempt on Franklin's part to demonstrate that Lucy was Law's companion, but Eleanor, who was to join the party, failed to meet them at the Washington Navy Yard. Although they had to sail without her, she was picked up downstream at Indian Head by a tender sent from the *Sylph*. Elliott Roosevelt, writing nearly sixty years later, speculated that although she felt that "swimming and playing in the sun . . . was not for her, at the last moment [she] changed her mind in order to watch over Father [and Lucy]."

As the heat and humidity in Washington became barely tolerable, Eleanor, with the Roosevelt children and staff, were scheduled to relocate, with the usual difficulties, to Campobello, while Franklin, but for occasional visits north, would return to summer bachelorhood. It was the traditional routine of officialdom in the District, yet more and more it rankled Eleanor. She resisted, and a quarrel ensued, as she was implicitly guarding her marriage; and despite the arrangements on the yacht in which Law squired Lucy, Franklin was under continuing suspicion. Reluctantly, Eleanor left on July 15, well into the sultry summer.

Franklin claimed war-related reasons for his absences, which, from Campobello, Eleanor began viewing as excuses, especially when his letters described outings not only to golf clubs, but further weekend sailings, usually on the *Sylph*. The cruises included such Harvard Gold Coast friends as Livingston Davis and Capital cronies like Nigel Law and Wilson's youngish physician Cary Grayson (now a Rear Admiral via relentless pressure from the White House). Also aboard were distaff invitees like the charming Lucy Mercer—always described by Franklin as being accompanied by the allegedly flirtatious Nigel Law.

Miss Mercer had become essential to Eleanor as social secretary, and as a reliable extra female at her dinner parties. Franklin's allusions to Lucy, concealing her openly, soon began stirring querulous letters from Campobello. Eleanor exploded on July 23, after he had reported "about 3½ feet of mail" which Lucy was working through, and about which she had sent responses for signature, "Your letter of Thursday is here and one from Miss Mercer. Why did you make her waste all that time [on] fool notes. . . . She tells me you are going off on Tuesday and I hope you all had a pleasant trip but I'm so glad I've been here and not on the Potomac!" Eleanor was clearly not at all glad, but because of the recurrent

Livingston Davis with FDR at Hyde Park, March 31, 1913. FDR LIBRARY

summer crises about polio in the Northeast, occurring as far south as Washington, she remained uneasily at Campobello into October.

JUST BEFORE THE annual family retreat to the island in 1917, Eleanor had been interviewed at home by a *New York Times* newspaperwoman about how the transplanted New Yorker's large brood was adapting to wartime food restrictions. Eleanor had signed, innocently, a pledge card from the Patriotic Economy League. When "How to Save in Big Homes" appeared on July 17, she suffered acute embarrassment. In Washington, Eleanor would have been exposed to more open mortification. Had Lucy Mercer assisted at the interview—not out of the question for a social secretary—Eleanor might have been more prudent, but before she departed for her Campobello summer, Lucy had been dismissed. Whether Eleanor's suspicions had been aroused by intuition or rumor, letting her go, if only during the season's social vacuum, would not keep Lucy distant from Franklin. A week later, on June 24, as one of 11,000 women recruited by Daniels, she enlisted as a Navy Yeoman (F), 3rd class at $28.75 monthly, plus $1.75 daily for meals.

By what seems no coincidence Lucy was assigned to the office of the Assistant Secretary, and on July 25 Franklin wrote to Eleanor breezily, not mentioning Yeomanette Mercer's new role, that a cruise on the *Sylph*, ostensibly a "visit to the fleet," included among others Lucy Mercer and Nigel Law, "and they all got on splendidly." The incautious letter arrived just as *The New York Times* interview appeared, multiplying Eleanor's anxieties.

The wartime "food-saving" regimen at the extravagantly staffed Roosevelt home, the article reported,

> has been selected by the conservation section of the Food Administration as a model for other large households. Mrs. Roosevelt on her pledge card said that there were seven in the family, and that ten servants were employed. . . . Mrs. Roosevelt does the buying, the cooks see that there is no food wasted, the laundress is sparing in her use of soap, each servant has a watchful eye for evidence of shortcomings on the part of the others. . . .
>
> No bacon is used . . . ; corn bread is served but once a day. . . . Meat is served but once daily, and all "left overs" are utilized. Menu rules allow two courses for luncheon and three for dinner. Everybody eats fish at least once a week.
>
> "Making the ten servants help me do my saving has not only been possible but highly profitable," said Mrs. Roosevelt today. "Since I have been following the home-card instructions, prices have risen, but my bills are no larger."

With unkind humor, Franklin wrote to Eleanor the next day that her embarrassingly unanticipated "newspaper campaign" was a "corker":

> I am proud to be the husband of the Originator, Discoverer and Inventor of the New Household Economy for Millionaires! Please have a photo taken showing the family, the ten cooperating servants, the scraps saved from the table, and the handbook. I will have it published in the [illustrations insert of the] Sunday Times.

Honestly, you have leaped into public fame, all Washington is talking of the Roosevelt Plan, and I begin to get telegrams of congratulations and requests for further details from Pittsburgh, New Orleans, San Francisco. . . .

Eleanor was beyond humiliation. The ten "servants" included the children's caretakers, and even Miss Mercer. Although now in the Navy, she had been going through, in Eleanor's absence, the piled-up mail about the *Times* article. "It was horrid of that woman [reporter]," Eleanor wrote to her husband. "So much is not true and yet some of it I did say. I never will be caught again that's sure and I'd like to crawl away for shame." At least she was in Campobello, remote from gossips but not from anxiety. "I don't think you read my letters," Eleanor charged, "for you never answer a question and nothing I ask for appears!"

The wartime summer of 1917 was a complicated one. At the same time that FDR was overseeing cantonment construction work directed by a new Engineering Corps lieutenant commander, Elliott C. Brown, he was privately employing Brown, at Sara's expense, to remodel and expand the "the Place," as the family called "Springwood" at Hyde Park. FDR was increasingly busy with the belated wartime buildup, especially frustrated, he wrote to Eleanor on July 25, by "old lady officers and lack of decision in the Department." He was the Navy representative on the Shipbuilding Labor Board, effectively coordinating all the burgeoning labor relations for the Navy—for which, happily, he had the astute and politically sensitive Louis Howe work on contracts and formulas for cost-of-living wage adjustments. Procurement remained a massive problem as unprepared factories, and yards yet unbuilt and unstaffed, could not keep up with the need for parts of every sort. Franklin arranged for hollow shafts for destroyers to be manufactured by having the Erie Forge Company in Pennsylvania construct a new plant at government expense. When lack of an appropriate generator delayed the opening of production, Howe commandeered a generator intended for the Hotel Pennsylvania in Manhattan, delaying the opening of the hotel by three months.

FDR's "Eyes for the Navy" campaign secured 50,000 binoculars from their owners for one dollar each plus the chancy promise of their return after the war. He signed (ostensibly) every acknowledgment of gift. His campaign for donations—token sales—of private oceangoing motorcraft for sub patrol, despite concerns from armchair admirals who never sailed them about their seaworthiness, would soon include delivery of his own *Half Moon II* from Campobello. In the *New Republic* on April 14, freelance magazine writer William Hard wrote that Roosevelt "is an effective young man because, among other reasons, he is an optimistic young man. Yet even he was obliged to tell the yacht-owners of New York that a motor-boat, to be an 'auxiliary,' should be at least forty feet long. Now how many motor-boats have we that are forty feet long? A large number. The Yacht Register says 1275."

Franklin appeared in the House of Representatives to press for $174 million in further appropriations, yet not every request sailed through. One that did authorized him to order eight million pounds of gun forgings for warships from the Tioga Steel & Iron Company of Philadelphia for which the government would pay 4½ cents per pound above cost. FDR signed the huge order on August 4, 1917.

With "Pitchfork Ben" Tillman, Chairman of the Senate Naval Affairs Committee, Franklin came to Daniels with an inventive chemist, John Andrews, who claimed to be able to supply the fleet's needs for oil at two cents a gallon. He wanted to demonstrate his method. "Chief, it is worth trying," Roosevelt argued. "I say he should be given the opportunity to prove he can do what he says." After Daniels gave in, Andrews drove to the Brooklyn Navy Yard in an open Packard, armed with an empty gallon can and a black satchel of unidentified chemicals, accompanied by a quiet gentleman he identified as his banker from McKeesport, Pennsylvania. A test under the supervision of senior engineering officers, during which the motor of a boat, set on a block, successfully "developed power" using water mixed with Andrews's ingredients, seemed to confirm that Andrews could in effect turn water into wine.

Returning to Daniels and Roosevelt after his apparent success, Andrews offered the Navy "exclusive possession" for $2 million, "but I will not give you the secret preparation that propels the engine until I get the money!" Daniels insisted that quantity of product had to be assured. He could not buy "a pig in a poke." Andrews took his black bag of unidentified ingredients, and his banker, and left. He was later located in a Pittsburgh suburb, but when sought the next morning he was gone. Captain E. P. Jessup, in command at the Brooklyn Yard, reported to the Department that he was convinced his visitor "had something, and it is a pity we could not have gotten it out of him." The formula, or the fakery, vanished with Andrews.

Daniels and Roosevelt were deluged with innovative if largely imaginary ideas for mechanisms to win the war. Some came from prestigious sources. Thomas Edison told Daniels that he felt "quite sure he could put an end to Fritz and the submarine menace." He was given working space at the Brooklyn Navy Yard but nothing useful materialized. Elmer A. Sperry of Sperry Gyroscope conceived but could not construct a "Flying Devil"—a pilotless torpedo that could cruise fifty miles; also a net with a buoy with light and whistle attached that allegedly could trap a U-boat and attract patrol craft. A crank came up with "a process by which he could bring down the power of a bolt of lightning, make it give its death-dealing blows where he chose & it would win the war." Daniels offered him space at Annapolis "& if successful to give him just compensation." Peter Cooper Hewitt of New York, a well-to-do scientist on the Naval Consulting Board, reported his experimenting to upgrade a German "bomb of gases." Others came up with unsinkable ships and anti-torpedo devices. Ralph C. Browne's proximity fuse for the mine barrage was the conspicuous success.

A delegation from France arrived to promote its ideas on gas warfare, which had added a new horror to war. Louis Howe wrote to Grace, who was at their summer cottage, "For the most part they were little, thin-faced, thin-whiskered, soft-voiced men and to hear them stand up and describe how they found one trench that was very deep with 2300 men in it and fired gas shells into it until every man was killed[,] and like tales seemed like a dream of some kind as if one were listening to some kind of play. . . ." The tale was indeed dramatic, and the exaggerated casualty figures absurd. The Navy did not pursue the weaponry. Roosevelt wrote to Philip Little of Salem, Massachusetts, who had proposed his ideas about submarine periscopes, and smoke screens for warships, that the Department "does not consider any mirror light or bright substance advisable for use on periscopes," and that Navy plans for smoke screens have already "been carefully worked out."

Ambitious to push the Navy forward above the sea, Daniels and Roosevelt backed a proposal to cross the Atlantic by air. (Obtuse as usual, Admiral Benson insisted, "The Navy doesn't need airplanes.") On September 4, 1917, Lieutenant Commander George C. Westervelt returned to the Department from Italy to report that the Italians were building "the largest air-craft in the world." The machine might fly as far as New York. Despite Benson, the Navy in July had requested an additional $45 million for aeronautics. Admiral David W. Taylor, chief of construction, prepared a crisp directive for Westervelt and M.I.T. wind tunnel engineer Jerome C. Hunsacker: "We want a plane designed that will fly across the Atlantic." Yet when, for oversight, Daniels wanted to put Roosevelt on the Aircraft Board, he declined. Franklin claimed he could not spare time for three additional meetings a week. Hunsacker became the design and procurement specialist for all Navy aircraft.

Among the inventors who called on Daniels and Roosevelt was aircraft pioneer Orville Wright, who recalled the first flight at Kitty Hawk, North Carolina. News came as they were conferring that the Germans had seized Riga in Latvia from the crumbling Russians, and that it was likely to be easy for the enemy to continue on to Petrograd, the former St. Petersburg. Franklin said, according to Daniels's diary, "We ought to have sent T.R. over to Russia with 100,000 men. This would not have happened." Also in the office then was Captain Josiah S. McKean, deputy to Admiral Benson, who scoffed, obviously referring to the Assistant Secretary, that "it was strange how many folks T.R. had fooled." Amid power struggles, Russia was tottering, and Theodore Roosevelt could not have rescued the increasingly unreliable ally had he tried, but Franklin brought him into any conversation where he thought the prosecution of the war lacked energy.

As Uncle Ted, advocate of the strenuous life, remained on FDR's mind, Franklin engaged Yale football coach Walter Camp to set up exercise routines for Washington bureaucrats, including Franklin himself. For workouts, Camp even rented a house in the District at Navy expense. When he made the mistake of calling Daniels a slacker for ignoring the regimen, Daniels (according to his then-teenage son, Jonathan) consulted his doctor, Sterling Ruffin. "Joe, you never took any exercise in your life," Dr. Ruffin said. "You never walked when you could ride. Stay away from that crowd and you'll live longer."* Seldom ready to relinquish a pet idea, the Assistant Secretary brought fitness up again after the war. The "FDR plan," Daniels noted in his diary, "of ½ a day each month in work-hours was not approved by any [in the Department]."

However debonair and energetic Franklin appeared in the summer of 1917, he was breaking down physically. Long subject to respiratory infections, he came down with another serious episode and spent a week in the hospital. Leaving the children with a governess and nurse, Eleanor rushed down to be with him. After he was released and she returned to Campobello, he recuperated briefly with his friends Caroline and William Phillips at their posh home on Woodley Lane. Back north after two weeks with Franklin, which apparently included Eleanor's raising further marital concerns, she wrote to him on August 15, "I hated to leave you yesterday. Please go to the doctor twice a week, eat well and sleep well and remember I *count* on seeing you [on] the 26th. My threat was no idle one."

Although evidence is lacking, Eleanor apparently assumed that during her long absences, Franklin and Lucy Mercer had become overly close, and that his fleeting allusions to her in his correspondence, always among others, were cautious cover. Eleanor had hardly unpacked at Campobello when a letter dated August 20 arrived describing a busy social Sunday beginning with golf and lunch at Chevy Chase, and an outing in Franklin's automobile to Harpers Ferry. "Lucy went and the Graysons and we . . . left at nine and got home at midnight." Quite obviously Nigel Law was not with them. Alice Roosevelt Longworth, probably just after the drive, telephoned Franklin (according to her memoirs), "I saw you 20 miles out

---

* Daniels outlived both FDR and Camp.

in the country. You didn't see me. Your hands were on the wheel, but your eyes were on the perfectly lovely lady."

"Isn't she perfectly lovely?" Franklin agreed—if one accepts the distant recollection of a compulsive gossip. Afterwards, in Eleanor's absences, Alice invited her cousin to bring Miss Mercer to dinner parties at the Longworths'—and he apparently did. Alice claimed to have spent delicious minutes on her telephone afterward regaling intimates about Lucy. Alice's younger sister, Ethel, remembered Eleanor weeping on her cousin's shoulder after her engagement to Franklin many years earlier and deploring, "I shall never be able to hold him. He is so attractive." That anxiety had lingered—and festered.

Franklin had been instructed to be at Campobello by August 26, and apparently kept to schedule, writing "Dearest Babs" that after he met with Lord Northcliffe on the twenty-second he would have "nothing more to do" in Washington. Alfred Harmsworth, now Viscount Northcliffe, controlled, with his younger brother, Harold, then Air Minister and soon to become Viscount Rothermere, such influential English newspapers as *The Times*, *Daily Mail* and *Daily Mirror*, and had just been named by Prime Minister Lloyd George to lead the British Mission to Washington. Obviously FDR received a different slant on events than he did from naval journalist Arthur Pollen of *Land and Water*, who told Franklin, while accompanying Northcliffe, that the Royal Navy "has done nothing of a constructive character since the war began," and castigated the "extraordinary folly of Jellicoe and the Admiralty." The Assistant Secretary was prepared to believe it. And he saw his own dilatory department as much the same. Also, the American military was making little real impact across the sea, although the French and English remained heartened by its potential.

Satirizing Allied hopes for quick American successes, George Grosz, collaborating on an animated film now lost, *Sammy in Europe*, pictured skyscrapers rising out of the French soil as Yanks disembarked. "Ludendorff is not afraid of America," *Graf* Kessler noted in his diary from Supreme Headquarters. "Up to now, they have sent [to the line], in total, thirty thousand men, so two divisions. That is as good as nothing on the

Western Front." (Even those troops needed much further training.) He also noted that October that German officialdom, recalling hopefully earlier American anxieties like those voiced by both naval Roosevelts, felt it "unbelieveable that they would commit the stupidity of bringing their army over here, for then they would offer Japan a never to be repeated opportunity to defeat them [in a denuded Pacific]."

When Roosevelt came back to Washington he immediately made return inspection visits to the inadequately performing First, Second and Third Naval Districts (headquartered at Boston, Newport and New York). Reporting to Daniels, he deplored, "I am sorry to say that the conditions are to all intents and purposes no better." At home he was exiting, for the family, the N street house, writing to Eleanor on September 9, "You are entirely disconnected and Lucy Mercer and Mrs. Munn are closing up the loose ends." Mary Munn, Eleanor's friend, who worked with her on Red Cross affairs, was an Astor heiress, which blunted whatever disquiet was raised by the Lucy reference. Apparently Franklin's continued allusions to her were to suggest that he was concealing nothing from Eleanor.

Lucy would be discharged from the Navy after only four months' service "by Special Order of the Secretary of the Navy" on October 5, 1917, just after the death of her long-estranged father, Carroll Mercer, a drifter and drunk who had run through his wife's money years before. Without identifying targets, as was its prudent practice, the local gossip paper *Town Topics* reported that a charming Washington girl—she was twenty-six— linked to an aristocratic young diplomat, apparently Nigel Law, had "recently gone into retirement because of family bereavement." Lucy could hardly have left the service on bereavement grounds as she had seldom seen her father and did not attend his funeral. Yet thanks to the upright and sanctimonious Daniels, who may have suspected that the Nigel Law connection was a facade, or felt that an enlistee had no business mingling with brass, Miss Mercer now had no income. Her yeomanette pay had abruptly ended. Minna Mercer, once a Washington socialite, and daughters Violetta and Lucy, lived in a small apartment on Florida Avenue on precarious remittances from a distant Carroll Mercer relative, Lucy's funds, and Violetta's small nursing salary. The sisters had paid the rent.

Whether Daniels and Roosevelt discussed Lucy's unexplained dis-
charge is unknown. Very likely Franklin could not contest, or even raise,
the matter, and his son Elliott would later write in a family memoir that
he assumed some quiet indirect support came afterward from FDR. When
Eleanor carefully sent Lucy a check for work done during the Campobello summer, Lucy returned it—twice. Even Violetta's income would di-
minish as she volunteered as an Army nurse and went to France with a
mobile hospital. Yet despite Eleanor's suspicions, she had Lucy return occasionally as social secretary at R Street.* With both Roosevelts at home
but for Franklin's brief absences on Navy business, no letters would mention Miss Mercer, even in passing.

REBUFFED BY DANIELS about employing retired Rear Admiral Cameron
Winslow, former commander of the Pacific Fleet, FDR tried another tack,
asking in October to employ for "special work" Livingston Davis, at
$3,000 a year. Davis, who was bored with his brokerage, and his wife, was
eager to come, and he had already accompanied Franklin to Haiti. "My
second pair of legs," FDR called Livy, whom Eleanor despised as much as
she once loathed the now-indispensable Louis Howe. Avoiding both as
much as possible, she put in hours at a Union Station railway canteen for
servicemen, often before dawn, and did other volunteering for the Red
Cross and the Navy Relief Society, including, soon, hospital visits. Livy
Davis left Boston, dutifully brought his wife, Alice, although he was
chronically unfaithful to her, and rented a house on New Hampshire Avenue. In addition to playing golf and tennis with Franklin, and accompanying him to men-only social occasions, Davis traveled on inspection
trips with the Assistant Secretary while Louis Howe minded the shop.

Another Alice popped in and out of the Roosevelts' lives. After asking
Eleanor how she could contribute to the war effort in Washington, Alice
Longworth poured coffee sometimes at Union Station, then claimed "can-

---

* Very likely FDR was not involved in Eleanor's decision. Decades later, the obses-
sively randy John F. Kennedy prevailed upon Jacqueline to hire as a press secretary
Pamela Turnure, one of his mistresses.

teen elbow" and stopped coming. Her ear for gossip, however, resulted in her enlisting Franklin in a spy hunt. In May 1917 the Webb-Overman Espionage Act had been passed, mandating fines and imprisonment for anyone in wartime who should "collect, record, publish, or communicate" information "useful to the enemy." A Washington socialite she knew, May Ladenburg, was the daughter of a partner in a German-American banking firm, and a bedmate of Wall Street financier Bernard Baruch, forty-seven, married with children, and a serial philanderer. Wilson leaned on Baruch's economic expertise and valued his judgment, yet was not above the anti-Semitic remark typical of his background. In the President's office on April 9, 1917, Daniels had commented about an appointment for Baruch that he was "somewhat vain." Wilson remarked, "Did you ever see a Jew who was not?"*

An adviser on commodity availability and prices, Baruch was suspected by intelligence sleuths of leaking sensitive information to Miss Ladenburg, allegedly relayed to a German uncle abroad. Approached by the Army intelligence chief, Colonel Marlborough Churchill, to help trap her friend, Alice persuaded cousin Franklin to furnish fake classified documents about shipping movements which Baruch might reveal during a tryst. Although Franklin liked Baruch, he fell for the caper. Listening devices were planted at 1831 M Street, NW, and monitored from an adjacent stable. "We did hear her ask Bernie how many locomotives were being sent to Romania . . . in between the sounds of kissing . . . ," Alice claimed long afterwards. "Of course we were doing a most disgraceful thing. . . . but it was sheer rapture." On discovering the bugs, May informed Baruch, who told Dr. Grayson, who told Mrs. Wilson, who informed the irate President. Yet Churchill was promoted and Baruch emerged unscathed, as he would from other bedroom episodes for decades after. In January 1918 he became chairman of the War Industries Board. And he would remain an FDR confidant into the next war.

---

*Yet Wilson, at great political risk and to the ire of many conservatives, had appointed the distinguished Louis D. Brandeis to the Supreme Court.

When Alice, on a chance meeting, offered unspecified "secrets" to Eleanor, she told her tattling cousin indignantly, as she reported to Franklin, "I said no and that I did not believe in knowing things which your husband did not wish you to know so I think I will be spared any further mysterious secrets!" The cousins may have been contemplating far different secrets.

Disloyalty of a different sort came up in a cryptic diary entry by Daniels which slightly misquoted Cato's memorable *Delenda est Carthago*—Carthage must be destroyed. When visiting Daniels, Grenville S. MacFarland, editor of William Randolph Hearst's *Boston American*, had warned that Roosevelt, in sharing his impatience about allegedly sluggish naval administration with novelist Winston Churchill in hopes of influencing Wilson, was plotting a coup that would put Franklin in the Secretary's chair. (If such a plotter existed, it was Colonel Thompson of the Navy League, a Daniels enemy, from whom FDR now kept his distance.) Also, MacFarland charged, Roosevelt had carried his dissatisfaction to the hostile Republican senator John W. Weeks of Massachusetts, a colleague of Cabot Lodge. "If not loyal sh'd not hesitate" followed in the Daniels diary—unclear as to whether it was MacFarland's advice to sack FDR, or that of Daniels to himself. Happily, the Secretary was a deliberative type—if much too deliberate for Franklin. Daniels knew he needed his deputy, and understood that Franklin was not out to oust him. To the President, no one in his Cabinet adhered more to Wilsonian principles than his Secretary of the Navy. They would last out the war, and the Wilson administration, together. If the Assistant Secretary was ambitious, that rise would not be played out under the mansard roofs.

Almost certainly Lucy Mercer was not at the table as an extra woman when Eleanor hosted a small post-Christmas dinner on December 28, 1917, attended by Addie and Josephus Daniels. The matriarchal Sara Roosevelt was present, and a visiting British naval captain. The occasion suggested that all was well in the Department. Daniels left on a late train immediately afterwards for Raleigh, leaving Roosevelt again to be Acting Secretary—but only until New Year's Eve.

7

"FDR Wishes to Go Abroad"

THROUGHOUT THE WARTIME months of 1918 there are scarcely more than a half-dozen entries in Secretary Daniels's Cabinet diary mentioning Franklin's name. Any implication that there was serious dissension between the two, or that the Assistant Secretary was not carrying his responsibilities, is unlikely. The two disagreed on many things, especially when Franklin's audacity came into conflict with Daniels's caution, yet they worked together effectively as the American war effort burgeoned. Roosevelt would complain about inaction, and Daniels would often concede, yet the Secretary would never go beyond what he thought the President wanted.

Feeling constrained by war, Wilson put aside his liberal leanings. He knew that further domestic reforms were precluded, and he took a tough line on dissent, fostering strict censorship and open propaganda. Both were managed by the hard-fisted George Creel, formerly a *New York World* editor and now director of the Committee on Public Information, for which he was effectively a committee of one. Among Creel's earliest ventures was to probe the covert backing of FDR to replace Daniels, surfacing in press opinion promoting more vigorous prosecution of the naval war. To deflect intimations of disloyalty, Franklin wrote to a Harvard friend, Edwyn Johnstone, who had informed him about such schemes, "Personally I have no use for a man who, serving in a subordinate position, is continually contriving ways to step into his boss's shoes. . . . I have worked very gladly under Mr. Daniels and I wish the public could realize how much he has done for the Navy." Franklin expected that his loftily loyal sentiments would at least indirectly reach the Secretary.

Creel traced the source to Louis Howe, who had been planting suggestions among old newspaper cronies. He warned FDR's deputy that Wilson would hear of any further treachery. Knowing nothing of Howe's machinations, Franklin remained zealously—although often insincerely—protective of the administration, and of Daniels. FDR worked with Secretary McAdoo on mail censorship to allay subtle communication with the enemy, authorizing the examination of letters ostensibly dealing with "Chess problems," route instructions to masters of merchant ships, likely strikes or labor agitation and attempts to evade censorship by posting mail across the Mexican border. When the *New York Sun* on March 24, 1918, published an article about an air-launched torpedo, Roosevelt warned the editor of the *Sun* privately that such experiments were being conducted for the Navy and that for military reasons, no further mention of the weapon should be made.

Restless with the sluggish bureaucracy of war, FDR wanted to be more closely involved. Commander Husband E. Kimmel, who earlier had been at Veracruz, shared drinks with Franklin and Livy Davis and "told us," Davis wrote in his diary, "about his experiences with [the] British fleet. Thrilling." Nigel Law had departed briefly for England, ostensibly on embassy business, wangled a visit to the front, and on returning regaled Franklin with his war tourist adventures. "FDR wishes to go abroad," Daniels noted in his diary of March 20. The Secretary himself was uninterested, although Newton Baker, on another floor, was eager to see what Yanks flooding into France were doing to ready themselves for the real thing. While Daniels preferred to leave the war to the admirals, Roosevelt reminded him that the Navy included the Marines, who were already preparing for action. Eight days later Franklin wrote to Sara disconsolately, "Not much likelihood of my going over, though they ought to send me."

"Several talks" with Daniels followed, and an FDR memo enumerating Navy activities "on the other side," which had "assumed such proportions and such a diversity that it is next to impossible for those over here without a close knowledge of affairs over there to form an intelligent opinion upon which to base appropriate action." Still, he was "over here." Aside from visiting shipyards and munitions plants, he was chairing a committee on postwar training and rehabilitation for the wounded to come and discussing patents and purchases with purveyors and contractors for everything from flying machines to munitions factories, and even types of paint. Daniels was interested in protective camouflage, learning from English sources that "it made the ship appear to be going in one direction while it was in reality going in another."

The frigid winter in late 1917 and early 1918 raised unforeseen problems. In New York, a parade of Army conscripts preparing for embarkation to France was hampered by a snowstorm. According to Daniels, Herbert Hoover, now Food Administrator, had difficulty getting supplies to Atlantic ports for lack of sufficient railway freight cars. Henry Garfield, son of the assassinated president and now Fuel Administrator, had trouble transporting coal. Edward J. Hurley, chairman of the Shipping Board, blamed cold weather for the slowdowns at private yards, and Secretary of Agriculture David Houston foresaw a downturn in crucial wheat crops.

Impatient to get going on projects so that, before it was too late, the United States would count for something in winning the war, Roosevelt became the target of unsavory as well as legitimate entrepreneurs. (He and Daniels continued seeing a succession of inventors.) The former type was much like the slippery Arthur Patch Homer of Sterling Motors, who was still lobbying in Washington. Emory S. Land, then a young officer (but three years older than FDR), as a naval architect on the Board of Devices and Plans accompanied the Assistant Secretary to motorboat shows to furnish advice on the construction of small watercraft. "There was always some friend of his who had his ear," Land remembered, pulling FDR back from hasty misjudgments. Eugene Sullivan, arrested in Boston in June 1918 for influence peddling, claimed that he "had to use a lot of bull on F.D.R. to get him to give a [raincoat] contract" to a firm not the low bidder, but the allegation vanishes from the record after a brief note in Daniels's diary. Commander John M. Hancock, overseeing Navy purchasing, claimed that Roosevelt "was a sucker for anyone who was a classmate or a member of the Newport [social] crowd." Land recalled "someone selling paint, a classmate perhaps: Valentine Paint Company. FDR was always talking up Valentine Paint." There was reason, however. Valspar Paint in New York City was a brand long in military use, even employed by Commander (later Rear Admiral) Robert E. Peary on his expedition toward the North Pole in 1909. Valspar may have furnished the camouflage paint which Daniels wanted.

Land soon was transferred to work with Admiral William Sims in England, and much later, by executive order of the President in February 1942, he became, as a vice admiral, chief of the War Shipping Administration, overseeing the design of four thousand Liberty and Victory ships.

Involving himself in everything he could, Franklin traveled about speechmaking for the Fourth Liberty Loan, promoting the sale of war bonds. A colorful and sexy Howard Chandler Christy poster even had a naval theme, "CLEAR THE WAY!"—with a beflagged, skimpily attired cover girl rising dreamlike above a warship's muscular battery crew, some bare to the waist, as they fired a salvo at sea. In Washington at a big Liberty Loan rally on April 14, Roosevelt appeared impassive in dark suit and broad-brimmed hat accompanying the film stars who ensured a big turnout—Douglas Fairbanks and Mary Pickford, Marie Dressler and Charlie Chaplin.

The Department had long outgrown its floors in the State, War & Navy Building. Almost too late to matter, construction was under way for a Main Navy Building, to consolidate offices which by early 1918 occupied twenty-seven locations throughout Washington. The Bureau of Yards and Docks, overseen by the Assistant Secretary, had responsibility for "shore construction." Various sites had been proposed, one—the Ellipse near the White House—objected to, reasonably, by Wilson. Finally a tract in Potomac Park extending from Seventeenth to Twenty-first Streets was approved, and under wartime urgency, work on the foundations began on February 25. It took until March 28 before an appropriations bill legalizing the project was enacted for separate Munitions (War) and Navy buildings,

*Clear the Way!! Buy Bonds.
Fourth Liberty Loan.* FDR
appeared often at rallies to
promote Liberty Bonds. This
time—1918—a naval theme
was utilized in the poster by
Howard Chandler Christy.
FDR LIBRARY, AND IN
AUTHOR'S COLLECTION

connected by a covered bridge, with State then to occupy all of the venerable Victorian structure. Little of the oversight, and even of the complex-
ities of moving in, beginning on August 17, 1918, appear in the papers of
the Navy's civilian executives. Yet, employing 3,400 men, with a shifting
labor force of 7,500 due to the mobility of unskilled workers paid 30 cents
an hour—increased to 44 cents to keep the work going—Turner Construction Company of New York completed the sprawling reinforced
concrete buildings in 5½ months. By early October, 1918, all bureaus were
ensconced in the new Navy building, its floors nautically designated as
decks. Secretary Daniels was in Room 2046 off the main corridor on the
second deck; FDR occupied the adjoining suite.

A rare public relations success as "Main Navy" construction continued was the first official air mail flight, on May 15, 1918, from New York
to Washington. Waiting on the White House lawn for the symbolic delivery were the President, Postmaster General Burleson, Daniels, Roosevelt and other dignitaries. Daniels and his wife received three letters,
each with a new square, red six-cent stamp featuring the "Flying Jenny"
biplane. "Give me one of the stamps," FDR—a compulsive collector—
requested of Mrs. Daniels. "I want to add it to my stamp collection." He
got it, Addie Daniels recalled to her son Jonathan. "Nobody could refuse
Franklin anything." Except, she might have added, Secretary Daniels.

One no-win task handed to Roosevelt was to do something about the
notorious naval base at Newport, which was reported to the Secretary as
a "festering place of ill fame" after a Navy chaplain was found guilty of
"immoral conduct." When the chaplain's Episcopal bishop refused to believe the evidence, an admiral was sent from Washington, who returned
to confirm that Newport was a "wide-open town" for prostitution, abetted by local officials who shared in the profits. On his way to Cambridge
in June as a Harvard overseer, FDR detoured to Newport and found that
conditions were as reported. Daniels ordered naval police "to stand before houses of ill fame and prevent Navy personnel from entering zones of
rottenness." The Secretary refused to permit prophylaxis stations—they
were "invitations to sin"—but during one of his absences, FDR as Acting
Secretary approved supplying condoms. As prostitution involved homo-
sexual enticement as well as the traditional trade, Roosevelt would find
the Newport issue haunting him, even after the war. He had suggested
(but denied) using young sailors as decoys for entrapment.

Among Franklin's more public problems in June was that his wartime
visibility had encouraged Tammany politicians to seek him out as a candidate for governor. He had been principal speaker at Boss Murphy's July
4 celebration the year before, and the party in New York was warming to
him. Although FDR was tempted, Louis Howe warned that it would be
risky and premature, and would mean relinquishing his Navy office to
run. If he lost, he would be nowhere. In mid-June, Wilson intervened
through Daniels, advising, "Tell Roosevelt he ought not to decline to run

for Governor if it is tendered to him." Feeling that it would appear that he was running away from the war, and that being in some equivalent of active service would better enhance his political future, he put the overture aside.

Franklin kept up the pressure on Daniels that one or the other should cross the Atlantic, not as a war tourist, but to validate what the Navy and Marine Corps were doing. The Marines were finally engaged with the enemy. "One of us," FDR persisted, "ought to go and see the war in progress with his own eyes, else he is a chess player moving his pieces in the dark." Wilson wanted Daniels close by, "for frequent conferences," the Secretary claimed after the Newport inquiry began. "You draw the inspection trip. See Navy operations at first hand, send frequent reports, and make recommendations as conditions demand."

Roosevelt promptly checked on warship departures and offered early in April to sail on "the cruiser that leaves on Sunday." He cabled Navy personnel in England and France. The *Half Moon II* was already operated by the Navy; his life insurance was paid, and 49 E. 65th Street in Manhattan had been rented to Thomas W. Lamont, a partner in J. P. Morgan & Co., for two years at an annual $4,500. Eleanor packed off the children to Sara at Hyde Park and, having found a local purpose, was devoted to the tin-roofed railroad canteen at Union Station, dispensing coffee, sandwiches and cigarettes to troops disembarking from eight or more trains day and night. She saw little of Franklin anyway. Even Mrs. Wilson turned up occasionally, in Red Cross uniform, to assist. "Yesterday late," Eleanor wrote about a memorable afternoon, "the President came down and walked down the tracks and all around and they tell me seemed much interested."

AMERICAN TROOPS COMMITTED to battle in France were none too soon. Mutinies suppressed by the demoralized French after the mutual carnage at Verdun, and terrible losses by the dispirited British on the Somme, left fewer and fewer reserves to bring forward. A massive German spring offensive would become possible as the imposed Brest-Litovsk treaty of peace with Bolshevik Russia on March 3, 1918, released hundreds of thousands of seasoned troops for transfer to the Western Front. Soon they would be more than matched. The inevitability of an active American presence meant that General Erich Ludendorff's armies had to force a solution before two million Americans, however inexperienced, and undersupplied because of transport bottlenecks from overburdened French ports, could alter the outcome. After another winter the war might spill onto German soil.

On the River Marne in early June, at Chateau-Thierry and Belleau Wood, east of Paris, American soldiers bolstered by a Marine brigade had beaten back the Germans, enduring the heavy losses their innocence of war made inescapable.* The Marines, included in Franklin's proposed oversight, were a land-and-sea adjunct to the Navy he had longed to join.

Daniels stalled FDR's permission to leave from April into early July. In the interim, Franklin prepared and published, in *The New York Times* of June 9, "U-Boats Off Shore!"—on Germany's intent to terrorize the enemy and force the withdrawal of destroyers and patrol vessels now in European waters "in order to protect our own coasts. To do this would be playing directly into the hands of the German Admiralty."

Some of Franklin's small civilian staff, including Livy Davis, who had been close at hand for work and play, sailed on the British liner *Olympic*. Franklin left three days earlier, on July 9, 1918, on the destroyer *Dyer*, commissioned on July 1. The voyage would be its shake-down cruise. The *Dyer* had been built in Massachusetts by Bethlehem Steel's Fore River Shipbuilding Company in Quincy, where its shrewd assistant manager, whom FDR got to know well, was the opportunistic Joseph P. Kennedy. Moving postwar into banking, cinema and lucrative evasions of prohibition, Kennedy would prove the knowledgeable if controversial candidate FDR injudiciously picked, when in the White House, to be the chairman of the new Securities and Exchange Commission.

In preparation for departure, according to Davis's diary, he and Franklin "worked until 1:30 A.M. over Sims' reports" from London. By the time

---

*Max Goertz, a German soldier wounded then, described his corps as having returned "in shreds. . . . That was the summit of the house of cards. Château-Thierry, that's where the storm struck and one piece after the other came crashing down."

Franklin and Livy sailed, with Marine captain Edward McCauley, Jr., Sergeant W. W. Stratton (as orderly), Lieutenant Commander Elliott Brown (a Harvard friend and architect), Navy captain Victor S. Jackson and R. H. Camalier as secretary, over a million troops had been ferried to France. Three months earlier, Admiral Strauss had initiated the operations FDR had long promoted—the mining of U-boat access to the Channel and northern approaches into the Atlantic. In January 1918 losses to submarines had been 318,000 tons of shipping, thanks to the convoy system the lowest in years, yet losses remained barely sustainable. The five camouflaged troop transports escorted by the *Dyer* were also accompanied by the destroyer *Macdonough*. Unexpectedly, the flotilla would encounter—a moment of concern at dawn on July 12—twenty-eight freighters headed across their bows en route to England. Convoy routes, FDR noted with alarm, were never supposed to cross and endanger each other. Ships blinkered cautiously toward the approaching vessels until a final "good-bye."

Minor distress occurred on Sunday, July 14. As the "tin can" carrying Franklin rolled in heavy seas—it was 315 feet long and displaced only 1,060 tons—"the crockery disintegrated and we thought a torpedo had hit us when a big drawer of knives, forks, spoons and dishes hopped out of the sideboard and bounded across the ward room, narrowly missing all of us at the table." To Franklin's disappointment there were no sub sightings, although later, for color, he invented one. As planned, the *Dyer* steamed toward Fayal in the Azores chain. Although one of its engines needed maintenance, Franklin dismissed it in his letter-diary intended for Eleanor. "This run was the ship's shake-down, and we must expect things like this to happen."

At Ponta Delgada the destroyer's officers struggled happily through the Portuguese high commissioner's ten-course dinner, and Franklin offered a toast, in French, to the Republic of Portugal. With the engines again running smoothly, the *Dyer* plowed north into squalls and through "the active submarine zone," testing its guns and a depth charge for readiness. On Sunday, July 21, the destroyer reached England. At Portsmouth, Admiral Sims, although loftily distressed by junketing politicians, was waiting to brief Roosevelt. In Admiralty Rolls-Royces the FDR party motored to

London, meeting Livy Davis and Renah Camalier at the Ritz at six. Afterward they went to a "big entertainment" for servicemen. "House packed with khaki and a few of my Navy men." FDR looked forward to France, where in a costly counter-attack in the Rheims salient, "our men have undoubtedly done well. One of my Marine Regiments has lost 1200 and another 800 men."

The next day Roosevelt and his entourage met with First Lord of the Admiralty Sir Eric Geddes and were shown a model the British had created for mining the Channel approaches. At a press conference on July 26, where his rank was explained as "corresponding to that of a Deputy First Lord of the Admiralty," he boasted as backer of the mining barrage that "anti-submarine measures had now been developed into a science," and that "there was no longer any possibility that the German submarine could become a decisive factor. . . . " Relieved to be, finally, abroad, he confessed to a group of ministers and officers at the American Luncheon Club in the Savoy Hotel that—so *The Times* reported—"it had taken him just four years to get to this country."

At another lunch, with Foreign Minister Arthur Balfour, Roosevelt raised his "worry about the Italian Naval situation," a problem which Balfour promised to take to Prime Minister Lloyd George. Despite high-level persuasion, Italian inaction endured. As Franklin would learn, Italy was only going to keep its fleet in being, rather than exposed to battle, to exert whatever postwar influence could be established in the Mediterranean. The Italians were not interested in fighting a war—only in exploiting the peace.

With Geddes the FDR party visited stations in Wales and Ireland. In England they toured "National Shipyards" turning out standardized freighters. In London he worked at "my office" in the Admiralty complex at 30 Grosvenor Gardens—which was actually that of Captain (later Rear Admiral) Frank H. Schofield, who complained in a letter to his wife, Claribel, that he had to "share" space with the Assistant Secretary, who was only there for "a look-see." (The office was adjacent to that of Admiral Sims.) At Viscount Astor's Thameside estate, Cliveden, Franklin and Livy visited the "big hospital"—1,100 beds, largely for Canadian wounded—which had expanded from its origins in Nancy Astor's roofed tennis court. Ironically, given the wartime intrusion of medicine at Cliveden, she had converted to Christian Science in 1914. The Virginia-born Lady Astor, Franklin wrote to Eleanor, was "just the same, enthusiastic, amusing and talkative soul as always"—and in 1919 would become the first woman elected to the House of Commons.

On July 30, having returned to the Ritz on the 8:15 train that morning, Franklin dressed formally for a royal audience at 10:30 at Buckingham Palace. Accompanied by Captain McCauley and British admiral Sir Alan Everett, he "passed through several corridors lined with paintings of naval actions that I would have given anything to stop and look at." (FDR collected naval prints as well as stamps.) Everett waited while an equerry in a frock coat conducted the Americans up a flight of stairs to King George's study, where McCauley, once introduced, retired with the gentleman-in-waiting. With FDR the King discussed nautical matters, George V confessing that as a former naval officer—he had to give up the sea on becoming heir apparent* after his father, the future Edward VII— he longed for "active naval service." Since "our troops had reoccupied Chateau Thierry and had found examples of wanton destruction," he hoped that the Yankee presence would convince the American people "that the stories of outrageous destruction were true."

The King told FDR of "a nice letter from Uncle Ted" he had received, and learning since of "Quentin's probable death" (his plane had crashed in occupied territory), he "expressed much sympathy." Discussing other war casualties, King George recalled his visiting a military hospital in Scotland caring for sailors wounded in the Battle of Jutland, and stopping at the bed of a burly casualty who had a tattooed portrait of the King on his bared chest. When he praised the sailor's valor, the tar turned to expose a tattooed image of the Queen between his shoulder blades, one of the Prince of Wales on his right arm, and another of Princess Mary on his left arm. As the King again lauded his patriotism, the sailor confided, according to

---

* George's elder brother Eddy, the sickly Duke of Clarence, had died in 1892.

FDR's reminiscence twenty-three years later, "That ain't the half of it, your Majesty. You should see me behind. I 'ave two other portraits—I am sittin' on the Kaiser and von Hindenburg."

The scheduled fifteen courtesy minutes had lengthened beyond forty when the King "made a move" signaling closure, and Franklin said his good-byes. Afterward, in a post-luncheon speech at the Savoy, he credited the Royal Navy for carrying and escorting American troops to Europe. In June alone, 60 percent had come over in British bottoms. "I much hope," he wrote to Eleanor, "that these figures will be telegraphed home, but I doubt it as the representatives of the [Creel] Committee on Public Information over here have done nothing."

At the Liberty Hut, a YMCA operation, Roosevelt spoke to "a great gathering of American soldiers . . . and our Blue-jackets." In the evening he was a guest at "one of the famous Grays Inn dinners, a really historic occasion in honor of the [Allied] War Ministers," where Lord Curzon, representing the War Cabinet, spoke at length. "To my horror the Italian Ambassador and I were called on without warning to speak at the close." To one listener, the Assistant Secretary's impromptu remarks seemed inadequate. The Minister for Munitions came up to Franklin afterward and—probably after imbibing too many toasts—grumbled something acerbic. Winston Churchill, who had met FDR only once before, in Washington, would not see him again until the summer of 1941, on the cruiser *Augusta* in Placentia Bay, off Newfoundland, and the Prime Minister would not recall the earlier episode. In his later memoirs he invented a warmly diplomatic recollection.

As luncheons, dinners and conferences followed, the FDR diary becomes a list of names, yet Franklin was more interested in experiencing the war. The German high tide reached in the spring was beginning, under pressure, to recede as resources were diminishing and disillusion about the outcome increasing. It now seemed likely, he wrote to Eleanor as July gave way to August, that

American troops are to be the deciding factor. Mr. Balfour said that everyone understands that it was the American Second Division with the

Brigade of Marines* which stopped the rush at Chateau-Thierry and which opened the definite counter-offensive at Soissons, which has pinched the [German] salient into untenability. . . . We are off in the morning, all of us, for France, and should have a wonderfully interesting time.

He also told Eleanor that despite rationing of nearly everything, he and Livy had found opportunity for shopping. (An Admiralty chauffeur was in attendance.) "My old friends, the silk pyjamas, have gone up from 30 to 60 shillings, & I only got 3 pairs instead of the six pairs I wanted!" FDR also reported—much differently—to Daniels, noting that he would write again from Paris "after we have seen the Flying Base at Dunkirk." It housed the first Navy Aviation Squadron—which operated on patrol with a dozen British-built flying boats. The Navy would soon have "night bombers" being manufactured by Caproni in Turin, and each "will start to fly over the Alps next week and will carry a bomb weighing 1750 lbs."

The Channel crossing on a British destroyer on July 31 left him proud of the apparent success of the mine barrage, which had increased the safety of commercial fishing and improved the food supply. Daniels telegraphed to Paris, "Get all information about the fighting of Marines with any special instances of more than usual courage. Destroyer builders working better and every energy employed for speeding up work on them."

After a night in a bomb-damaged chateau near Calais, the party was motored in several vehicles to Paris. Bulky Renah Camalier bounced about alone in one vehicle with all the luggage. To Franklin's delight they proceeded indirectly through Clermont, Creil and Chantilly, past fought-over trenches and barbed-wire entanglements, before being installed luxuriously in the Hotel Crillon. He conferred with French officials, including the Minister of Marine. Once Franklin called on Marshal

---

*After two weeks in command, Major General James G. Harbord had been reassigned to a headquarters post and ordered on July 25 by General John J. Pershing to turn over his command of the Second Division to Marine brigadier general John A. Lejeune, now raised to major general. It was a remarkable position to be held by a Marine.

Joseph Joffre, who confessed his "discouragement" with American preparedness when in Washington just after war had been declared; he went to a luncheon at the Elysée Palace given by President Henri Poincaré for Herbert Hoover. FDR visited Premier Georges Clemenceau, still wily and energetic at seventy-seven, who regaled Franklin with dramatic, first-hand war stories. (Happily, Franklin's French was adequate.) "He did not wait for me to advance to meet him at his desk, and there was no formality such as one generally meets. He almost ran forward to greet me and shook hands as if he meant it; grabbed me by the arm and walked me over to his desk and sat me down about two inches away."

On August 3 Franklin looked up his cousins Ted (Major Theodore Roosevelt, Jr.) and Archie (a lieutenant) in a house in Paris where they were recovering from their wounds. Both had earned decorations. Archie was "looking horribly badly" and Ted "still has one leg on the sofa." They were "wonderfully interesting" and "both have splendid records." In the evening FDR's staff went to a "Revue" at the rowdy Café de Paris where "nine men out of ten" were in uniform and, he claimed, there was "wonderfully little intoxication. Nobody in uniform can be served with spirits, and French beer and wine are even weaker than in pre-war days." Apparently the Roosevelt party were all in civilian clothes, as nightlife was for them was a spirited exception to the ban.

At six the next morning, Sunday, August 4, his entourage, some like Livy badly hungover, were motored to the front in three vehicles. At Chateau-Thierry, with forward lines now twenty miles east, General Pershing was setting up headquarters for the First Army, which he expected would be succeeded in numbering as reinforcements arrived by "a second, third, etc." Refugees were returning to wrecked villages in one direction while the inadequate roads were clogged in the other "by an American artillery train, French guns, mostly 155's, but American-manned." A gun carriage "had broken down, of course at a narrow turn, and all traffic was held up in both directions. I got out and walked to the scene and found two very junior youngsters [in uniform] making a bad mess of the tangle." Communications were even more tangled. Although troops had proceeded well beyond Chateau-Thierry in the previous two weeks, neither rail trackage nor bridges disabled by the withdrawing Germans had "been advanced [by the French] one mile."

When the local French general sent an emissary to invite the Americans to dinner, Franklin realized that Captain V. S. Jackson, assigned by Daniels as naval attaché, had arranged for the party to be as far from "the actual fighting" as possible. Franklin was furious. It was "the final straw" for Jackson as guide. He preferred a good war. Roosevelt took over.

> From now on for four days I ran the trip, especially as I had discovered that the [Jackson] plans called for late rising, easy trips and plenty of bombed houses [now] thirty miles or so behind the front. We were to have slept in a comfortable hotel at Chalons, but I accepted the General's invitation to dine here . . . and to sleep on the floor of some unoccupied house. We left immediately [afterward], passed . . . over the ridge just in front of where the Marines first went into action when they checked the advance, and thence on a couple of miles to the eastern edge of Belleau Wood. . . . In order to enter the wood itself we had to thread our way past water-filled shell holes and . . . up the steep slope over outcropping rocks, overturned boulders, down[ed] trees, hastily improvised shelter pits, rusty bayonets, broken guns, emergency ration tins, hand grenades, discarded overcoats, rain-stained love letters, crawling lines of ants and many little [burial] mounds, some wholly unmarked, some with a rifle stuck bayonet down in the earth, some with a helmet, and some, too, with a whittled cross with a tag of wood or wrapping paper hung over it and in a pencil scrawl an American name.

Returning to their vehicles, they traveled north and east through shattered villages until they came to a clump of woods shielding "a great pit, ten or fifteen feet deep, containing the steel turntable and mechanism for a gun of very large calibre." It had been intended as mount for a long-range "Big Bertha" artillery piece (named for Bertha Krupp) to fire toward Paris, then abandoned as the Germans were forced to withdraw.

Soon, to the north they saw exploding shells and white puffs suggesting fire at a "Hun plane probably doing photographic work." It was their first encounter with action. Three or four miles farther on it became "quite evident that we are on the battlefield. To our sensitive naval noses the smell of dead horses is not only evident but very horrid." More than the corpses of horses were soon visible. "Dead Boche" were still sprawled in the fields "and in one place a little pile of them awaiting burial."

They passed a French division, with its equipment, moving to the rear "to recuperate," and German prisoners with them who, as they were the enemy, had a "stolid, stupid look" on their faces. At nine, in the growing darkness, they returned, exhausted, toward the headquarters of General Jean Degoutte, with FDR's party beginning "to realize," he wrote smugly, "what campaigning, or rather sight-seeing, with the Assistant Secretary means, and Captain Jackson is still visibly annoyed because I upset his comfortable plans. . . . " Crossing a pontoon bridge over the Marne, they reached a shelled village with two houses still intact. With their one "electric torch" to ascend the rickety stairs they located two former bedrooms. "By using six matches I discovered a table, chair and a bed with a mattress and a *duvet* on it. I managed to get my boots and leggings off and fell in—1:00 a.m. and a thoroughly successful day."

Before six on Monday, August 5, they were again on the move and visited a French hospital across a cratered road which had been bombed by an enemy plane despite two white crosses visible from above, then motored through Mèzy and Dormans seeking the Marine regiment to the east. Beyond Châtillon-sur-Marne and barbed-wire entanglements where the Germans had been, they stopped to try to locate the Marines "by long distance telephone." Finally, in the southeast of the St. Mihiel sector, they learned that the brigade was billeted near Nancy, and that General Lejeune was with Second Division headquarters in the city itself. Franklin knew all of the senior Marine officers and some of the [prewar] regulars. "Orders have just been received sending part of the Second Division up to the trenches," he reported in his letter-diary to Eleanor. "I am a little surprised, and I think the Division was, too. They were due to go the rear after the Belleau Woods fighting, during which they had about

40 per cent. of casualties.* Instead they were sent into the attack again at Soissons and lost over 20 per cent more. At last they were taken out, only a week ago, and sent here to Nancy to rest and take in their replacements. Now part of their resting is to be done in the front line trenches." The implication was clear and clearly unpublicized. More than a million and a half soldiers in the American Expeditionary Force had already crossed the Atlantic to France, but their readiness was minimal. Lacking ground transport, many were still in the clogged replacement pipeline from the crowded harbor in Brest. The division in the line, especially its Marine component, was "the most tried and true unit of the A.E.F."

Accompanied by General Lejeune and brigade commander Colonel Wendell C. Neville, Roosevelt inspected a battalion of the 5th Marines. Drawn up the length of a narrow street in a suburb of Nancy, they looked "wonderfully well" rather than exhausted and drawn. "The majority were in the khaki of the army, their own olive drab having been worn out long ago. The replacement troops were easily recognizable by the olive drab. It gave one a pretty good idea of the heavy casualties which had taken place. . . . " At a sloping field a mile further, a machine gun battalion was drawn up, and in the next village a battalion of the 6th Marines. Again many were in army khaki. According to Lejeune, they could be identified as Marines if they could wear the Marine Corps device on the collar points of their army shirts, but he lacked the authority. "I told him," FDR wrote, "that I would assume responsibility and then and there issued an order."

On Tuesday, August 6, after an early breakfast, the Roosevelt party "started on another breakneck motor spin" toward Verdun on the *Voie Sacrée* over which troops and supplies were rushed during the horrendous siege in 1916. The road was now widened to allow streams of traffic in both directions. Wearing French helmets and carrying gas masks, the group was escorted past hundreds of shell craters** by Colonel Dehaye, governor of Verdun, "into the tunnel which leads to the citadel, for the

---

*The Marines lost more than 100 officers and 5,500 men killed, wounded and missing.
** As trenches collapsed under incessant artillery fire during the siege, communications were often forwarded in empty shell cases thrown from crater to crater.

4000 men forming the garrison line live 60 feet under ground in vaulted galleries laid out like streets. . . . As for sanitary and toilet arrangements, they are practically non-existent." Air was forced into the tunnels by pumps, always arriving stale. Above was "a scene of colossal destruction" with "detached and jagged walls" everywhere. Back again below ground in a vaulted, "close and damp" canteen, the visitors had a spare lunch.

Afterward they were escorted to the "Valley of Death" at the Fort Douaumont ridge ("it is probable that over a hundred thousand men were actually killed in this little stretch of valley"*). As Colonel Dehaye pointed toward the village of Fleury, Boche observation balloons rose in the near distance. "The Colonel hurried us on . . . and said that we undoubtedly had been seen and that they would begin shelling the road in a minute or two." As they reached the south slopes a quarter-mile beyond, "sure enough the long whining whistle of a shell was followed by the dull boom and puff of smoke of the explosion at the Dead Man's Corner we had just left." Dehaye explained that the German battery had orders to aim "at that angle in the road every six minutes . . . in case traffic is reported as passing that point. As he spoke, a second whistling shell came over and exploded at the angle, and was followed by another." For Franklin it was his key moment abroad. He had been under actual fire.

At dark they had "a delightful dinner" in the dank canteen, slept in tunnel rooms, and left by motor the next morning, arriving at the Crillon in Paris late in the afternoon, "just in time to hear the last shots from the long range gun." One shell exploded north of the Louvre, and, Livy Davis wrote, "We saw the dust and debris." It was the last firing of the big Krupp artillery piece. The Germans had to move it out of range as they withdrew from the forest of St. Gobain.

That evening, accompanied by Captain McCauley, Franklin left by overnight train for Italy, reaching Turin at six in the evening the next day, Thursday, August 8. A private Italian government carriage had been

---

*French casualties at Verdun between February and July in 1916 were more hideous than FDR then knew—between 600,000 and 700,000 dead—and roughly equal on both sides.

attached at the border, where an Italian aide joined them. On the morning of the ninth "an enormous delegation" led by Admiral Del Bono, the Minister of Marine, met them at the railway station in Rome, and FDR began several days of frustrating discussions about "the lack of practically any offensive operations" and encouraging "more activity in the Mediterranean and Adriatic." In his introduction to serious international negotiations (for which he assumed authority he did not possess), Roosevelt pressed for a joint Allied naval command, but the Italians wanted no British or French involvement whatever, in part an excuse to do nothing but wait for Austrian collapse and then seize coveted territorial spoils.

On Saturday, August 10, Roosevelt reported in a letter home that he

remarked . . . in our conference that the Italian Battleship Fleet had not gone outside Taranto Harbor for over a year, that they had no fleet drill and target practice. [Admiral] Thaon di Revel leaned forward and said, "Ah, but my dear Mr. Minister, you must not forget that the Austrian Fleet have not any either." This is a naval classic which is hard to beat, but which perhaps should not be publicly repeated for a generation or two.

The Italians would earn his continued disgust in several further wars, yet he wrote to Daniels when back in Paris that his visit was "very successful" and "well worth the long trip." The Italian government could not be expected "to make the same sacrifices as France and England have made, and . . . some of their demands may be a little unreasonable. . . . " In effect, to Roosevelt's disappointment, Italy wanted material American aid, but offered nothing in return.

The results were even worse than he inferred. At a luncheon he gave for journalists, replying to a welcoming from Signor Gallenga, Minister of Foreign Propaganda, FDR announced, intoxicated by his sense of self-importance, or perhaps by something alcoholic and Italian, "I can tell you that fresh American troops will be sent to Italy, for henceforward the unity of our single front is as it should be, recognized as complete, solid, and indivisible." Since he was accepted as a Minister, he had asserted prerogatives he did not have in proposing a joint Mediterranean naval command and in offering troops he did not direct. Learning of it from Daniels only late in September, the President was furious, as had been English and French officials. Wilson ordered the Secretary to furnish names and missions in future regarding those "who go over assuming to speak for the Government."

Roosevelt's party returned to Paris in mid-August, then left for Bordeaux. At Pauillac, near the mouth of the Gironde, was a base entirely built by American personnel and materials. They lunched at a huge new mess hall "built almost entirely out of seaplane packing cases." Franklin "said a few words to the [3,000] men and [a] splendid entertainment was furnished by a jazz band, quartette and others." The ranks were filled with talent of a sort—"actors, musicians, professional ball players, etc." That was the "good war" aspect of the "wonderful location." As for why they were there, "Our Navy Dept. has fallen down rather badly. This base receives and assembles all airplanes . . . from the U.S. Part of the material, such as the Liberty Motors, has arrived in bad condition, showing faulty inspection at home and necessitating much work here; . . . for instance, we have in France over a hundred seaplanes but only two self-starters." Roosevelt reported to Daniels "scandalous conditions" which he blamed on lax administration of the Departmental bureau "overseeing the air arm." (Admiral Benson, FDR knew, had no use for aircraft in his Navy.) Daniels noted in his diary, "Held conference and wired that all diligence would be used, but that 148 [aircraft cases] had been shipped & others would go forward." He had praised Liberty engines as a bargain at $3,500.* Elsewhere in France, FDR was more satisfied. On August 25 he telegraphed, "Have completed inspection west coast ports. Conditions on the whole excellent."

Franklin expected to leave for home early in September but found reason to delay. He visited a radio station the Navy was constructing at Croix d'Hins and the docks at Bordeaux. He even swam off the chilly French coast and may have picked up there the beginnings of another

---

*The Liberty Engine had been designed over four days in a hotel room in Washington by J. G. Vincent of Packard Motors and E. J. Hall of the Hall-Scott Motor Company. Its simplicity made it useful for mass production but oversight and shipment had been hasty and sloppy.

FDR observing the unloading of Navy war materiel at the docks in Bordeaux, France, August 1918. He is top center, right. FDR LIBRARY.

FDR boarding a plane at the U.S. Naval Air Station, Pauillac, France, August 14, 1918. FDR LIBRARY

FDR at Rear Admiral Charles Plunkett's 14-inch railway naval cannon being readied for
travel to the front on a flatcar at Ste. Nazaire, France, August 17, 1918. FDR LIBRARY

upper respiratory infection, which progressively worsened. On the way to
Brest, from which he planned eventually to depart, and where most supplies and troops from the U.S. were offloaded, he paused at St. Nazaire on
the Loire. There, Navy 14-inch guns designed for big warships were being
mounted on railway carriages for transport to sectors on the front where
they could fire a 1,400-pound shell more than twenty miles. The flatcars
had "U.S. Navy" painted boldly on their sides.

Big batteries on warships were of little use in a conflict fought far inland, and when capital ship construction was being delayed to give priority to destroyers, Roosevelt had urged alternative ground deployment by
rail. As the transition was finally in progress, and the war might drag on
into winter—no German territory had yet been reached—Franklin wrote
to Eleanor cryptically, "Somehow I don't believe I shall be long in Washington. The more I think of it the more I feel that being only 36 my place
is not at a Washington desk, even a Navy desk. I know you will understand." He closed with "A great deal of love from / Your devoted / F."

Eleanor shared the message with Louis Howe, who reassured her, since the war seemed to be winding down, "I wonder if he knows that it has been practically decided to accept no new volunteers whatever under the new draft [regulations], and also that married men with children are not going to be called. I fear that he will have a somewhat strenuous time getting the President to waive regulations, particularly as I feel the President has sufficient judgment to know that things would go very badly here if [FDR] should leave. . . . "

At St. Nazaire, Rear Admiral Charles P. Plunkett, overseeing the railway emplacement of the naval batteries, wore an Army uniform. He and his crews were going forward. Roosevelt asked whether a role could be found for him. When Plunkett joked that Franklin had to be able to "swear a French train onto a siding and let my big guns through," he produced a plethora of French maledictions (some perhaps imagined) which impressed the admiral. Plunkett promised Roosevelt, should he return, the rank of lieutenant commander.

The railway artillery would gain mythic proportions. In rare humor, Wilson would tell a postwar meeting of his Cabinet, on returning from a visit to France still to come, that the Navy guns "created a great sensation as they were carried about the country to the battle front. One crewman said: 'Kills everybody within 100 mi[les] & hunts up [all] his next of kin & kills them.'"

In Paris, after conducting a press conference for the Creel Committee in his barely adequate French, while sitting informally on the edge of a table and asserting that the mine barrage against subs had begun to work, and that the Allies were "over the hump" in the war, he returned to the Crillon. At his breakfast with Clemenceau the next morning, the Premier commented that if he had to conduct press conferences he would resign. Another courtesy call again took Franklin close to the front. He met with General Douglas Haig, traveled into what remained of Belgian Flanders, observed an artillery exchange, experienced two German air raids of no consequence and lunched with King Albert of the Belgians.

An influenza pandemic, often combined with pneumonia, was already raging across Europe and had reached North America. Eventually the plague would kill more than twenty-one million worldwide. Franklin was feeling increasingly ill; his temperature had reached 102 degrees, alarming Livy Davis, who was accompanying him by rail to Paris. As Roosevelt persisted on following his schedule, his fever, he claimed, but not his persistent aches, abated briefly, enabling AEF chief John J. Pershing to visit him. Franklin then paid a courtesy call on Marshal Ferdinand Foch, the Allied commander, bringing up, to the obvious disinterest of Foch, who only cultivated his own ideas, the potential of the naval batteries. As a British destroyer ferried his party across the Channel, two German planes made bombing passes, which pleased FDR as he was again under fire.

Although he had telegraphed Daniels that he would be returning on September 5, he made no mention of that in a penciled message apparently written from London a day earlier:

> private for the secretary:
>
> For your information only, I have long thought of my proper duty in the war and now after organization work is nearly completed I am certain that I should be in active service in some capacity. . . . I naturally prefer Navy if possible and therefore will ask you about October 1 for a commission in Navy or Marines that will insure service at front. I do not need to tell you how hard it will be for me to end our work together, but know you will understand.
>
> Roosevelt

"In September 1918," he recalled to Daniels decades later, "I think I wrote you or cabled that after I had come home and reported to you, I wanted to go back to Europe with an assignment in uniform, to the Naval Railway Battery." Daniels did not remember it and told his son Jonathan, then working for Roosevelt, that he had no record of it. But Louis Howe knew.

Reluctant nevertheless to abort his mission despite increasing illness, he traveled by rail overnight from London to Scotland to visit the Navy's Battleship Division Nine in the Firth of Forth, where it was part of the rather useless post-Jutland Grand Fleet. He went even farther north, to

Inverness, to review the North Sea mine barrage, about which he took great pride. He could not have known of German commercial banker Paul von Berger's new pessimism, conceded to intimates in Berlin on August 29, about "the insane expectations regarding the submarines." Berger saw reasons he did not identify to "suspend" the U-boat campaign. His bleak outlook for the *Kriegsflotte* was at odds with a new propaganda play opening in Berlin, *Stand-by to Fire*, which implied future successes at sea.

The Assistant Secretary's party was four hours late for the mining inspection, blamed entirely on a tire puncture rather than their halting for the "brew of hot Scotch, honey, and oatmeal served in beakers" described by Livy Davis. They had also fished for salmon, and at Strathpeffer, a former spa taken over for wounded sailors, quaffed quantities of the national beverage, especially Livy, who also praised the "real chartreuse." With the weather outdoors "dour," Livy reported in his diary, they "had to keep it out with copious draughts of Scotch."

Back in London, although overwhelmed by what seemed increasingly to be acute bilateral pneumonia rather than influenza, FDR stubbornly reoccupied the Admiralty desk he had poached and prepared reports for Daniels. Giving in to his debilitation, he also wrote from bed in his hotel room. At a club for American officers in what had been Benjamin Disraeli's last home, on Curzon Street in Mayfair, some of the party, including an insistent Roosevelt, paid alcohol-fueled farewells to locally based friends. One of them, Langdon Marvin, a Congressman on leave, was now with a Red Cross unit. Realizing that the wan FDR had been pushing himself through serious illness, Marvin offered to help him pack his bags. Once home, Franklin assured him, he would resign his desk job and "get assigned to the big guns at the front."

Roosevelt returned across the Channel in a storm which pitched and rolled the destroyer about. When, with Davis* and McCauley, who were less ill, perhaps somewhat immunized by their alcohol intake, Roosevelt reached Brest by rail, he was pallid, weak and becoming incoherent. His fever was high, his muscles ached; his lungs were congested; his head

---

* Soon after disembarking, Livy Davis would be hospitalized with double pneumonia.

reeled; his ears roared. The immense *Leviathan* was loading. A Reuters dispatch in the September 20 issue of *The Times* reported that "Mr. Franklin Roosevelt, who has arrived at an Atlantic port, is suffering from a light attack of pneumonia."

Prior to embarking, the tottering Franklin and his group attended—it was almost unavoidable—a dockside mass funeral in the rain. Seventy-seven soldiers awaiting departure had already died. The mortality rate of the "Spanish flu" pandemic was more than thirty times that of the "normal" annual strain.

Franklin was taken to a cabin and put in a bunk to await the sailing, which became delayed and further delayed. The large transport *Covington* had been torpedoed and sunk when homeward bound from Brest in July, but the *Leviathan*, an even more formidable target, steamed west without incident, but for the ravages of the influenza catastrophe. On the floating hospital, 1,540 passengers and crew were suffering from flu, 1,067 from pneumonia. In the absence of anything else, the chief medication supplied aboard was quarts of whisky. Many victims were buried at sea as the *Leviathan* churned forward. Sixty-eight arrived dead. Of the 130,000 troops carried home on thirty-eight ships, 2,000 died. Many more died after debarkation.

Eleanor was at Hyde Park with Sara when, on September 12, they received a cablegram. They were to meet the liner with an ambulance and a physician. The dock would be crowded with ambulances. On September 19, 1918, with Dr. George Draper, whom Franklin had known at Harvard, in attendance, he was carried from the liner on a stretcher and down a gangplank. Seeing signs of recognition, Eleanor at first did not think he was "so seriously ill as the doctors implied." An ambulance took him to a guest bedroom in his mother's townhouse, as his own, adjoining, was still tenanted by the Lamonts. Utterly listless, he was unable to fend for himself, and when his baggage was unloaded and deposited at East 65th Street, Eleanor had to do all the unpacking. It was then that she discovered a packet of letters to him from Lucy.

8

"As the Rules Dictate"

Early in 1904, a year before the Roosevelts married, Eleanor went to see Bernard Shaw's *Candida* in Arnold Daly's production at the Madison Square Theatre in Manhattan. Daly played Eugene Marchbanks, a naïve and romantic young poet whom Candida Morell, at thirty-three the wife of a popular and attractive minister, teaches (ambiguously, according to the clever script) the facts of life. When the curtain closed, the temperature as Eleanor emerged on 24th Street near Broadway was minus-four, but she was exhilarated, and returned to see the play several more times. The dramatic comedy hinged on its "auction scene," in which Candida must choose, according to the callow Eugene and her distraught husband, James, his career at stake, between them. She elects to stay with James, who, she claims, needs her most. (Eleanor would once admonish her husband, "Boy dear, do you realize that you have not written your mother in over a week?" In the play, Candida explains to Eugene, "Now I want you to look at this other boy here—my boy—spoiled from his cradle. . . . Ask me what its costs to be James' mother and three sisters and wife and mother to his children all in one. . . . ")

The New York Times critic conceded, "I confess that this is one of the few occasions on which a naturally censorious disposition found nothing to cavil at." Although the setting is 1890s London, "The young things in front," according to another critic, James Huneker, "weep to see the poor boy going out lonely and broken-hearted into the cold night to save the proprieties of New England Puritanism."

The real-life triangle in September 1918 had a different arrangement of the sexes—two women and a man—but again the proprieties were at stake, and more. As Franklin was gravely ill, Eleanor, without asking his permission, opened the explosive packet of Lucy's letters and read them with increasing dismay. Very little is known, other than from possibly unreliable third parties, about the immediate aftermath of the impasse, and how the Lucy Mercer issue played out. Since Eleanor was too impatient, she told her son Elliott much later, to wait for her husband's condition to improve, the painful realities were first aired in Sara's townhouse on Friday, September 20, the day after the *Leviathan* docked. Franklin would have been too ill to say much, but he could not dispute his passion for Lucy. The letters were evidence enough. Eleanor's denying Franklin her bed (and opening him to other alternatives) seemed to her no excuse for his duplicity.

Wounded and betrayed, she again confronted Franklin with the letters when he was sufficiently recovered to be moved to Hyde Park at the end of the month. Then, he may have downplayed to its believable minimum the extent of his infidelity which Lucy's correspondence suggested. Marital "duty," the ordeal which Eleanor had renounced, very likely was never raised then, or later in the library at Springwood where she and Sara sat as judge and jury.

Although the commodious study at Hyde Park, built to Franklin's plans, was intended, with its rows of bookshelves, model ships, and nautical prints, to reflect him, it is very likely that the imperious Sara—it was her property—took pride of place by the fire, and Eleanor and Franklin sat where they could. In the "auction" scene in *Candida*, the denouement takes place in James Morell's library, where he is diminished by the paradox of place. ("*Morell, quite lost, takes the chair by the fireside: the children's chair.*") All three Roosevelts recognized their roles in their own drama. Sara and Eleanor had little need beyond Lucy's letters to imagine what might have occurred, and Franklin, humbled, had to plead his weak case as best he could.

Often together, the guilty pair—there was no question of that—had opportunities to go to whatever amorous limits they desired. They had no need for concealment in a hotel under a false married identity, and in any case, celebrity would have been a handicap to secrecy. Roosevelt was so well known in Washington and environs that they would have had to travel to a remote location for discreet romantic trysts. Subterfuge seemed hardly necessary, as Eleanor was often away with the children and servants at Campobello or Hyde Park, and the Roosevelt homes on N Street and then R Street were accessible to Lucy as social secretary, even after Eleanor had let her go. Other than Franklin, no one else knew of that perilous freedom.

Humiliating gossip from acquaintances who had seen the couple may have reached Eleanor, and even Franklin had noted, recklessly, yet cagily, in his letters to her, Lucy's occasional presence on weekend outings. Eleanor's outrage, in a letter to Franklin, at Lucy's seemingly well meaning assistance at R Street during the summer of 1918 suggests more than dawning suspicion of violated trust.

With the incriminating letters in hand, Eleanor (as she later told her daughter, Anna), "questioned him, offered him a divorce and asked that he take time to think things over carefully before giving her a definite answer." She had warned Franklin sternly about the effect of a divorce on their children. For the sake of their brood and their livelihood—and the societal decencies—they might continue to live dispassionately together. When Eleanor was seven, in 1892, her mother and father had separated. His alcoholism was stigma enough; divorce would have been unthinkable.

Like Candida Morell, Eleanor realized that divorce, or, in their case as Franklin was an emerging public figure, even public separation was impossible, and that she held in her hands all the trump cards, including Franklin's present and his future. He may no longer have wanted Eleanor, but he needed her. Very likely he recognized his predicament. Without divorce he could go off to Mexico or Jamaica with Lucy, if she would go with him, but how would they live? What could he do? The political ascent he dreamed of and already had begun planning for, and his sources of income to support it, would have vanished in scandal.

Although Eleanor ostensibly offered him his freedom to choose, under New York matrimonial law the sole cause enabling divorce was adultery. In New York it remained unlawful for the party guilty of adultery "to re-marry any person whatsoever" although the innocent partner might enter into another marriage "as if the party convicted was actually dead." Mari-tal mistakes could not then be undone by divorce. A compassionate state law passed in 1813 had made desertion grounds for legal separation for mistreated or deserted wives. In 1880 the statute was extended to hus-bands. Yet it was not divorce. Only in 1922 did the New York legislature pass an "Enoch Arden" act, authorizing decrees of presumed death once a missing spouse had not been heard from for five years. The conspiratorial device for divorce, employed for decades in stage comedies, was for a husband, even if not the guilty party, to enact an ostensible adultery by registering at a hotel with a female paid for her role, and having their pseudo-affair confirmed by the documented registry or by the testimony of the participant.

It seems possible, from the questionable memories of Mercer relatives, that Lucy was contacted by someone other than Franklin or Eleanor—perhaps Sara, or even Louis Howe—to learn her wishes. Could she, as an observant Catholic, marry a divorced man? Her Church did not recog-nize divorce. As in the case of the Episcopal formula under which the Roosevelts were married, the husband had vowed before God "to love and cherish her until death do us part." Lucy could have been relentless in her cultivation of Franklin short of matrimony. Religious scruples sug-gested that she could only accept the Church formula of annulment, which was hardly possible after thirteen years of the Roosevelts' marriage and the birth of six children. There was also the possibility, with priestly assent but without conversion, of a divorced spouse agreeing, on remarry-ing, to rear any children from the new marriage as Catholics. Living in sinful cohabitation, with her soul in jeopardy, was for Miss Mercer very likely impossible. Love in a bower did not exist for them, however it was celebrated in song and story. Nonetheless she would tell intimates forthrightly decades later and then long widowed that Franklin had been "the love of her life." Yet she could not have him as her husband.

Lucy's mother had already been divorced when she married Carroll Mercer in London, in a Church of England ceremony which to her later Catholicism was no marriage at all, as the Anglican persuasion, like Roman Catholicism, did not recognize divorce. Minnie Mercer came to Rome only after parting with Mercer, taking her daughters with her. All three remained with Rome, and its authority over their lives.

Impatient for freedom from her family, Eleanor's cousin Alice Roosevelt had wed a compulsive adulterer and rising Republican politician, Nicholas Longworth, and by 1912 wanted to free herself from him by divorce. The family reputation, she was warned, would be in jeopardy. Since the elder Roosevelts, although powerless in the circumstances, were opposed, the couple lived thereafter in mutual deceit. Despite a history of family raffishness and infidelities, no Roosevelt, on Franklin's side or Eleanor's, had ever divorced. The implicit rules of their privileged class, which might have populated an Edith Wharton novel, did not permit it. When Alice Longworth bore a daughter outside her marriage, the father a widely known senator, Nick accepted the child and she bore his surname.

HYDE PARK WAS the appropriate stage for the final scene in the melodrama in which Eleanor and Franklin were trapped, as the imperious Sara held the purse, and its strings. Franklin may have had two properties as gifts from his mother and one of his own, but he could not afford to keep them without her. Nor could he afford much else. "It is all very well for you, Eleanor," Sara is reputed to have said, "to give Franklin his freedom." But both had to confront the consequences. Whatever his qualms of conscience, if he broke up his marriage, even with Eleanor's reluctant consent, his mother warned, he would be disinherited. He would never again inhabit his beloved "Springwood." He would lose his children, who, in his stead, would become her heirs. Although he would never have "another dollar" from her, he would legally retain his $6,000-a-year trust income; yet how would he be able to pay for the upkeep of his residences in Manhattan and Campobello, his children's private school education, his own expansive lifestyle, his club memberships, his taxes, his medical bills, even his life insurance premiums? What prestigious law firm would employ a figure of public disrepute, and what fashionable society would not exclude him? His financial anxieties would continue to escalate. His political future would plunge to zero. Eleanor herself risked social suicide.

The only person with whom Roosevelt could confide was the reliable Louis Howe, who in times of stress had become close to Eleanor. Whatever Elliott Roosevelt's later sources of information, he would write after his father's death that "it was Louis Howe going back and forth and just reasoning, convincing father that he had no political future if he did this." Of even more immediate concern was the future for both FDR and Howe at the Navy Department. Josephus Daniels's puritanical rigidity was a byword in Washington.

The first priority of departmental as well as family business was to cut ties with Lucy. Franklin might not have sent Louis Howe as intermediary, yet Howe may have been involved anyway, as well as Franklin himself. Anna Roosevelt, who came to know Lucy Mercer much later as Mrs. Rutherfurd, disclosed that "L. M. hinted to me that there were a couple of such meetings to wind up loose ends." At one of them Franklin apparently brought his European diary with him to describe what he had seen and done abroad that he could not have detailed in brief letters to her. He may have claimed, then, that Eleanor had refused a divorce, and he may have offered Lucy temporary financial support from what little resources he had. According to Anna, Lucy reaffirmed her love, but understood that the relationship was over.*

Were these personal sacrifices in the grand tradition of the romantic stage? Not if the box office mandated happy endings or sanguinary tragedies. As columnist Murray Kempton would write, the Roosevelts "had all acted as the rules dictate." Franklin promised not to see Lucy

---

*Thanks to intermediaries, including Anna, later, it was not over. They exchanged occasional messages of a familial nature, and for his first inaugural in March 1933, Franklin quietly arranged for a limousine and seating for Lucy. For years they did not meet.

again. Eleanor destroyed the compromising letters and very likely Lucy did likewise. One person she seems to have confided in then was Elizabeth Henderson, a cousin originally from Salisbury, North Carolina. Elizabeth was married to Captain Lyman A. Cotten, a member of the General Board of the Navy who was known to the Assistant Secretary as well as to Lucy. As the Cottens lived in Washington near Minnie Mercer's apartment, Lucy, rather than remain with her mother during the wrenching aftermath, moved in temporarily with her cousin's family. The Cottens claimed that Lucy told them that a marriage with Franklin would have taken place, but "Eleanor was not willing to step aside." So Franklin may have told her.

According to Elizabeth Cotten, the situation was "hopeless," but she was "sure neither one of them ever loved anyone else." Although Lucy became devoted to her future husband, her emotional attachment to Franklin would outlast her wedding vows. Whatever FDR told Lucy at the time, Eleanor's purported willingness to step aside was unrealistic. Elizabeth Cotten suggested, breezily, "Nothing is easier in the Roman Catholic Church than annulment, especially among those occupying high places," but her remark ignored the theological complications—a long Roosevelt marriage and a large brood. Once when Alice Longworth was doing bitchy "imitations" of her cousin Eleanor for their aunt, Corinne Roosevelt Robinson, "Auntie Corinne looked at me and said, 'Never forget, Alice, Eleanor offered Franklin his freedom.' And I said, 'But Darling, that's what I've wanted to know about all these years. Tell.' And she said, 'Yes, there was a family conference and they talked it over and finally decided that it affected the children and there was Lucy Mercer, a Catholic, and so it was called off.'"

In effect, it was never on. However passionate the relationship had been, however dashing Franklin seemed to Lucy, the abrupt end saved the Roosevelt marriage, such as it had become. Much later James Roosevelt described the aftermath for his parents as "an armed truce." Although the marriage would never return to what it had been, and was physically over—the couple would never again share a bed, and apparently had not done so since Eleanor's last pregnancy—it rescued a political career of immense promise. Whether or not Louis Howe was asked, he apparently reminded his chief of the jeopardy in which that promise hung. It could not be repatched after public catastrophe. To appease destiny, FDR needed his increasingly purposeful spouse.

Eleanor wrote of that time "obliquely," as her biographer Blanche Wiesen Cook put it. "I think I learned then," Eleanor would confess, "that practically no one in the world is entirely bad or good, and that motives are often more important than actions. I spent most of my life in an atmosphere where everyone was sure of what was right and what was wrong, and as life progressed I have gradually come to believe that human beings who try to judge other human beings are undertaking a somewhat difficult job."

In 1982, the centenary year of FDR's birth, Murray Kempton fashioned a "fugitive fantasy" of what seemed to him a "splendidly eternal" myth of what might have happened. Together, he wrote, Franklin and Lucy

> had sacrificed her immortal soul and his own high destiny. There, these two will endure in the imagination, growing old together, say near Newburgh [on the Hudson], he languidly farming and dimly drawing wills and litigating country quarrels and she stealing now and then into the dreary little [Episcopal] church to grieve a while for the spiritual loss that had bought their happiness. The Depression is hard on him, but, when he dies, he has [by then] managed to recoup by selling his remaining acres for a postwar housing development. . . . She lives a long while afterward, is restored to the [Roman] Church, and works in the library and always thinks of him tenderly. They would, we may be certain, have brought it all off better than the Windsors,* and hardly anyone would have known they had.

Although Franklin could not have left for a problematic new life with Lucy, the resentment about his faithlessness would never leave Eleanor,

---

*Edward VIII, on his abdication in 1936 to marry the twice-divorced Wallis Warfield Simpson, relinquished his throne for love and melancholy exile as the Duke of Windsor.

however loyal she would remain to him, to his career ambitions, and to the rules of their class and time. Among the papers she kept all her life was a faded newspaper clipping of "Psyche," by Virginia Moore, a Virginia writer who published three books of poetry between 1926 and 1936, and one on lives of literary women from Sappho to her own century. It was found after her death in 1962:

> The soul that has believed
> And is deceived
> Thinks nothing for a while
> All thoughts are vile.
> And then because the sun
> Is mute persuasion,
> And hope in Spring and Fall
> Most natural,
> The soul grows calm and mild. . . .

At the top of the tattered clipping she had written "1918."

IN A LETTER to Sara, dated February 14, 1920, Eleanor wrote to her mother-in-law, in a line cautiously buried among updates about the children and political gossip in Washington, "Did you know Lucy Mercer married Wintie Rutherfurd two days ago?" Both knew him. Lucy had met Winthrop Rutherfurd, a striking, immensely rich widower in his late fifties, at Corcoran House, on 1607 H Street, home of Edith Morton Eustis and her husband, William. When Eleanor was away, Lucy had often visited them with Franklin, and when Alice Longworth had seen Franklin and Lucy out driving, the pair may have been motoring to Oatlands, the Eustis country estate. A wealthy Virginian, William Corcoran Eustis was a Harvard man a decade prior to Franklin, and Edith—a few years older than FDR—was a daughter of Levi Morton, once Republican governor of New York and Vice President under Benjamin Harrison. Despite differences in politics Levi Morton was a country crony of James Roosevelt.

The Mortons of Rhinebeck, only a few miles from Hyde Park, were Dutchess County friends and neighbors, which gave Franklin entrée to the lavish, art-filled Eustis home in Washington. Winty Rutherfurd, a descendant of Peter Stuyvesant, the Dutch governor of New York, and John Winthrop, the first governor of colonial Massachusetts, was Edith's brother-in-law and a friend of Theodore Roosevelt. Rutherfurd's wife, Alice, Edith's sister, had died in 1917, leaving her husband with six children—five sons and a daughter. The youngest was then four years old. Before Alice Rutherfurd's death she had converted to Catholicism and was loyally joined in the faith by Winthrop.

Apparently through Edith Eustis's intervention, Rutherfurd in mid-1919 asked Miss Mercer, who was without a job, to look after his children in some undefined way. She left her mother's apartment, for which she somehow paid the $35 a month rent, on July 30, 1919. Although no governess, she had all the other necessary attributes. She was competent, attractive, Catholic, and possessed credentials as Eleanor Roosevelt's former social secretary. Early in 1920, the oldest Rutherfurd son, the teenage Lewis, died of pneumonia. Winthrop was shattered. But he had already asked Lucy, half his age, while he was only a year younger than her mother, to marry him. The Roosevelts found out when their friends Frank and Lilly Polk—he was Undersecretary of State—visited for tea. As they were leaving, Lilly Polk (who knew Lucy Mercer) asked Eleanor loudly enough that Franklin would hear whether they knew that Miss Mercer was going to marry Winty Rutherfurd. Reportedly, Franklin winced "like a horse in fear of a hornet."

The marriage took place quietly, given the circumstances, at the home of Lucy's sister, Violetta Marbury. (While an army nurse in wartime France she had met William B. Marbury, a battlefield physician from a venerable Maryland family.) On February 13, 1920, the *Washington Post* reported in its social notes that Lucy Page Mercer had been married "yesterday morning" to "Mr. Winthrop Rutherfurd of New York. . . . On account of deep mourning only the immediate family were present." Rutherfurd had estates in New Jersey and South Carolina, and homes in

Washington, New York and Paris. When the letters predicament had arisen, both her destiny and Franklin's were in doubt. Lucy's future was now assured.

ELEANOR MET HER Uncle Ted at a family funeral late in 1918 while Franklin was recovering, and the subject came up as to what young Roosevelt would do next. The war was ending. Attempting to avert internal chaos, Germany's allies had been quitting. Germany was probing President Wilson about peace, and at first he was failing, in his imperious manner and to his later cost, to consult England and France. TR wrote afterwards, possibly seeking some intimation of FDR's future, or hoping to involve himself in manipulating destiny,

> Dear Franklin:
> We are deeply concerned about your sickness, and trust you will soon be well. We are *very* proud of you.
> With love,
> Aff. Yours
> Theodore Roosevelt
> Later, Eleanor will tell you of our talk about your plans.

What plans niece and uncle shared remain unknown. The elder Roosevelt wanted a bright future for Franklin, and may have felt that his remaining under Wilson, whom TR thought would soon be discredited, would be a mistake. FDR had to cut himself loose. Publicly, the Colonel was for "complete victory and unconditional surrender"—and he felt that in the interest of a quick peace, Wilson would bargain both away.

Leaving Franklin with her mother-in-law, Eleanor took the children to Washington to begin school, commuting back and forth until he was able to travel. He worked on a long report for Daniels about his inspection journeys, dated October 1, which impressed the Secretary with its precise details and shrewd recommendations. Franklin also spent some evenings with Eleanor to work on revising the letter-diary from France for possible publication, very likely hoping for some healing togetherness, but the project and the goal both remained unfinished.*

In a Cabinet meeting Daniels praised Roosevelt's report to Wilson. From Hyde Park, FDR wrote to Charles McCarthy, who undoubtedly had learned of Roosevelt's yearnings for active duty from Howe, "You are quite right in guessing that I am probably going to get into the fighting end of the game, but if I do so I suppose it will be the Navy and not the Army." Howe kept in touch by telephone and told Eleanor, "Do assure Mr. Roosevelt that things are really going smoothly, and you might tell him that I showed [the office] the seemingly impossible by being ready for his arrival without a single unanswered letter or unattended to piece of work. . . . Politically speaking, he is taken ill, which is the usual Roosevelt luck. . . . "

As the midterm election cycle was in progress, Franklin was freed by illness from mounting the stump for the beleaguered Democrats. "If you have approved my leadership," Wilson appealed to voters, "and want me to continue to be your unembarrassed spokesman in affairs at home and abroad, I earnestly beg that you will express yourselves to that effect by returning a Democratic majority to both the Senate and the House of Representatives." Republicans, he charged, "have been unquestionably pro-war, but they have [also] been anti-administration. . . . Republican leaders desire not so much to support the President as to control him."

Franklin returned to work on October 18. Livy Davis met him, with Eleanor, at Union Station and realized that he was wan and not yet well. His proverbial buoyancy had vanished. At R Street a telegram arrived from Hyde Park for him from "Sis"—twelve-year-old Anna. She had won, as a door prize at a Red Cross benefit in Rhinebeck, where Laura Delano, "Aunt Polly," lived, a German Shepherd puppy. Could she keep

---

*Togetherness continued, but tenderness did not. But for an occasional and perfunctory "dear," only after FDR's sweeping reelection victory for governor of New York in 1930 could Eleanor write to him warmly, as she was leaving for the Todhunter School in Manhattan, "Much love and a world of congratulations. It is a triumph in so many ways, dear, and so well earned. Bless you and good luck these next two years."

him? "Yes," her father replied. It was obviously a family necessity. "Major" would come with her to Washington.

However tottering, Franklin remained stubbornly eager to get into uniform before the war ended, and from his office exploited his reports on the Navy in England and France for an appointment with Wilson. A story probably planted by Howe to push his chief's cause had already appeared in the press suggesting absurdly that Roosevelt, if it came to that last resort, would enlist in the Navy as a common seaman. But Wilson didn't read newspapers, and Howe had already warned Franklin that enlistments of any kind were now canceled.

The White House appointment was set for October 31, but the self-absorbed President remained busy all day. Ignoring his wartime partners, he was trying to dictate his own peace terms to the desperate Germans. Roosevelt had to wait until 11:00 PM for a meeting. Daniels, like Howe, realized that Franklin's unending desire for a uniform was more bizarre than ever, but to put an end to the impossible dream he had encouraged the appeal. "In his judgment," FDR recalled of Wilson, "I was too late— that he had received the first suggestions of an armistice from Prince Max von Baden [the new German Chancellor], and that he hoped the war would be over very soon."

The interchanges with Prince Max at first were foolishly kept secret from Britain and France, but their intelligence services would pick them up. Although the Allies had practiced their own dark diplomacy throughout the war, their anger at Wilson's failed subterfuge would not be useful to the President, who publicly claimed high ideals. Wilson did not even inform his military commanders in the field, determining in his Calvinist confidence that he had succeeded in arranging how the war would end and how he would manage the peace. After all, he did not need to consult the Allies, as the United States in his professorial wisdom was only an "associated" nation not legally bound to them.

In the midterm election on November 5, the Democrats lost six seats in the Senate and thirty in the House. Wilson's ebbing ability to lead was more fragile than ever. The Republican insistence on a punitive peace seemed more in line with the public mood, and that of the Allies, than the President's more liberal policies already offered, on his own, to Germany. The day after, Theodore Roosevelt declared that Republicans had won "on the unconditional surrender issue, and their victory serves notice on Germany that Foch will dictate the terms of the Armistice." Seeing the results as a vote of no-confidence in Wilson's accumulation of wartime domestic powers, Senator Lodge claimed a "country-wide revolt against dictatorship and a desire to return to constitutional limitations." Both views suggested little future in Washington for FDR and the Democrats.

ILLNESS REAPPEARED AT R Street. Three of the Roosevelt servants came down with influenza, then the five children, and Franklin. "There was little difference between day and night for me," Eleanor remembered. A doctor came twice a day. Little John was especially sick, with bronchial pneumonia as well as "Spanish flu." His crib was moved to her bedroom. Many in Washington went about on the streets wearing gauze surgical masks; about 3,500 in the city died. Worldwide, the Navy was swamped, operating hospitals from the Azores to the Philippines, including Strathpeffer in Scotland, where FDR, once more out of the picture, but again recovering, had visited. Thirty-one Navy nurses died during the pandemic, which continued into the new year.

STILL HOPING FOR a curtain-call opportunity in uniform if peace negotiations failed, Franklin on November 9 wrote dispiritedly to Lathrop Brown, now in the Tank Corps, that "the consensus of opinion seems to be that the Boche is in a bad way and will take anything, but I am personally not so dead sure as some others. If the terms are turned down and the war continues, I think I shall get in the Navy without question." Yet the hapless Germans could not turn any terms down. The war was about over.

Two days later, just after five in the morning in France, an imposed Armistice was signed in Marshal Foch's railway carriage in the forest of Compiégne, to take effect six hours later, affording time for cease-fire messages to reach most troops. Despite Wilson's personal preliminaries, no U.S. representative was present in Foch's negotiating party. At 6:25 AM, General Hunter Liggett received instructions for his I Corps that hostilities were to end at eleven (twelve by Berlin clocks) and he urgently ordered front-line commanders to obey. Some American units were beyond reach, and futile casualties mounted.

Franklin and Eleanor awoke in their separate bedrooms to the sounds of jubilation and newsboys crying "Extra!" in R Street and beyond. The first bulletins had arrived in Washington at 2:45 AM. Everyone who read newspapers knew the shooting was about to stop, and emotions had not been quieted by the premature Armistice reports of November 7, triggered by an erroneous United Press report from Brest, purportedly from Paris. Eleven o'clock Paris time was five in the morning in Washington.

The Roosevelts hastily dressed and soon were in the dawn-dim streets themselves, joining the happy, makeshift processions. The ravages of "Spanish flu" were temporarily forgotten. As in many cities and towns, effigies of Kaiser Wilhelm, who had abdicated and fled to Holland two days earlier, were ceremoniously hanged, beaten, blinded, burned or dismembered by delirious—and often drunken—throngs. For Eleanor, "The feeling of relief and thankfulness was beyond description." It was not the same for their Uncle Ted, for whom the cacophony of screaming sirens and automobile horns meant an ambulance journey from Oyster Bay through traffic jams across Long Island to the Roosevelt hospital in Manhattan. Edith wrote to her children, "Father is flat on his back with gout. . . . He is having a horrid suffering time." A hospital spokesman would downplay the former president's problem as a flare-up of lumbago, concealing, for a time, his last illness.

On the Western Front, many American soldiers held up their watches to check the time and kept firing until the Armistice became effective. The rail crew of one fourteen-inch naval gun whom FDR so wanted to join received the cease-fire order on schedule, then rifled a 1,400-pound shell deep into German lines, timed to land and explode precisely at 11:00 AM French time. Captain Harry Truman's battery had fired its last barrage at 10:45. "When the firing ceased all along the front lines," he remembered, "it seemed . . . so quiet it made me feel as if I'd suddenly been deprived of my ability to hear."

With Eleanor, Franklin walked gingerly through the noisy, crowded streets to watch the impromptu parades passing the brightly lit White House. He had missed out on the action. Now all he could do was wind up his segment of the war.

9

Aftermath

W EAK AND WAN but on the job after the Armistice, Roosevelt found looming in "Main Navy" a bewildering tangle of demobilization affairs, foreign and domestic. Although he knew that Daniels had no interest in personally attending to the European phase of the winding-down, both Sims in London and Benson in Washington had already urged "immediate action," and Daniels had shared their memos. On November 14, FDR reminded him "that an enormous number of [overseas] contracts, claims, both personal and property, readjustments, etc., etc., had been laid on one side pending the termination of hostilities."

Franklin argued that a civilian representative of the Navy was necessary to conduct government business inappropriate for careerist high brass, or for the inexperienced young officers they might designate. There would be political implications in dealing with other sovereignties, and, cagily, he wanted "your administration of the Navy to continue without scandal or criticism" as much of the business was financial. For example, he wrote in a memo to Daniels that shipping home all military vehicles seemed ridiculously expensive. "How can we tell in Washington as to whether it would be better to send some automobiles home or sell them on the other side?" The Navy even had to dispose of long-range radio stations used to contact ships at sea. "This civilian does not need a large staff. He should have one or possibly two good lawyers, one first-class Paymaster, and one first-class Civil Engineer." As Roosevelt was the only assistant secretary and civilian executive in the Navy Department, he was not concealing his eagerness to undertake the job himself.

Daniels was reluctant to let his deputy go. Postwar departmental business was piling up, and kept accumulating. Formulated long in advance, war contracts cancellation orders had already been wired by the hundreds on November 12, with many more to follow, offering thirteen cents on the dollar for closure. Many contracts would take years to settle. In a self-congratulatory stretch, Louis Howe wrote to a friend after both he and Franklin left their posts, "At this moment, thirty-two naval officers [are] doing the work which was my job in the old administration."

The Army, almost immediately, discharged 600,000 soldiers not yet abroad, each with a meanly small stipend and a ticket home. British vessels which had ferried troops to France charging for each American soldier, although Britain would owe the United States borrowed billions it would never pay back, were now being withdrawn to satisfy national needs, additionally burdening homeward transit for overseas draftees upon the Navy. Army indiscipline in France on news of the Armistice required prompt, often makeshift, solutions. Most of the nearly two million Yanks abroad had seen no action and were still in ramshackle training camps far from the war. Placards they raised read "Hell, Heaven, or Hoboken by Christmas"—or used stronger language. The Navy began converting all available vessels with any troop-carrying potential into temporary transports—battleships, cruisers, tankers, freighters and confiscated enemy ships—174 in all, conveying 419,000 doughboys westward in their initial voyages. Processing took time, and funding, and multiple circuits for each reused vessel. Many troops would have to wait, with increasing impatience, into the spring and summer of 1919.

Perhaps to soften Daniels, Roosevelt invited him to lunch a few days after the Armistice, hoping that Eleanor would be additionally persuasive. Franklin needed her physical support after his illnesses, and he wanted to demonstrate after the Lucy debacle that Eleanor was inseparably vital to him. He had no idea that on some days, whatever the weather, while he

The Clover Adams memorial in Rock Creek Cemetery, known as *Grief*, but actually untitled, sculpted by Augustus St. Gaudiens for Henry Adams in 1892. Visited alone and often by Eleanor in 1918–1919 in the aftermath of the Lucy Mercer affair.

was busy settling into Main Navy, finished too late for the war, she would be driving, always alone, to a secluded grove of pines in Rock Creek Cemetery where Augustus St. Gaudens, with architect Stanford White, had sculpted at a nameless gravesite a brooding bronze figure shrouded in a cowled robe. Eleanor would sit on a stone bench and, according to caretakers, contemplate what St. Gaudens had wrought.

"Wisdom," Henry Adams said, "is silence." Commissioned by Adams, the image was an unforgettable memorial to his unidentified wife, Marian "Clover" Adams, who in severe depression had killed herself, at forty-two, on December 6, 1885. A skilled photographer, "Clover" had consumed a vial of potassium cyanide, a developing fluid she used. Known since as *Grief*, St. Gaudens's bronze figure was gloomily provocative. "As I looked at it," Eleanor later wrote, "I felt that all the sorrow humanity ever had to endure was expressed in that face. Yet in that expression there was something almost triumphant." In his crusty, pessimistic third-person memoir, *The Education of Henry Adams*, which Eleanor had yet to read, Adams had written, obliquely, "The interest of the figure was not in its meaning but in the response of the observer."

Eleanor would turn her melancholy into a reconstituted marriage inwardly as cold as the statue. Her first of many lonely visits may have been impelled by the anniversary of Clover's suicide, attributed by her friends to lingering despair over the death of her beloved father, but reflecting, too, her quiet desolation over her husband's infatuation with Elizabeth Cameron, the beautiful second wife of loutish former Pennsylvania senator James Donald Cameron.

Marian may have believed she had been betrayed. Both Adams and Cameron, who had long been estranged from Elizabeth, had died in 1918. Eleanor had learned in gossip-ridden Washington of Adams's love for Lizzie Cameron. Although it was apparently unrequited, he remained devoted to her all his life, and visited Elizabeth whenever he was in Paris, where she had lived for many years.*

FRANKLIN WAS AGAIN ill early in December, which may have given Daniels an excuse to delay authorization for the Assistant Secretary to undertake the Department's winding down of business abroad. Daniels preferred permitting Admiral Sims, whom he despised, and who stiffly protected his perquisites, to administer demobilization from London. Although still "laid up in the house" on December 7, FDR again pressed, in

---

* Although Mrs. Cameron was pregnant at the time of Clover's death, Elizabeth and Adams, who was childless, were geographically distant from each other at the likely time of her daughter's conception. Busybody speculation about Martha Cameron's parentage arose anyway.

a longhand letter, for permission to travel, this time claiming that he wanted personally to be absolved of guilt "in what I believe to be a failure to handle the problem rightly." Politically sensitive, Daniels gave in. An undated penciled note by Franklin to Admiral Benson, who would be sailing to France separately, confirmed, "Assistant Secretary of the Navy will leave for London Dec. 15 and will be in full charge of all questions in Europe involving disposal of all navy property, etc." Yet Daniels stalled further in signing travel orders until Christmas Eve, after a visit at his office from Sara, noted in his diary cryptically as "Mrs. James Roosevelt—." Was she on a mission to level confidentially with Daniels about the Lucy affair and its closure? Did she merely want to see Main Navy?

Whether or not Sara had anything to do with the turnabout, that afternoon Daniels gave Franklin "full authority to ascertain the status of all outstanding contracts . . . and to settle such obligations incurred by the Navy and claims arising from Naval operations abroad."

Amends at home were in order for Franklin as he again bounced back from illness. The Roosevelts gave a party to celebrate the approaching marriage of Sallie Collier, daughter of Sara's younger sister Kassie. "It was really wonderful and I enjoyed it," Eleanor wrote to Sara. Franklin added that Eleanor talked to "heaps and heaps of people, and I actually danced once." Daniels was there, and declared, with guests assuming that he meant the engaged couple, "No woman marries the man she really married." The Roosevelts understood. Franklin, Eleanor wrote, was postponing his Sunday golf mornings at Chevy Chase to afternoons, in order to accompany her to St. Thomas's Church, "which I know is a great sacrifice to please me."

They were home around the Christmas tree with their family on Christmas Day. They also invited twelve sailors from a convalescent home run by their friend Anne Lane, wife of Secretary of the Interior Franklin Lane, and twelve sailors from the Naval Hospital. Alice Roosevelt Longworth came late, having traveled to Oyster Bay for her father's homecoming to Sagamore Hill after forty-four days in the hospital. TR was worn but stoic; hospitalization could do no more for him. He talked, but without conviction, of recapturing the White House in 1920, and fighting off Wilson's "visionary" League of Nations scheme, which would link the United States in a peace treaty to the selfish interests of the European vic-tors. "I have only one fight left in me," he told his sister Corinne.

With Sara remaining with the children, who were recovering from flu, Eleanor and Franklin took the train to New York City, where the next day, despite falling snow, the Assistant Secretary and Eleanor in freezing cold reviewed the returning "Victory Fleet" from the bridge of the de-stroyer *Aztec*. FDR stood bareheaded at attention with his bowler hat clamped against his chest and his hair whitened by snow; Eleanor was shielded by a broad-brimmed black hat. Prominent in the fleet were the sister battleships *Florida* and *Utah*, which had done convoy duty on the approaches to Ireland. (On December 7, 1941, the *Utah*, relegated by obsolescence to target vessel, was nevertheless bombed to the bottom of Pearl Harbor, where its hulk remains.)

From Hoboken, Eleanor and Franklin sailed for France on January 2, 1919. Heavy winter seas pitched and rolled the *George Washington*, just returned from taking President Wilson to Europe. Although weakened by midterm election losses in November, he had George Creel's wartime Committee on Public Information, not yet shut down, mount a futile campaign in his absence to persuade "all the world" that "hope for the fu-ture lay in Wilson alone."

Aboard with FDR as his legal adviser was Thomas J. Spellacy, a federal district attorney in Connecticut, who was accompanied by his wife; Commander John M. Hancock, Navy purchasing chief, as FDR's business aide; Captain Charles McCauley as military aide; and the inevitable Livy Davis, detested by Eleanor, as "special assistant." While at sea, Eleanor wrote to Sara that Franklin was exercising daily with coach Walter Camp, aboard as a recreation specialist; playing shuffleboard; and begin-ning "to do a little work." Davis and Mrs. Spellacy were soon seasick, and Eleanor wrote to Sara that she wished both unnecessary travelers were "safely at home." Brought aboard as a Christmas gift for Franklin from Eleanor was the first commercial printing of *The Education of Henry Adams*. It occupied, for her, some of the rough hours at sea while he dealt with paperwork. Although the memoir carefully left Clover Adams un-

FDR bareheaded to take the salute from the homecoming fleet in the falling snow, aboard the USS *Aztec* in New York harbor, December 26, 1918. FDR LIBRARY

mentioned, reading it aware of what it left out apparently, for Eleanor, substituted for her homage at the somber sculpture site.

Shipboard entertainments featured a musical skit by crewmen in drag. Films, then still silent, included Charlie Chaplin's hilarious *Shoulder Arms*; and an orchestra, quartet and singers performed. The liner was crowded with American business elite, including steel magnate Charles Schwab, now head of the Emergency Fleet Corporation, and Bernard Baruch, former chairman of the War Industry Board. FDR and Schwab spoke at a gala dinner on January 5. Also aboard were tourist families—at least mothers and daughters—in hoarded finery, and released from wartime restraints. "Just wait until I get home and tell you what these respectable people now let their daughters do," Eleanor, her less-than-amorous feelings now aroused more than ever, wrote to Sara. "Your hair will curl as mine did!" The voyage seemed prewar Atlantic travel suddenly restored.

En route, a radio message arrived from Daniels that the Roosevelts' Uncle Ted, only sixty, but enfeebled by inflammatory rheumatism, had died at Sagamore Hill on January 6. "The old lion is dead," Archie cabled his brothers in France, still recovering from their wounds. To reporters aboard Franklin described TR as "the greatest man I ever knew." Wilson, in Europe drawing delirious crowds who acclaimed him as the saintly American bringing peace, was in Italy, but his press secretary at home, Joseph Tumulty, released a message of sympathy to TR's family. (Wilson himself cabled Edith Roosevelt that he was "shocked," rather than, as he first dictated, insincerely, "grieved.") Secretaries Baker and Daniels ordered all units on land and sea to fly flags at half-mast. As a tribute to TR and his son Quentin, killed in air action in France, General William Keily, army director of aeronautics, ordered two four-plane flights from Hazelhurst Field at Mineola, Long Island, to drop laurel wreaths and hover, in turn, over Sagamore Hill until the former president's burial.

The *George Washington* docked at Brest on January 9, 1919. Since accommodations ashore were poor, FDR and Eleanor at first remained on board in their luxurious suite, with two staterooms and bath. Conditions for troops awaiting return passage were appalling. Marine brigadier general Smedley Butler, Franklin's old friend from Haiti, ran the overcrowded evacuation camp as best he could, but was unable to alleviate the ankle-high mud and what Eleanor described in a letter to Sara as "savage and constant rain that had washed out roads." Butler had been sent 60,000 returnees but had accommodations for only half that number. The influenza epidemic had abated among the men, but their frustration and misery had not. To prying visitors from the other side of the Atlantic they shouted, "We want to go home!"—and less printable complaints. Reportedly, Eleanor wrote, only those troops on occupation duty in Germany "are at all contented."

By the eleventh the Roosevelts were in Paris, in a suite at the Ritz. The city was "full beyond belief and one sees many celebrities and all one's friends! . . . The prices are worse than New York for everything"—and so were the women, "who all look exaggerated, you wonder if any are ladies, though all look smart and some pretty." As Eleanor wrote to her

FDR on his postwar trip to France, early 1919, with Commander John M. Hancock, Livy Davis, and F. T. Kilgore of the Marines. ARMY WAR COLLEGE AND FDR LIBRARY

mother-in-law, Yanks on leave, attached to accessible Frenchwomen, did not suit her ascetic tastes. "The scandals going on would make many a woman at home unhappy." Some reminders of the war, other than men in uniform, remained. The Champs-Elysées was lined with captured German artillery pieces and a lone tank.

On Sunday the twelfth, while Franklin continued on Navy business, Eleanor went to the American Church for the service and a sermon on "Uncle Ted." The disposition of naval property occupied Franklin, and the task went quickly and efficiently. "The most successful thing I pulled off in Paris," he wrote to Daniels, "was the sale of the radio station [at Croix d'Hins, near Bordeaux] to the French Government. They had backed and filled. . . . " Roosevelt finally warned that if the French didn't want the high-powered "Lafayette Station" for overseas communication themselves, he would order it dismantled and shipped home. Represented by André Tardieu, a future premier, the authorities who had hoped it would be abandoned to them paid the asking price the next day. En route in Marine vehicles to the Channel, and England, the Roosevelt party visited trench systems, canals, ruined villages, and the skeletons of shattered churches. Appalled by the carnage, which included still-unburied corpses, and debilitated by bleak weather and the jolting travel, Eleanor developed pleurisy in her right lung, but insisted, Franklin wrote, on "getting out of the car at all points of interest." When a British officer assigned as escort told Eleanor that women were not yet permitted in the war zone, Franklin wrote to Sara, "I told him we had already visited the entire battle area," and "he almost fainted and had visions of [his] court martial." At shell-ravaged Cathedral Square in St. Quentin, too ill to eat the canned beef-paste sandwiches furnished by the Army commissary, Eleanor discreetly tucked her rations into the cathedral rubble.

Despite the preliminary work of Admiral Sims, who resented interference, in London Franklin found financial problems with the British government "pretty heavy." They were largely due to "loosely drawn" Army agreements with the Air Ministry, which had furnished most American flying machines actually used. He expected protracted negotiations "for several years to come." Many contracts also involved the Navy. Downplaying FDR's concerns—he suggested possible postwar investigations by a Republican Congress—Sims insisted sourly that affairs in England could be settled without further input from Washington. Still with a rasping cough, Eleanor was visited by a doctor at her suite at the Ritz, recovering sufficiently to pick out an "Alice blue"* velvet dress for Anna at Liberty's and to write gossipy letters home.

With Livy Davis (who had little official role and was forbidden most military sites), and without Eleanor, Roosevelt then recrossed the Channel to Ostend on a destroyer to deal with closing down the operations of the Northern [Flanders] Bombing Squadron. He was scheduled on arrival

---

* "Alice blue" was a shade of light blue with a hint of gray named for Alice Roosevelt Longworth. It became a fashion rage, inspiring a hit song ("Alice Blue Gown") in a 1919 musical.

to dine with King Albert, but the USS *Farnell*, skippered by William F. Halsey, whom FDR knew from a Campobello journey, lingered cautiously in a coastal fog bank. After two hours, Franklin brashly commandeered a motor launch, took his chances on mines and murk, and made the royal luncheon in Brussels. Following a visit to shattered Liege, he was motored into the Rhineland, where, on the east bank opposite Koblenz, American troops occupied the venerable fortress of Ehrenbreitstein which he had first seen on boyhood visits to Germany. Inspecting a Marine brigade there, he noted how fortunate they were in their posting. Patting a pocket where he claimed he had his steamship tickets for home, he confided that he would be happy to trade his vouchers for a Marine uniform. A private allegedly shouted, "*I'll* swap you!"

Returning with trunks of battlefield memorabilia and old histories from struggling German shops along the Rhine, Franklin arrived in Paris after midnight on February 9 to work on the remainder of naval business in France. (Livy Davis would recall only a strikingly beautiful but unfortunately married American lady he met while café-hopping.) While FDR completed his final business rounds, Eleanor, who had arrived without him, relaxed her asceticism to be fitted for a gown at fashionable Worth's, and visited friends and relatives, including Ted, Jr., still undergoing repairs on a knee. He would see action again in another war, dying of a heart attack on a beach in Normandy in 1944.

Conferring with General Pershing in Paris, Franklin reported learning that because of possible offense to German sensibilities, the American flag did not fly from the *Festung* on the Rhine. Pershing ordered the Stars and Stripes to be hoisted at Ehrenbreitstein "within the hour." Happily for Eleanor, who had chafed at waiting for Franklin, Livy decided to remain briefly in Europe with Herbert Hoover's food administration. Often loud and drunk, and parasitic upon FDR's work and leisure, he had contributed to Eleanor's coolness toward her husband, who seemed blind to Livy's failure to outgrow his playboy compulsions. Thirteen years later, Livy Davis would slip into the woodshed at his home in Brookline, Massachusetts, and put a gun to his head. "He was a good companion," Franklin would write for the annual report of their Harvard class.

The *George Washington* sailed from Brest on February 15 with President and Mrs. Wilson aboard. As a gesture to history, Franklin, who had arranged for Wilson's sailings, had acquired from the Wanamaker Department Store in Philadelphia a replica of a desk presented by Lafayette to President Washington for use in Wilson's stateroom. When Edith Wilson discovered later that Roosevelt had quietly purchased the desk after its employment aboard and shipped it to his study in Hyde Park, she protested that she had wanted it for her husband. "You're not going to get it," the Assistant Secretary, an inveterate collector, declared.

"I told him he was nothing but a common thief, and I should have sued him for that desk," she recalled with lasting bitterness—but the replica remained at Springwood until acquired decades later by James Roosevelt.

With the war won, the President was returning home to popular, if not political, plaudits. The fractious new Republican majorities in Congress were openly dissatisfied with Wilson's internationalist bent, especially the proposed League of Nations, which he hoped would be his legacy. Wilson had appealed that Democratic losses would "certainly be interpreted on the other side of the water as a repudiation of my leadership." One of TR's last, post-election attacks on the President had validated that. "Our Allies and our enemies and Mr. Wilson himself," the Colonel claimed, "should all understand that Mr. Wilson has no authority to speak for the American people at this time." Wresting approval for the League from greedy and vindictive allies had required conceding much of his visionary solutions for European peace and for disposition of enemy provinces and colonies. On blatantly national interests, the victors were bargaining away whatever unity in war had masked the mean realities below its surface. Already abroad too long, and out of touch with discontent at home, Wilson counted hopefully upon a functioning League to mitigate, over time, the injustices already written into the draft peace treaties.

At sea on February 21, FDR wrote to Daniels at length about the settling of claims and the closure of fifty-four bases and stations in Europe. Aboard ship during the eight-day homeward crossing, the President rested, slept, wrote, walked about the deck with Mrs. Wilson and dined in his suite with a few of the passengers he felt useful to him, including, despite Edith's animosity, Eleanor and Franklin. Defending the League of Nations charter, to Wilson the essence of the treaty, he used messianic language that he would employ, and re-employ, for months. "The United States must go in, or it will break the heart of the world." It was "the only nation that all feel is disinterested and [that] all trust." To their surprise, as Franklin had met with him at the White House on many urgent issues, Wilson confided to the Roosevelts that since the beginning of the war he had read no newspapers—only summaries furnished by Joe Tumulty, who in effect chose what Wilson would know before he met with others or made decisions. It was a disastrously lax practice that FDR, later, would never follow.

Anticipating no solace in political realities at home, Wilson largely sulked while aboard, agreeing only to attend an entertainment which turned out to be a bevy of cross-dressed sailors in a chorus line. One gob in pink tulle slithered up to the Commander-in-Chief and chucked him under the chin. Wilson was startled but did not walk out. Briefly out of character, he even autographed the program for Eleanor.

The President planned to be back in Washington only long enough to sign bills and secure votes in Congress he needed. He would gain few. The League to him was the anchor of the peace, but its draft Covenant, already released in the press, seemed to unmoved makers of contrary opinion to be alien to the Monroe Doctrine and certain to link the United States to the vicious politics of unstable Europe. "If the Saviour . . . should revisit the earth and declare for a League of Nations," Senator William Borah contended, "I would be opposed to it." However hostile, Senator Lodge promised to withhold debate in the Senate until Wilson had a chance to contend that the League document was not a surrender of sovereignty.

A longshoremen's strike in New York prompted Tumulty to recommend that Wilson dock instead at Boston, to stir the plaudits of citizens in Cabot Lodge's domain and possibly influence votes. Plowing toward shore, the *George Washington* had to proceed cautiously in heavy fog, nearly running aground northeast of Marblehead before making harbor

FDR (center, left) marching in a military homecoming parade, Poughkeepsie, New York, 1919. FDR Library

in Boston. FDR later claimed that as a yachtsman familiar with the approaches, he assisted from the captain's bridge in repositioning the ship. Evidence for that, other than from Eleanor, is lacking.

The liner tied up on the evening of February 23. Boston officials put together a public greeting and grand parade the next day. Senator Lodge was absent from the ceremonies, but at Mechanic's Hall, Governor Calvin Coolidge, usually a man of very few words, lauded Wilson (as he never would again) as "a great statesman . . . to whom we have entrusted our destinies, and one whom we are sure we will support in the future in the working out of that destiny." After a brief response, Wilson and the Washington-bound party boarded a train which stopped briefly at Providence. From the platform the President maintained passionately about the League his mantra that "if America disappoints [Europe] the heart of the world will be broken."

Early on the morning of February 25 the special train reached Union Station. The weeks abroad for the Roosevelts, which Franklin hoped would contribute to marital healing, had failed. "Dined alone," Eleanor wrote in her diary from home. "Franklin nervous and overwrought and I very stupid and trying. Result a dreadful fracas." Lucy still haunted R Street.

THE OLD CONGRESS was about to expire. The newly elected Senate would be in Republican hands, and the peace treaty would require an impossible two-thirds majority for ratification. Thirty-seven Republican senators had already signed a manifesto that if the treaty included the Covenant of the League of Nations, they would not vote for it. In a tactical blunder that Franklin would not repeat when in another wartime White House, Wilson continued to spurn the political opposition. No Republicans sat in his Cabinet;* no Republicans of any stature participated in war making or peace making; few opponents were ever consulted about anything. The vindictive Treaty of Versailles was handled no differently by the Allies. As with the Armistice, the defeated would be presented with a *diktat*. A young British officer with the Supreme War Council in Paris, the future Field Marshal Earl Wavell, would be realistically cynical, remarking, "After the 'war to end war,' they seem to have been pretty successful . . . at making a 'Peace to end Peace.'"

After ten days in the White House, Wilson returned to Europe for four frustrating months, into the signing process and beyond, eliciting further empty acclaim until, on April 3, he suffered a calamitous physical breakdown. However alarming, his cerebral hemorrhage was kept hidden from the newspapers, as was Wilson himself. One side of his face became numb; his physical and mental faculties were impaired. Although some symptoms eased, his personality, already dismaying, became more rigid and petulant. On the day he left seclusion and returned to Brest for his second voyage home, Colonel House urged him to "meet the Senate in a conciliatory spirit." Wilson refused.

---

* In another wartime, FDR's appointee as Secretary of the Navy would be Frank Knox, the GOP candidate for Vice President in 1936; his Secretary of War, Henry Stimson, had been a distinguished former member of two Republican Cabinets. As a roving ambassador worldwide, he would appoint Wendell Willkie, the feisty Republican who had run against him in 1940.

The Senate Committee on Foreign Relations debated the treaty for two months, its rejection predictable. Article X in the League Covenant, which raised the most Republican objections, called for the signatory nations "to respect and preserve . . . against external aggression the territorial integrity and existing political independence of all State members of the League." The President would oppose all amendments, and stubbornly planned an exhausting campaign trip by rail to energize popular support that would not be forthcoming.

WHILE WILSON WAS abroad and largely uncommunicative, Daniels and Roosevelt were engaged in the frustrations of postwar retrenchment. Every base, yard and factory closure ordered was inevitably in a location represented by a job-protective Congressman. Daniels spent more and more time away, leaving the dirty work to the Acting Secretary, and through FDR to Louis Howe. Enjoying his peacetime perquisites, Daniels sailed on the thirteenth crossing of the *Leviathan* to Europe, traveled about the Atlantic and the Pacific coasts, and enjoyed an "inspection trip" to Hawaii. Franklin ran the Department, occasionally exchanging cables with the Secretary. Promoting the Navy's role in the war, he encouraged William Fox,* head of the pretentiously titled William Fox Film Corporation of America (later 20th Century Fox), to exploit the Navy and Marines to cinema audiences, which FDR promoted to station chiefs abroad as "special work." He was always aware that government, to succeed, had to pass muster by the public.

Postwar partying in the Capital resumed, with Eleanor alternately putting on a gown and mending the marriage, or pouting in continuing martyrdom. In a recasting of priorities, she was also shifting from a white corps of servants to a black cadre, more in keeping with Washington ways, and far cheaper for her budget. She was also spending more time apart from the children, and Franklin, at Hyde Park. On March 2, 1919, a social evening without Eleanor brought Franklin together with Nigel

---

* Born in Hungary in 1879 as Vilmos Fried, he bought his first nickelodeon in 1904.

FDR at his desk in the New Navy Building, Washington, DC, 1919. FDR LIBRARY

Law for the last time. He was being reassigned to London. Although many years later he would recall Roosevelt warmly as the American epitome of the English country gentleman, apparently they never talked, or met, again. Possibly Franklin had suspected for some time that Law's worshipful intimacy had been integral to his rather vague embassy assignment. Was he posted to learn what he could from the inside through FDR and his many contacts in government? Intelligence gathering was often the covert activity of Third Secretaries.

Along with Departmental downsizing came modernizing. Franklin bought steel for continued new construction and pushed for further emphasis on aviation. Blimps and the much larger dirigibles, with rigid frames, seemed increasingly attractive for long flights and submarine patrol. The Navy's new blimps—gas-filled inflatable bags with a motor and rigid keel below for crew—had been employed for coastal patrol since

1917. FDR was eagerly overseeing the venture of the first postwar blimp, the C-5, which resembled a whale with rear flippers, and was intended to cross the Atlantic. In early May 1919, the C-5 flew from Cape May, New Jersey, to Montauk Point, Long Island, and on May 14, on toward St. John's in Newfoundland, sending voice-radio transmissions en route. Encountering fog and then rough weather, by radio it contacted the cruiser *Chicago*, which in preparation was anchored at St. John's. Guided down, the C-5 was cabled to the ground to secure it. But while the four-man crew caught up on meals and its engine was being overhauled, a violent storm arose and tore the blimp loose. Lieutenant Charles Little, checking conditions, jumped clear and the airship drifted eastward. The destroyer *Edwards* was dispatched to follow the C-5, losing sight of it before it deflated and crashed. "Sad news just came," Franklin wrote to "Dearest Babs," in Hyde Park, "that the C-5 broke away from her moorings and is drifting over the ocean, no one on board. This ends one of our hopes of crossing the Atlantic."

The Navy strove to beat the British, but on the same day as the C-5 crashed, the Admiralty announced that it would send the more rigid R-34 in the opposite direction, to Cape May, the home base of the C-5. It would be the first crossing of the Atlantic by airship. Yet, as Franklin wrote, the blimp was only "one of our hopes." On May 8, three Navy Curtiss seaplanes had flown from Rockaway Naval Air Station on Long Island indirectly toward Plymouth, England. The trimotored biplanes NC-1, NC-2 and NC-4 (NC-3 had been cannibalized for spare parts) made intermediate stops en route to Trepassey, Newfoundland. The operation was complex and expensive, made possible in part by development of the compact and lightweight Westinghouse GN4 aircraft radio alternator and transmitter for contacting ships below. Twenty-two Navy destroyers in the Atlantic began stationing themselves along the planned path, while the *Aroostook*, a minelayer converted to a seaplane tender, would be sent from Newfoundland to England to await the planes and return them. A quarter-century later, Richard E. Byrd, then a retired rear admiral, would write Franklin, "Do you remember the miles of red tape you cut through to make this first transatlantic flight possible?"

FDR (left) and Daniels (right) with the NC-4 crews at New Navy in 1919 to go over plans for the NC-4 crews' transatlantic flight. This photograph was presented to Roosevelt by Richard E. Byrd in 1944. FDR LIBRARY

The first ocean leg, to the Azores, proceeding in thick fog, took the *NC-4* more than fifteen hours and 1,200 miles. Both the *NC-1* and *NC-2* made forced ocean landings in rough weather. The crews were picked up unhurt. (In Washington, Franklin had busied himself by radio trying to locate the missing planes.) Alone, the *NC-4* refueled and flew on to Lisbon, and then to Ferrol, in Spain, adding nearly twenty-seven hours in flight time. From Ferrol, the seaplane made it to Plymouth on May 31, while more Navy vessels were posted below. The venture had taken nearly fifty-four hours in flying time, 4,513 miles—and twenty-three days, three aircraft, and fifty-three ships beneath.

All three crews were welcomed at Main Navy on June 30, 1919. Daniels and Roosevelt had their pictures taken with the aeronauts. "I said a few words," Daniels noted succinctly in his diary. The Navy had little opportunity to savor the mixed success. The six crewmen had been feted in London and Paris before returning on the *Aroostook* to New York, and then Washington. In prewar 1913, the London *Daily Mail* had offered a prize of £10,000 "to the aviator who shall first cross the Atlantic in an aeroplane from any point in the United States, Canada, or New-foundland to any point on Great Britain or Ireland, in 72 consecutive hours." War had delayed any attempt, and the NC-4 had not attempted to earn the prize. On June 14, 1919, Captain John Alcock and Lieu-tenant Arthur Whitten-Brown, in a Vickers Vimy twin-engine biplane built for the challenge, yet quickly losing radio contact aloft, flew from Newfoundland to the dark, sodden bogs of Ireland nonstop in sixteen hours and twenty-seven minutes.

While Acting Secretary, Franklin met with Owen D. Young of General Electric, the firm that had developed much of the long-range radio trans-mission expertise employed by the Navy. Rather than unload the wartime technology to the eager British, Admiral William H. G. Bullard, director of communications, suggested creating an American company to acquire rights and facilities. Although the Navy, citing national security, wanted continued government control, Republicans in Congress had objected. With Franklin's encouragement, Young formed Radio Corporation of America. FDR wired Daniels for advice and consent. RCA became the motive force of American radio.

After FDR left Main Navy, his éclat intact, he brought off the largest-scale radio transmission to date. Heavyweight boxing champion Georges Carpentier, a Frenchman, was to fight Jack Dempsey at Jersey City on July 2, 1921. Efforts were under way to broadcast the event everywhere possible, for which permission was needed to use the Navy radio facilities built by General Electric and soon to be the property of RCA. The equip-ment was set up in Hoboken. Theaters, halls and auditoriums within two hundred miles of the four-hundred-foot tower were engaged by the Navy Club of New York to receive the voice broadcast, admission fees going to the American Committee for Devastated France, as well as to maintain the Navy and Marine servicemen's club in New York City. (Almost no one yet owned a personal receiver.) Two days before the event the Navy, now under Republican management, objected that the transmitter's first public use should not be to communicate a prize fight. Defying Washing-ton bureaucracy, FDR, now president of the Navy Club, declared, "It is against Navy regulations, but I will O.K. it. Go ahead." The fight was aired by radiophone. Dempsey won by a knockout in the fourth round; and certificates of appreciation went to the combatants, who both signed the documents, as did Tex Rickard, the president of the National Amateur Wireless Association, and Franklin D. Roosevelt.

Much of Franklin's time during the early summer of 1919, while Eleanor and family were at Hyde Park and Campobello (the Manhattan house was still occupied by the Lamonts, with a rent increase), was taken up outside the Department by futile speechmaking to promote the League. Not yet having left for Canada, Eleanor was still in Washington late on the evening of June 2. As the Roosevelts returned from a dinner party, parked their Stutz in a garage several blocks from R Street and were walking home just after eleven o'clock, they heard an explosion from the direction of their house. Of the children only James was there, studying for his Groton School entrance examinations; the others were at Hyde Park.

The pair hurried along the sidewalk, Eleanor struggling in a long dress. Policemen had closed off R Street, which was strewn with bricks and glass. The curious were already gathering, and in Clint Eastwood's film *J. Edgar* (2011), but not in reality, a wide-eyed young J. Edgar Hoover, twenty-four and an ambitious Special Agent of Attorney General A. Mitchell Palmer, appeared on his bicycle amid the rubble. The house across the street was Palmer's. Hoover, twenty-four, and deferred from the draft thanks to an influential relative, would shortly head Palmer's new Radical Division, to track down "alien subversives."

Since Palmer's appointment by Wilson in March, his nearly paranoid preoccupation with radicalism had eclipsed everything else on his agenda. Stretching the law, enforcement of the Espionage and Sedition Acts had continued beyond the war, and aside from perennial superpatriots who were minor functionaries or self-appointed zealots, Palmer would become the most despised official in America. Sinclair Lewis would represent his type in the delusional General Edgeways of the sardonic *It Can't Happen Here* (1935), who would rant to a sympathetic women's group, "Our highest ambition is to be darned well left alone. . . . We must be prepared to defend our shores against all the alien gangs of international racketeers that call themselves 'governments.'"

Palmer's brick front was near collapse, its windows blown in, the front door swaying off its hinges. Branches of trees along the sidewalk were splintered and down. The panes of the Roosevelt house were also shattered, and on the front steps lay bloody bits of human flesh. They could hear Nora, Eleanor's cook, shrieking hysterically. Franklin rushed in and ran up to the second floor. James, eleven, was in his bedroom, barefoot and in his pajamas, gazing from his broken window at onlookers clustering in the street. Relieved that he was unhurt, his father embraced him. More slowly, Eleanor came up, clutching the hem of her long skirt. "What are you doing out of bed at this hour?" she shouted at James. "Get yourself straight to bed!"

Franklin crossed to the shattered house, where, until the blast, the Palmers had been safely upstairs in a rear bedroom. Now, amidst the chaos, they appeared awed. Nearby, Alice and Nick Longworth, returning from a party, found

> Loftus, the colored policeman on the beat, and an old friend, waiting for us at the doorstep with the news that Attorney General Mitchell Palmer's house had been blown up, so, taking Loftus on the box of the motor, we proceeded to R Street. The pavement in front of the house was matted with glass and leaves. . . . We went in to see Franklin and Eleanor Roosevelt, who lived just opposite. A leg lay in the path to the house next to theirs, another leg farther up the street. A head was on the roof of yet another house. As we walked across, it was difficult to avoid stepping on bloody chunks of human being. The man [with the bomb] had been torn apart, fairly blown to butcher's meat. . . . When we left, a large number of pieces had been assembled on a piece of newspaper.

Hardly ready for bed, Franklin joined the police in gathering parts of the unidentifiable bomber and his anarchist pamphlets scattered by the blast. Remnants of a suitcase, with a battered Italian-American dictionary and a brown fedora with a Philadelphia hatter's "De Luca Brothers" label seemed a clue to the assailant's origins. He had apparently tripped in the darkness close to the house. "The man probably fell with the bomb," suggested another neighbor, Senator Claude Swanson. The title pages of the pamphlets read "Plain Words," and the closing pages were signed "The Anarchist Fighters."* Before daylight came the house was roped off by police, who, Eleanor wrote to Sara, "haven't yet allowed the gore to be wiped up on our steps and James glories in every bone found!" Franklin came to the breakfast table with an object he found on the lawn, which proved to be a piece of collar bone. He took it to the police. His appetite gone, he never returned to his uneaten breakfast.

At about the same time, bombs also exploded in eight other cities, with little damage, but escalating what would be known as the "Red Scare," a relentless assault on civil liberties directed by Palmer. He blamed Russian Bolshevism for protests against "war profiteers" and whatever expressions of postwar discontent, from labor unrest as wartime gains were threatened, to political speech from splinter parties, that could be characterized under illiberal war legislation still in force as sedition. Through 1919 and 1920 Federal agents would arrest and indict thousands of alleged anarchists, Socialists and Communists, and conduct deportation proceedings against many of them who were not yet citizens, overriding their First Amendment rights—or any rights. Even the Supreme Court, in an opinion delivered on March 3, 1919, by Oliver Wendell Holmes, Jr., had upheld under the expanded wartime Espionage Act the abrogation of free speech. In that climate Franklin himself justified injunctions against strikes by workers in railroads, mines, shipyards and other industries performing "public service," although they were not government employees. He would earn the decades-long enmity of United Mine Workers boss John L. Lewis.

A WEEK AFTER the anarchist outbreaks, the enfeebled Wilson returned from France a second time, with the Treaty of Versailles. On July 10 he proceeded to the Capitol to present the document, League of Nations charter included, before the Senate. "We cannot turn back," he declared. Yet the nation had already turned back. Every give-away to greed in the document

---

*The printer, picked up months later, in early 1920, was Andrea Salsedo, affiliated with an anarchist group in Lynn, Massachusetts. Held in a building in lower Manhattan for questioning, he gave little away, and one night jumped from his 14th-floor room to his death.

seemed a betrayal to those who wanted to promote amity by peaceable give-backs. Ethnic aspirations confronted ethnic animosities. Punishments were insufficient to some, as, to others, were rewards. American attacks on the Treaty were often disguised responses to prewar domestic and economic reforms, as became obvious when big bankers, industrialists and press barons made ultra-wealthy by the war financed anti-League spokesmen across the nation. If Republicans recaptured the presidency, as Congress had been re-won, Wilson warned, the country would return to 1912.

Twenty-five race riots during the summer of 1919 emphasized that the war had continued to segregate the military by color. Temporary jobs performed by blacks and now returned to white veterans had also changed nothing for the better. For many the "New Freedom" espoused by Wilson had little or no impact. Washington itself was rigidly segregated, and arms were increasingly accessible and plentiful. The usual rumors of black outrages upon white women led to vigilante shootings by soldiers and sailors still in uniform, abetted by supportive civilians. Blacks, male and female, were dragged from segregated streetcars and beaten. When Franklin wrote to Eleanor at Campobello on July 23 that as only one person was killed the night before, he considered the violence in the Capital "about over."* He did not urge Daniels to restrain Navy men, and Daniels on his own seemed to have no interest in doing so. The President, a Virginian, had other concerns.

By then, Wilson's plans to appeal for the League across the country had jelled. No Lodge-inspired amendment to the document modifying American responsibilities was acceptable. Wilson had lingered abroad, and then at the White House, until he and Admiral Grayson felt he could be seen again. The President's left cheek and eye still twitched, his hands still trembled. Grayson warned that an exhausting campaign for the League would put Wilson's life in jeopardy, and he tried to abort the venture. A newspaperman asked solicitously if the President felt well

---

*The day before, after heavy rain, serious leakage had flooded several rooms at R Street, and Franklin, in pyjamas at 6:00 AM, vainly applied bath towels. He summoned assistance.

enough to endure dozens of whistle-stop speeches. "I don't care," he claimed, "if I die the next minute after the treaty is ratified."

Since Franklin was alone in Washington, and still traveling on occasion to make pro-League appeals, Eleanor left Campobello at the end of July, the children remaining with staff, and returned to R Street. She was being supportive, but still not above harboring suspicion. Observing the unpromising shift in public mood about the treaty, FDR began tapering off his speechmaking, using the excuse of pressing Navy business.

Opening his missionary campaign for the League, the weakened President boarded his special train, the blue-painted *Mayflower*, on September 3, with Edith Wilson, Grayson and Tumulty. In twenty-two days, increasingly drained, Wilson traveled across fourteen states, giving forty impassioned speeches and many more impromptu whistle-stop rear-platform appeals. At Cheyenne, Wyoming, he extolled the flawed treaty as a "people's peace." Stubbornly, he persevered despite breathing difficulties, throbbing headaches and dizziness. Realizing his increasing loss of control, he may have gambled that his possible martyrdom might stir popular pressure for adoption of the League Covenant.

At Pueblo, Colorado, on September 23, Wilson employed death as metaphor in urging that rejection of the treaty would be a disservice to "those dear ghosts who still deploy upon the fields of France." Very likely identifying himself with the war dead, he paused, his eyes filling with tears. His voice became hoarse. In sermonizing mode he depicted "pastures of quietness and peace such as the world never dreamed before." When he stopped, somewhat abruptly, and failed to continue, in the lengthening silence the puzzled audience began to disperse. Wilson stumbled with difficulty to his compartment aboard the *Mayflower*, where that evening he suffered another stroke. At the insistence of the Wilsons—apparently Edith—Admiral Grayson announced to the press the next morning that because of the President's "nervous exhaustion" the remainder of the tour was canceled. Wilson remained in curtained seclusion as the train steamed slowly and quietly back to Washington.

Three days after his return to the White House, Wilson fell unconscious to his bathroom floor. A cerebral thrombosis had paralyzed his left side. His mind wandered; he could speak only in brief whispers. When Secretary of State Lansing recommended that Admiral Grayson, with Tumulty, certify the President's incapacity so that under the Constitution Vice President Thomas Marshall could function in his place, Tumulty in misguided loyalty rejected the proposal and declared, "I am sure that Dr. Grayson will never certify to his disability." Lansing was soon fired, and replaced by a nonentity. Effectively the presidency became a hidden triumvirate of Tumulty, Grayson and Edith Wilson, with the distraught, stubborn and unsophisticated Mrs. Wilson* in charge, relaying ostensibly dictated messages from the President in her own hand.

WITHDRAWN, IN THE paralysis of the Administration, from the treaty controversy, Roosevelt cautiously avoided talking about it, even privately. When Daniels, often now away as Wilson remained inaccessible, returned to Washington, Franklin in late October journeyed off during the political hiatus on a nineteen-day moose hunt in New Brunswick with Livy Davis, still hanging on, and with Lieutenant Commander Richard E. Byrd, who had been an officer on the *Dolphin*, and would later gain fame as an explorer by air over both poles. Franklin proved to be no Uncle Ted. He lodged one shot at a distant moose but bagged nothing as he roughed it with his party, which included a cook and two guides, playing rubbers of bridge and sipping bourbon at cabin fireplaces in the evenings.

This time, Eleanor tried some mending of the frayed marriage. A letter to him, even using "dear," hoped that he was enjoying his holiday and deplored their leading "such a hectic life. A little prolonged quiet might bring us all together and yet it might do just the opposite! I really don't know what I want to think about anymore!"

FEW IN WASHINGTON were permitted to see the incapacitated President or learn anything about his condition. Rumors flew. The New York *Herald* reported that Wilson, like the "Sleeping Princess," was "alive, yet of sus-

---

*Raised in the impoverished post–Civil War South, Edith Bolling Galt Wilson had only two years of formal education but had risen into Washingtonian society circles.

pended animation." A royal visitor, Albert, King of the Belgians, told Daniels on November 1 that the listless Wilson now "had [a] full beard and it was white." On November 18, according to Edith's memoirs, she asked the frail President to accept the Lodge reservations on the treaty "and get this awful thing settled." He appealed, "Little girl, don't desert me!" He dictated to her a message for Senator Gilbert Hitchcock of Nebraska, the Democratic minority leader, hoping that supporters of the treaty "will vote against the Lodge resolution of ratification." (When Hitchcock had visited, the invalid had lifted his head from his pillow long enough to croak, "Let Lodge compromise!") At dinner with the Roosevelts on the evening of November 19, Daniels brought the expected news. "Senate defeated the treaty. Lodge has one passion. Hatred of Wilson."

Following King Albert, the Prince of Wales arrived, a fashion-plate Peter Pan who later became Edward VIII (and after abdication Duke of Windsor). The Prince nearly had his Washington visit canceled when George V, his father, learned of Wilson's stroke. Once the voyage materialized, the Prince dutifully saw Wilson briefly at his sickbed, was a guest at official entertainments, reputedly dancing diplomatically with Senators' daughters; and even meeting two delighted (and white) household employees of the Roosevelts, who were British subjects. Eleanor had obtained introductions for Ada Jarvis, a nurse, and Elspeth Connachie, a longtime Scot governess. Daniels and FDR accompanied the Prince to Annapolis, where he wore the honorific uniform of a captain in the Royal Navy. He told the midshipmen that he thought their austere quarters were palatial. "When I was at naval school I lived in a trunk."

Soon out of action again, Franklin remained susceptible to throat and bronchial tract ailments and underwent surgery for inflammation of the tonsils, normally a childhood ailment. It was not his only trouble. While he was still hospitalized, a letter addressed to Eleanor arrived, but intended for him—from Anne Sims. The admiral, her husband, had learned that sailor decoys had been used in ferreting out "the sad business" in Newport, and that the Assistant Secretary, rather than Daniels, was involved. A second trial for Samuel Kent, the Episcopal chaplain ensnared in the scandal, was set for January 4. Sixteen other Navy men were arrested. Apparently

FDR with cane, next to Daniels, also with cane, at a formal review in Washington, DC, for the visiting Prince of Wales, third from right, November, 1919. FDR LIBRARY

without her husband's knowledge Mrs. Sims was alerting Roosevelt. On Christmas Eve he replied cautiously that on the recommendation of the Bureau of Navigation he had given instructions "to conduct an investigation. . . . The means were neither ordered nor discussed." The sleazy Newport affair would keep dogging him.

A British arrival resulting in still further trouble for Roosevelt was Viscount Grey of Fallodon, who as Sir Edward Grey had been Foreign Minister until December 1916. He had disembarked in New York on the same day as Wilson had collapsed in Colorado. Since Lord Reading, incapacitated by severe gout, had to be replaced at the Washington embassy, Grey, despite his own increasing debility, had been appointed as replacement. Feeble and already nearly blind, he was nevertheless president of the League of Nations Union, an organization thought dear to Wilson's heart. As necessary support he brought with him Sir William Tyrell, once Grey's principal private secretary and then head of political intelligence. Grey's mission, which failed, was to persuade Wilson to accept whatever Republican reservations there were and to sign the Treaty including the League. The Roosevelts became fond of Grey. But the Viscount also brought back Major Charles Craufurd-Stuart, a war hero at Gallipoli who had been secretary to Reading and had left with him. Although the Major's embassy experience was useful to the handicapped Grey, Craufurd-Stuart was already notorious in Capital circles as a bon vivant and as a compulsive gossip about Edith Galt Wilson. His most unquotable, yet often quoted, quip about her allegedly puritanical new husband was "What did Mrs. Galt do when the President proposed to her? [*pause*] She fell out of bed."

Socialites talked. The First Lady found out. She tried to have Craufurd-Stuart declared *persona non grata* and sent home. Her voyages with Wilson to Paris, and Reading's exit, with his staff, seemed to close the matter. Yet the Major was back. Employing Admiral Grayson as her intermediary, Edith Wilson again tried to expel Craufurd-Stuart. Brandishing his hauteur, Lord Grey brooked no interference with his entourage and merely immunized the Major's status from embassy attaché to personal staff. Given the President's incapacity, Mrs. Wilson, who informally reigned, denied embassy officials access to the White House. Grey was not even permitted to accompany the Prince of Wales on his token visit to the bedridden Wilson.

1919 WAS A year of disappointments. Although the peace would move frontiers about, it solved nothing and created new tensions and anxieties. The Wilson administration was on life support, as was the Roosevelt marriage. The Navy Department was under a siege that it had provoked by continuing to investigate moral turpitude at its Newport base, FDR seeking, for Daniels, evidence for "perversion and drugs." Further besieging the Department was the returning Admiral Sims, renamed to the presidency of the Naval War College at Newport although outraged by Daniels's refusal (as Wilson had called it "unwise") to permit him to accept an honorary Admiralty title. Sims wrote to a friend that he looked forward to the day when he could reveal "a number of rather disagreeable facts" about the Department. Then, in December, the recurrent troublemaker was further put off by the Secretary's culling of allegedly unworthy, deskbound, candidates from Sims's recommendations for meritorious service in his command. With hostility, Sims declined a Distinguished Service Medal from Daniels. Roosevelt, who indulged the arrogant, Anglophile Sims and had shrugged off obvious rebuffs in London, hoped for reciprocity of favor and backed him indirectly (and unwisely) by writing to Mrs. Sims, "Strictly between ourselves, I should like to shake the Admiral warmly by the hand." Recklessly prefacing any remark by "strictly between ourselves" was a guarantee it would not remain that way.

Even Louis Howe, who had intervened to help keep Eleanor and Franklin together, by October was living apart from Grace at the less-than-posh Hotel Harrington in downtown Washington, as one of their intermittent domestic disputes had festered. "I've had plenty of time to lie still and think everything over," he wrote to her. " . . . Forgive this scrawl but writing comes a bit hard yet. Nothing seems to matter anymore." He had been ill and felt sorry for himself. He hoped his son, Hartley ("Bub"), would write, as his rejection "would be the last straw. He is the only person in the world that cares for me. . . . Everybody else is indifferent or hates me or is afraid of me or uses me to get what they want." Apparently Franklin, for the moment, fit into one or another of those categories.

Out of favor at the White House because of continuing friendship with the shunned Viscount Grey, the Roosevelts nevertheless invited Grey, with cane and blue spectacles, and Tyrell to Christmas dinner at R Street. Warned in advance that young Jimmy had measles, Grey said he wasn't worried as he didn't think that he was subject any longer to "childish diseases." Sara was also present, and the reconciled Howes, with their son and daughter. Since Howe's apparent intervention on Eleanor's behalf in the Lucy affair, he had become "family" to her and to Sara, but all knew that the Washington interlude would be ending in a year. There were only the leavings to sweep up. The Wilson era had effectively ended for the Roosevelts, but for the long goodbye.

10

Running toward the Future

WALKING HER DOG along R Street early in the new year, Franklin's Hudson Valley friend Bertie Hamlin, now long in Washington, passed by his house just as he was emerging. "He has just had his tonsils out and has been ill, too," she noted in her diary for January 10, 1920, a Saturday; "he looks poorly. . . . He had two of his boys and a dog with him. Several of the children have had or are having chicken-pox—James is to have his appendix out—Eleanor was getting out 2,000 invitations for Navy teas. He said he did not expect to run for the Senate—that even if he wanted it or could get it—he thought it stupid." It appeared to be another bad election year looming for Democrats. Roosevelt was also, as usual, short on funds, and had to wait for his annual birthday check from his mother, on January 30 (he would be thirty-eight), to pay the doctor "for removing James' insides."

He wrote to Sara that she was, as usual, "an angel," as aside from his medical bills he had to pay "the gas man and the butcher lest the infants starve to death." He was far from broke, but his income, including that from his and Eleanor's trusts and other holdings, had fallen in 1919 from $26,725.70 to $24,401.78. Substantial as that seemed in postwar 1920 dollars, he and Eleanor lived well beyond their earnings. And in a year he would be out of a job.

Later that Saturday, Louis B. Wehle, an old friend from Harvard *Crimson* days, visited at R Street. Now a Kentucky attorney, he had been on the War Industries Board. He knew that the November outlook was gloomy for Democrats, but he had come to pitch an enticing ticket— Herbert Hoover for President, FDR for Vice President. The electoral votes in a close contest might hinge on the two big states showcasing a Californian and a New Yorker. "Frank," Wehle recalled saying, "you have everything to gain and nothing to lose. . . . Whether you win or lose," he argued, putting the most persuasive, yet paradoxically negative, spin on the outcome, "you would suffer the stigma of mediocrity that seems to attach to the Vice Presidency or to one who tries for it. But you are young and could live it down for several reasons: first, your bear the name Roosevelt; second, you have a first-rate record of public service . . . and third, in your campaign tours you would make a number of key acquaintances in every state."

Without pausing for second thoughts, although the "mediocrity" aspersion fit many forgettable vice presidential candidates, Franklin conceded that the gamble was worth checking out. "You can go to it as far as I am concerned. Good luck! And it will certainly be interesting to hear what the Colonel says about it."

As Colonel House remained a power in the party, Wehle took the train to New York and saw House that Sunday. "It's a wonderful idea," the Colonel agreed, "and the only chance the Democrats have in November." But that meant wooing Hoover, who seemed to have no party affiliation yet was far too flush to be anything but Republican. Roosevelt left that to Wehle and went about his Departmental business. The candidate at the top of the ticket was likely to be someone else. Franklin saw nothing politically promising at any level.

"I can tell you . . . perfectly frankly," Roosevelt wrote to his old friend Langdon Marvin on February 14, 1920, "that I do not propose to make an early Christian martyr of myself this year if the Democratic Party does make some fool mistake at San Francisco." What nominating convention foolishness he feared was left unstated but for identifying one perennial aspirant. "I would not run this Autumn for Dog-catcher," he told another enthusiast, "if the Democrats nominate a party hack or a reactionary or a Bryan. . . ." An even more dire prospect was faintly possible. Wheelchair bound at best, Wilson was telling his few intimates, stubbornly if feebly, that he might attempt a run for a third term, to fight for his rejected League of Nations Covenant. He was openly hostile to his party's strongest possibility, his son-in-law William Gibbs McAdoo, the resigned Treasury Secretary. Also in the picture was the controversial A. Mitchell Palmer, still darling of the party's conservatives. Roosevelt expected to be back in a desultory law practice, to make some money and relieve dependence on his mother. And to await a more propitious political moment.

Partisan attacks on the Navy Department were inevitable early in 1920 as both parties approached the quadrennial presidential campaign. Abetted by the chronically vindictive Admiral Sims and *Providence Journal* editor John Rathom, Republicans continued, to little effect, to exploit the sleazy Newport sex-for-sale affair. On the floor of the Senate, Boies Penrose, the wealthy, paunchy GOP boss of Pennsylvania, inveighed against the alleged encouragement of moral laxity by Daniels and Roosevelt. (After his death, *TIME* noted about Penrose, "Never married. He never kept a mistress. When he wanted a woman, he rented one—a professional. He scorned amateurism in everything.") The Senate Naval Affairs committee, majority Republican, probed the roles of both Daniels and Roosevelt in obtaining evidence of vice by using sailors as entrapment bait, and both suspects hoped for an inconclusive finding—and soon. Daniels pulled the teeth from the waning scandal by appointing his own three-man investigating committee, with Franklin as senior member.

The campaign against vice (although the gender was different) recalled Uncle Ted, who, as an audacious young chief of the New York City Police Department, ordered patrolmen to stop and frisk women unaccompanied on the streets at night on suspicion that they were embarked on selling themselves. (One newspaper mocked the predatory tactics by suggesting that sooner or later the Statue of Liberty would be arrested.) Prostitution flourished anyway, and Roosevelt risked his ouster, but, helpfully, politics intervened. President William McKinley on taking office in 1897 rescued TR by naming him Assistant Secretary of the Navy.

Franklin worried to Livy Davis that Newport would "hurt the Navy," but he was worried even more about the impact upon his future. Despite the Secretary's obvious protection of his deputy, Franklin saw them, post-Wilson, going their very separate ways. To promote his interests, Daniels had his newspaper in Raleigh. Outside politics, he could inveigh in print against John Barleycorn. On January 15, 1920, the Eighteenth Amendment mandating Prohibition had gone into effect. At midnight, the abstemious Daniels was in the First Congregational Church in Washington, in a pew with William Jennings Bryan, singing the Doxology at a celebratory service. Roosevelt dined at the Metropolitan Club, champagne glass in hand, where members of his Harvard class of 1904 were mocking Prohibition. Although he enjoyed bourbon at home, it was an American product, likely to flourish illegally. Recognizing future social needs, he had planned ahead, ordering four cases of Glenfiddich "Old Reserve" Scotch for delivery to Sara's address on E. 65th Street.

Two weeks later, Franklin's defiance of the times looked further backward. Speaking to an audience of fifteen hundred at the Brooklyn Academy of Music, he boasted of his evading, in the interest of prewar preparedness, the pacifist strictures of Daniels and Wilson. Boosting his own stock at the expense of the courtly Southerner who had made him, Roosevelt was seeking distance from the unloved outgoing administration. Yet he needed the party regulars for his own future, unless he planned to do a TR-style exit, which in the case of his Uncle Ted, even with the presidency behind him, had failed.

Daniels read the Eastern newspapers, which prominently covered Franklin's claims. So did the loyal Livy Davis, who was baffled at the indiscreet wounding of the Secretary. "What in the world is the matter with you," Davis wondered, "for telling the public that you . . . committed enough illegal acts to keep you in jail for 900 years?" Acidly, Daniels noted in his diary that FDR had charged that "the President had not made preparation for war prior to our entrance," and that Franklin "had risked impeachment for spending $40 [million] for guns sixty days after we entered the war. I sent for [Admiral Ralph] Earle who said I had given orders in March for guns for merchant ships while F.D.R. was in Haiti—& all orders had been made after conferences by me." Roosevelt had overstated his risks, yet Daniels and Earle were persuading themselves with less than half-truths. Franklin had returned from Haiti as the Navy was belatedly gearing up. He had spent many frustrating months before that, battling vast policy differences on readiness for war, including urging upon Wilson and Daniels and the admirals the arming of freighters. The President, and Daniels, had long impeded preparedness as akin to belligerence.

Although the emplacement of shipboard armaments had been legalized by Wilson's executive order only after the fact, FDR's claim served no purpose other than brag. The war was over and the preparedness issue dead. When the Assistant Secretary returned from further speechmaking, all Daniels recorded—and there was anger in his brevity—was "F.D.R. came in as usual." Impulsively, Daniels considered sacking him, and on February 17, visited the feeble President to consult on the matter, but Wilson needed no additional crises, and in his diary the Secretary only mentioned his own forbearance. Wilson and Edith were already sufficiently livid about Roosevelt's closeness to Viscount Grey. On February 21 Daniels noted in his diary, "F.D.R. persona non grata with W." Then he added, "Better let speech pass."

In March, FDR set up, with two friends, a law partnership at 52 Wall Street, in which he could become active when he relinquished his Navy appointment. Langdon Marvin was a loyal Harvard classmate with whom he had a nominal Wall Street partnership in 1911. Roosevelt had known Grenville Temple Emmet, a Spanish-American War veteran five years FDR's elder, from his early law beginnings; Emmet's wife, Pauline, was Eleanor's friend. In the 1930s he would be Roosevelt's ambassador to the Netherlands, then Austria, where he died suddenly in Vienna in 1937, the year before the *Anschluss*.

The law practice was among many Rooseveltian schemes to supplement his income. Most expedients would be unrewarding and stillborn. An exception would be a vice presidency to head the New York office, at 120 Broadway, of the Fidelity and Deposit Company of Maryland. Van Lear Black, a millionaire Baltimore financier, was a friend, a Democrat and a fellow sailor. Black's yacht, the 140-foot *Sabalo*, had visited Campobello, with

Franklin at the helm in familiar waters. Black's surety bonding firm, the nation's third largest, planned to purchase, at $25,000 a year, then a considerable salary, the Roosevelt name and contacts in New York among business, labor, politics and government. FDR would begin undemanding part-time duties in January 1921. (Into 1928, the position would furnish income and help him look occupied beyond politics.) Without a Manhattan address, as the Lamont lease at 49 E. 65th Street still had some months to run, the Roosevelts would camp as necessary in Sara's adjoining town house.

Based on his Navy experience, Franklin also looked, restlessly, at investing in the newly commercial radio industry, in dirigible passenger service, and in the risky possibility of licensing retail shops in Haiti and Santo Domingo. He had long dreamed of harnessing the powerful tidal flows of Passamaquoddy Bay, off Campobello, for electric power, and invested a modest sum in bank financing for shares. Further, the irrepressible Arthur Patch Homer had already popped up to promote an oil drilling venture in Oklahoma. Roosevelt bought 500 shares at ten dollars each. Abetted by Louis Howe, Homer intended refining cheap Mexican crude at Fall River, Massachusetts, freeing the Navy from dependence on the price fixing of processing giants like Standard Oil. Daniels was dubious, predicting in his diary on April 3 that the only person to profit would be Homer. Although Department admirals warned against it, Daniels reluctantly approved a deal with Homer's New England Oil Company, and Roosevelt would boast in a speech in New Bedford that the new refinery promised prosperity in the area. When the postwar market for oil collapsed and investors lost money, so did the Navy, which had to pay the agreed-upon price per barrel.

Earlier, in March 1918, the promise of fuel accessibility had prompted Franklin to explore the acquisition of petroleum-rich Curaçao, in the lower Caribbean, from the Dutch, using as precedent Wilson's purchase (as the renamed Virgin Islands) of the Danish West Indies in January 1917, ostensibly to protect approaches to the Panama Canal. Despite the disapproval of Daniels, who read imperial designs on the order of TR into the proposal, Roosevelt suggested that Marley Hay, a submarine expert he knew, who was planning to travel to the Netherlands, raise the matter there. Concerned that the Germans would view a sale as a violation of Dutch neutrality, the Netherlands foreign minister declined to discuss it. It was yet another example of FDR's venturing beyond his brief.

Franklin's business future as his Navy job wound down seemed based upon his executive experience in wartime Washington—and the fact that he was a Roosevelt. His political future depended upon how he could further exploit the Roosevelt aura, which had served him effectively. Helpfully, the Sims-inspired investigation of the Department was fading. And the Lucy episode seemed buried under St. Gaudens's bronze. FDR also spent time away from Washington to explore opportunities in New York politics, which appeared dim. In the gloomy outlook Tammany bosses saw him as a vote-getting possibility. The post-Wilson Democratic ticket seemed sure to lose almost everywhere. Former New York governor Martin Glynn objected to Daniels that Irish Catholic Democrats, a major political base, were ignored by the allegedly snobbish President. "None of our people are deemed worthy to sit in the [Wilson] councils," Glynn charged, "and it is about time to let the Democratic Party leaders know what a great defeat means. If we are not good enough to hold positions of [national] importance we ought to assert we will not vote the ticket. Frank Polk* and Frank Roosevelt carry no votes and no strength and yet they are recognized. Woodrow Wilson is an ingrate."

Party power brokers and prospective financiers, ignoring Wilson, and dismissing petty Navy controversies with a vanishing shelf-life, had long been suggesting FDR, who had a magic name, for the second slot on the presidential ticket—and even for the first. Seeing inevitable defeat, and oblivion thereafter, Louis Howe had long tried to warn off such conjecture. So had Franklin, although the prospect of early fame teased him. Eleven months before the nominating convention, reluctant to be exploited and then discarded, he had written to Judge Henry M. Heymann of New York to stop sending "Roosevelt for President" promotional material to newspapers. (Since the boosts were unsigned and postmarked from Washington, some editors wondered if FDR was concocting, on his own,

---

*FDR's Groton and Yale friend, Counselor at the State Department.

a naïve self-promotion.) "Thanks for your action in nipping my Presidential boom in the bud," he wrote breezily to Heymann on December 2, 1919. " . . . I sometimes think we consider too much the good luck of the early bird, and not the bad luck of the early worm."

Encouraged by Louis Wehle, Eleanor and Franklin envisioned the ideal Democratic candidate as Herbert Hoover. A successful manager, he had run Wilson's Food Administration and European relief programs efficiently, and seemingly without political ambition. Wealthy, and without open enemies, he was cultivated by both parties. "He's the only man I know," Eleanor wrote to her friend Isabella, "who has first hand knowledge of European questions & great responsibility & understands business, not only from the capitalistic point of view, but also from the worker's standpoint." For Eleanor it was a rare venture into political opinion.

"I had some nice talks with Herbert Hoover before he went West for Christmas," FDR recalled to a friend. "He is certainly a wonder, and I wish we could make him President. . . . There could not be a better one." Given later events, Franklin's appraisal of the "Great Engineer" would prove a rueful irony.

The party identity question would crop up again after another world war, when Dwight Eisenhower, with no known political affiliation, was sought after, and President Harry Truman confided that he would not run in 1948 if the general would seek the office as a Democrat. (Deviously, Eisenhower—like Hoover, earlier—was already flirting with wealthy and influential Republicans.) Although Hoover publicly shied away from what he described as party "entanglements," that ostensible aloofness concealed rising ambition.

Roosevelt's caution was also evaporating as he sought a role to play in a Democratic vacuum created by the eroding Wilson imperium. Millions of war veterans and millions more laid-off workers in war industries were still unemployed. The purchasing power of a 1913 dollar had declined by half, with food costs up 84 percent and clothing up 114 percent. Strikes spread across the country. Under government controls, wages had hardly kept pace with inflation, and even those holding jobs struggled. The postwar blame for the slowdown obviously fell on the Administration.

Pragmatism required Franklin's party loyalty, as name recognition was not enough; nevertheless being a Roosevelt resulted in a speaking invitation at the annual banquet of the Democratic National Committee in Chicago on May 29, where he avoided references to the faltering economy. Long friendly, through Uncle Ted, with Republican power broker Henry Cabot Lodge, FDR knew that Democratic political leaders longed for a roasting of the senator. Franklin furnished it. "When Mr. Lodge reads his morning paper . . . and sees what the President has said or done," Franklin charged, "his policy for the next twenty-four hours becomes the diametrical opposite." He even included praise for William Jennings Bryan, whom he loathed, as the tireless Nebraskan inspired a personal, if fading, following. "We must remember," Roosevelt noted, "that many of the ideals and principles enunciated by Mr. Bryan . . . are now the law of the land." The key word, which withdrew some of the faint praise, was "many." The Democrats, he declared, had "carried through more great measures for the good of the whole population than any other party in any similar period," and became a major factor in winning "the most stupendous war in history." Now they were "approaching the campaign of 1920" with "liberalism, commonsense idealism, [and] constructiveness" while the unnamed other party remained the bulwark of "conservatism, [and] special privilege."

The keynote address by Red-baiting Attorney General Palmer, preceding FDR's talk, was a bold bid for the presidential nomination, but it received unenthusiastic press coverage. Gossip resumed about Roosevelt for senator or governor, depending upon the office for which the sitting New York governor, Alfred E. Smith, a presidential aspirant himself, chose to run. In its June 19, 1920, issue the popular *Literary Digest* went even farther about FDR after Chicago, summing up his hard-hitting address by suggesting even higher office for him. Yet the widespread assumption was that Wilson's eight years were ending catastrophically and that any Republican could win the presidency.

As the practice in both parties held that aspirants had to wait their turns in the candidacy queue, Herbert Hoover, however talked about by Republicans, would have to win his place by subordinate service while his seniors sought the office. Other than favorite-son nominees, the leading

GOP candidates were Major General Leonard Wood, who bore the Rough Rider association with Theodore Roosevelt and whom Wilson had kept from wartime action; Senator Hiram Johnson of California, a populist former governor in the TR mold, and his Bull Moose running mate in 1912; and Governor Frank Orren Lowden of Illinois, an efficient administrator who had married a Pullman heiress, and was a backer of female suffrage, the Volstead Act enabling prohibition and Lodge's League reservations.

On June 8, with Senator Lodge as chairman, the Republican convention convened at the Chicago Coliseum, torridly hot and despite strong olfactory precautions still redolent of cows and pigs. Delegates stayed at the Blackstone Hotel. Corinne Roosevelt Robinson's seconding speech for General Wood overshadowed all the routine addresses but stirred no momentum for him. TR's sister—Eleanor's "Auntie Corinne"—was the first woman to address a major party conclave.

The balloting soon deadlocked without any of the twelve placed in nomination obtaining as much as 30 percent of the votes. Just after two in the morning on June 12, fifteen sleepless party stalwarts in what would become the proverbial smoke-filled hotel room compromised on Senator Warren G. Harding of Ohio, a silver-haired conservative mediocrity who looked presidential and considered William McKinley of his home state his political hero. Few knew of his financial irregularities or his sexual adventurism. (His wealthy campaign political director, Albert Lasker, quietly bought off the elder of the ladies. The younger mistress would write about her own affair after Harding's sudden death in 1923, to support her—and their—illegitimate daughter.) On the tenth ballot the reconvened delegates accepted the nominee, but when the customary motion to make the tally unanimous was proposed, Harold Ickes, a Bull Moose Republican from Chicago who had supported Hiram Johnson,* rose in protest, and others followed. Ignoring them, Henry Cabot Lodge declared the nomination unanimous.

---

*In 1933, when FDR wanted a Republican in his Cabinet, Hiram Johnson declined and the feisty Ickes would become Secretary of the Interior, a position he held for thirteen years.

As Harding's running mate, although the nominee recommended Irvine Lenroot, a bland Wisconsin senator, for the second position, party leaders picked the taciturn, tight-fisted governor of Massachusetts, Calvin Coolidge, who had gained widespread attention by ordering the National Guard in his state to break a strike by Boston policemen. "Silent Cal" had no domestic sins to hide and opened New England for the GOP.

As the ticket was parented by Senator Lodge, Wilson's implacable enemy, the enfeebled President pushed himself into the campaign, giving the *New York World* a wooden interview six days later and permitting a carefully staged press photo at his desk to appear that he was still managing affairs. (He was physically carried there, and placed in his chair.) Although the Democratic convention was imminent, Wilson, as earlier, refused to endorse a candidate. The League of Nations, he insisted, was still the primary issue before the country, and the only way to ensure its survival was to furnish him another term. Also, if the convention were deadlocked, he told Dr. Grayson, "I would feel obliged to accept the nomination even if I thought it would cost me my life." Although there was no chance of his being endorsed in San Francisco, Democrats realized that no pairing they concocted could win. At best the nominees would gain some national exposure, and perhaps another opportunity if the promised Republican economic boom failed.

HOWEVER RELUCTANTLY, THE Navy was pushed into the convention. In the main corridor on the second deck of the Department, Roosevelt encountered Lieutenant John L. McCrea, aide to Vice Admiral Hugh Rodman, new commander of the Pacific Fleet. Knowing that Rodman was about to leave for San Francisco, the Assistant Secretary asked McCrea to deliver a message. The Democratic convention was to open on June 28. Since FDR claimed difficulty securing a hotel room—certainly a fiction—he requested quarters for himself and for an aide on Rodman's flagship, the *New Mexico*. Rodman had sparred with Roosevelt over small patrol boats early in the war and was now peeved by the questionable use of a warship. "I don't like it one damn bit," he told McCrea. " . . . Can you beat it?"

Although Rodman gave in, the Secretary himself would complicate the improprieties. After the admiral left for Texas, to take the *New Mexico* through the Panama Canal and up the Pacific coast, he received a demand for accommodations from Daniels. When Rodman wired back that the only suitable stateroom aboard had been reserved by Roosevelt, Daniels telegraphed firmly, I SHALL STAY ON NEW MEXICO MAKE OTHER ARRANGEMENTS FOR ASSISTANT SECRETARY SIGNED DANIELS. Evicted, Franklin did not fault McCrea, who as a captain at the time of Pearl Harbor would be FDR's own naval aide, and as a vice admiral and commander of the *Iowa* in 1943 would take the President across the Atlantic and through the Mediterranean to a conference in Cairo with Churchill. FDR found other accommodations in San Francisco, arranging for a cabin on the battleship *New York*.

On the eve of the convention he impressed state politicians by presiding over a quarterdeck dinner on the *New York* for the delegation and his entourage—his secretary Renah Camalier; his new law associate Grenville Emmet; his Harvard pal Lathrop Brown; Tom Lynch, a Poughkeepsie florist who was his golf partner when at Hyde Park; and Dutchess County judge John E. Mack. Judge Mack had first proposed FDR for office because he was a Roosevelt and his mother could afford the campaign expenses. Ten years before, during that first run, Tom Lynch in a premature surfeit of optimism had put aside two bottles of champagne to await Franklin's becoming President.

Prohibition would be flagrantly flouted in San Francisco. Despite the dry amendment now in technical force for five months, the festivities overflowed with alcoholic conviviality. *Baltimore Sun* reporter H. L. Mencken, a compulsive imbiber, feared that no substitute for spirits would be available but "paint remover and sheep dip." Rather, he discovered, "No matter what a delegate ordered, he got bourbon—but it was bourbon of the very first chop. . . ."

After preconvention politicking, the delegates learned to their relief, and drank libations to the news, that Woodrow Wilson would not be placed in nomination. A token tribute to the broken President was substituted, and led by the Virginia delegation, representing the state of his origins. The aisles filled with marchers as spotlights played upon a huge portrait of the absent Wilson. Although Franklin wanted to demonstrate his party regularity, Boss Murphy, who was hostile to the President, ordered his delegates to remain seated. With George R. Lunn, the former mayor of Schenectady, FDR after a brief tussle seized the state standard from Judge Jeremiah Mahoney, a Tammany die-hard. To loud cheers, Franklin pushed into the crowd with his trophy. The scuffle, allegedly including a fistfight ("a clean upper-cut") which never happened, grew to something "spectacular" in wired press accounts, one of which Eleanor read. "You & Tammany don't seem to agree very well," she wrote. "Mama is very proud of your removing the state standard from them. I have a feeling you enjoyed it, but won't they be very much against you in the State Convention?"

Tammany's Al Smith, a first-term governor, would be a favorite-son nominee. His Catholicism and his reputation as a "wet" in a dry decade branded him unelectable, yet at the state delegation dinner on the *New York* quarterdeck he asked Roosevelt to deliver a seconding speech for him. New York delegate Frances Perkins, who would become FDR's Secretary of Labor in 1933, recalled his "vaulting over a row of chairs to get to the platform in a hurry." Looking buoyant and vigorous at thirty-eight, he would gush about the florid, cigar-chomping Irishman he hardly knew, "I love him like a friend; I look up to him as a man; I am with him as a Democrat; and we all know his record throughout the nation." To enthusiastic applause he added, "The nominee of this convention will not be chosen at 2 a.m. in a hotel room."

Roosevelt was almost wrong. Although Smith withdrew after eight unpromising ballots, the two-thirds rule was in force. After forty-five ballots, no candidate could break the deadlock among McAdoo, Palmer, and Governor James M. Cox of Ohio, who had ducked questions about the League. From the White House, Wilson, hardly conciliatory about anything, called Cox's candidacy "a joke." A Dayton newspaper publisher before election to state office, the governor's contribution to the war effort had been to ban the teaching of German in Ohio public schools.

Ballot after ballot, McAdoo and Palmer shed delegates whose commitments had lapsed, most votes picked up by the uncontroversial Cox.

On the forty-fourth ballot over four days Cox prevailed. As a running mate, Cox's floor manager obtusely suggested Edwin T. Meredith, Wilson's Secretary of Agriculture and a colorless Iowa publisher of farm periodicals, but Cox, who had stayed away and kept in touch by telephone, recognized the appeal of the Roosevelt name. "Young Roosevelt," he proposed. Although he had never met Franklin, Cox had his Ohio crony, Judge Timothy T. Ansberry, place the more visible FDR in nomination that noon.

Josephus Daniels advised Franklin to slip out of the hall—a customary convention tactic. Among the seconding speakers, Al Smith, repaying Roosevelt's gesture, came forward. Once all the seconders had droned through, the other aspirants, recognizing reality, withdrew. It was July 6, 1920, already a very long day. Convention rules were suspended to expedite the ending, and FDR was nominated for the vice presidency by acclamation.

Requesting the floor as a courtesy, Daniels, scotching any rumors, however accurate, about antagonism between him and FDR in their departmental partnership, claimed effusively that "to me, and to five hundred thousand men in the American Navy, and five million men in the Army, it is a matter of peculiar gratification that this Convention unanimously has chosen . . . that clear-headed and able executive . . . Franklin D. Roosevelt. And I wish to add that his service during this great war . . . was chiefly executive only because, when the war began and he wished to go to the front, I urged him that his highest duty was to help to carry the millions of men across and to bring them back." Franklin was then invited in to receive the traditional ovation.

From Campobello, Eleanor wrote to Sara, "This certainly is a world of surprises. I really think F. had a better chance of winning for the Senatorship but the Democrats may win, one cannot tell and at least it should be a good fight." The New York *World* sent a reporter from Eastport, Maine, to interview Eleanor. "While he may not have looked for the honor," she said, "I am proud of his nomination and hope he will be elected." A newsman from the New York *Evening Post* who went to Hyde Park to interview Sara at Springwood, and was obviously more familiar with urban settings than with the family retreat, claimed awe at "the stamp of ancient solid things, of good beginnings which have persisted well." Sara would only talk about her son's connection with Hyde Park, the place he loved best, where a village welcoming was already being prepared. In such surroundings, the city reporter wrote discreetly, with nothing political to impart, "there is no necessity ever to speak of what is one's belief; it is so certain and so sure."

Congratulatory telegrams to FDR poured in, "more than 2500," he estimated when back home. Under the premature caption "Another Roosevelt Headed for the White House," *The Literary Digest* in its July 30 issue ran a photograph of Sara at Hyde Park embracing her returning son. "If the name 'Roosevelt' looks a bit strange up among the head-liners on a Democratic national ticket," the story began, "there is some reassurance that the strain runs true." A wire from Herbert Hoover, calling himself graciously "an old friend," declared that he was "glad to see you . . . in such a prominent place." Although a Republican and unable to wish a Democrat success in the election, he considered Roosevelt's nomination "a contribution to the good of the country" in that it would "bring the merit of a great public servant" to public recognition.

Now as nominee, Roosevelt traveled homeward by rail, pausing in Utah, Colorado, Kansas and Missouri to confer diplomatically with Democratic politicians and to garner local press coverage. In Columbus, Ohio, he stopped to meet with James Cox for the first time. At a news conference they exuded the required optimism. Privately they accepted the necessity of meeting jointly with President Wilson. Only then, in their home districts, would come the formal notifications of their nominations.

On the warm afternoon of July 11, the Knickerbocker Express steamed in at Hyde Park. Bunting and pennants flew from the little brick depot. Sara awaited Franklin on the Springwood portico, as did a newsreel cameraman. Eleanor was traveling alone from Campobello. She had become used to that. She also avoided newsreel cameras.

Sunday, July 18, in Washington proved sunny and clear. Wilson was surprised by the appearance of FDR at the White House as, thanks to Edith, his dislike of Franklin had increased. Yet acceptance of the courtesy visit was necessary, and both candidates anticipated that they would have to make gestures toward the lost cause of the League. Cox arrived in a gray business suit and straw hat. Intending to call press attention to his nautical past, Roosevelt wore yachtsman's attire of white shoes and trousers, and dark blue jacket and tie. Joseph Tumulty escorted them from his office to the south portico facing the lawn. Edith Wilson, the power behind the disintegrating presidency, stood quietly in the background. In the warm sun, the President huddled in his wheelchair, a shawl concealing his paralyzed left shoulder and arm. The left side of his long, sunken face seemed dead. As senior nominee, Cox dissembled his shock, greeting Wilson warmly. The President, looking up weakly, whispered, "Thank you for coming. I am very glad you came." He did not, or would not, notice Franklin.

"Mr. President," Cox said, "I have always admired the fight you made for the League."

Struggling painfully, Wilson responded, "Mr. Cox, that fight can still be won!"

As Roosevelt watched, his tears welled as Cox assured Wilson, "Mr. President, we are going to be a million percent with you, and your Administration, and that means the League of Nations."

"I am very grateful," Wilson murmured almost inaudibly, his jaw sinking toward his chest. "I am very grateful."

Roosevelt cautiously said nothing other than joining in a goodbye, after which the two escaped into Tumulty's office. There, Cox penned a short statement for the press, maintaining their intentions to campaign for the League. FDR added, "I wish that every American could have been a silent witness at the meeting of these two great men. Their splendid accord and their high purpose are an inspiration." The encounter was far from splendid and the public would have been appalled by the wraith that was Wilson; yet the fiction for the newspapers was necessary.

All but out of office, Franklin, who knew better, wrote to Eleanor, "Reports are distinctly encouraging about the sentiment throughout the nation." He ordered the destroyer *Hatfield* to take him to Campobello. Lashed to the deck was his new *Vireo*, replacing the *Half Moon II*, given to the Navy for wartime patrol duty. Roosevelt piloted the *Hatfield* through the Lubec Narrows himself, earning a slap in the Hearst's *New York Journal* for his personal extravagance. He had no "right" to use a warship to "carry his 165 pounds . . . to a summer resting place. . . . Is a first-class ticket . . . not good enough?" Unfortunately the *Vireo*, not carry-on luggage, needed more than a first-class ticket.

While FDR was away, Daniels pondered a successor. "After cabinet [meeting]," he wrote in his diary on August 3, "I talked of FDR's resignation & asked if President had any man in view for vacancy. No. 'I resent & deeply resent' &c he said." What the "&c" disguised after the obvious "Roosevelt" can only be surmised, but the deteriorating Wilson had long cultivated resentment. The next day, a Wednesday, Daniels noted, "FDR & wife to dinner. They leave for Columbus and then for Hyde Park, & he resigns on Monday. He is full of campaign and goes West at once."

In Main Navy on Friday, August 6, Franklin proposed to Daniels that no replacement be appointed—that Louis Howe, who allegedly had high-salaried external offers, be moved informally into the Roosevelt slot. "He believes it," Daniels wrote. "I have a great big swallow but I cannot swallow that." (Howe would remain, but under a new appointee whose job would soon expire.*) It was the day of Roosevelt's formal farewell. A Navy band played in the second deck corridor. The head of the Metal Trades Council at the Washington Navy Yard presented him with a teakwood gavel fashioned from a replaced rail of the presidential yacht *Mayflower*. Harry T. Morningstar of the Association of Master Mechanics of Navy Yards and Stations presented FDR with an engraved silver loving cup. "We are looking forward, with gladness," he said, "to the fourth of March next, when we shall witness the inauguration of our beloved Assistant Secretary as Vice President of the United States, in whose election we all hope to have a most welcome part." The Chief Electrician at the Washington Navy Yard asked Daniels to do the parting honors, and the Secretary "spoke"—he would write—"of only two compensations for men in public office—consciousness of giving one[']s best to the public weal & the appreciation & friendship of co-workers. FDR had both."

---

*Gordon Woodbury, editor of the *Manchester [N.H.] Union*, would succeed FDR.

Standing on a flag-draped table to be seen by the crowd, Roosevelt vowed, "No matter what happens on November second, my heart will always be with the Navy. If things go right on that date, I feel quite certain that the Capital is going to hear a whole lot more of the Navy than it has ever heard before."

As Roosevelt was leaving the office he gave Daniels a handwritten letter:

Dear Chief:

This is not goodbye—that will always be impossible after these years of the closest association—and no words I write will make you know better than you know now how much our association has meant. All my life I shall look back—not only on the *work* of the place—but mostly on the wonderful way in which you and I have gone through these nearly eight years *together*. You have taught me so wisely and kept my feet on the ground when I was about to skyrocket—and in it all there has never been a real dispute or antagonism or distrust.

Hence, in part, at least, I will share in the reward which you *will* get true credit for in history. I am very proud—but more than that I am very *happy* to have been able to help.

We will I know keep up this association in the years to come—and please let me keep on coming to you to get your fine inspiration of real idealism and right living and good Americanism.

So *au revoir* for a little while. You have always the

Affectionate regards of

Franklin D. Roosevelt

The band struck up a farewell as he left for Union Station, and the next phase of his life.

Daniels would write a long, affectionate response, and prepared a formal letter accepting Franklin's resignation which would be signed by Woodrow Wilson. "FDR . . . left in the afternoon," the Secretary noted in his diary, "but before leaving wrote me a letter most friendly & almost loving wh. made me glad I had never acted upon my impulse when he seemed to take sides with my critics." The next day, although a nonworking Saturday, Daniels, in his reply, warmly papered over their prewar differences. To "Dear Franklin," he went back to their "first acquaintance," confiding that although "Love at first sight is rare with men," his "intuition" in recommending him had been fully justified. "I always counted on your zeal, your enthusiasm, your devoted patriotism and your efficient and able service, and always found you equal to the big job in hand. My thought and feeling has been that of an elder brother . . . and we will be brothers in all things that make for the good of the country."

Daniels was fifty-eight, Roosevelt thirty-eight. They parted as unlikely brothers, the elder looking back toward the past, and his newspaper in North Carolina to which he would return, the other toward the downs and ups of his unknowable future.

11

Postscript

WHEN JAMES COX'S deputy in San Francisco had awakened Tammany boss Charles Murphy at dawn to tell him that the nominee's choice for the second slot was young Roosevelt, Murphy's sleepy, unenthusiastic response was, "He is not well known in the country." FDR intended to reverse that perception. He knew he was "window dressing" for the Democrats, but he was only thirty-eight and he was thinking ahead. Although he felt finished with the political treadmill of appointive office, there was a beyond. "No man," he would later confide, "ever willingly gives up public life—no man who has ever tasted it."

On August 8, 1920, Franklin, Eleanor and Anna, now tall, blonde and fourteen, were in Cox's hometown, Dayton, Ohio, where formal notification of his nomination as Democratic presidential candidate was tendered. Warren Harding had already announced confidently that he would campaign in the comfortable manner of his fellow Ohioan, William McKinley, and Roosevelt spiritedly evoked his wartime experience by promising, in a brief address, a campaign that would "drag the enemy off the front porch."

At Hyde Park the next day, an audience estimated at five thousand filled the lawn at Springwood for Roosevelt's village, and national, blessing, with about five hundred invitees crowding inside. Every kind of conveyance was

FDR in Dayton, Ohio, August 8, 1920, to meet with Democratic presidential nominee
James Cox. FDR LIBRARY

employed to bring in visitors, and business in town was suspended for the
day. As a Dutchess County squire, Henry Morgenthau, Jr., managed the notification agenda, which included words from such party notables as Governor Smith and former Treasury Secretary McAdoo, and FDR's chief of only
the week before, Secretary Daniels. At hazard to the ship models and nautical prints beloved by the candidate, Senator Joe Robinson of Arkansas,
chair of the Nominating Notification Committee, performed his official
mission before a standing throng in the library.

Despite her pride in her son, Sara later grumbled about what tram-
pling crowds had done to her immaculate lawns and long veranda, the
Democratic "front porch." During the event, however, she hovered over
servants who offered lemonade and cake to onlookers outdoors, and more

FDR at the Hyde Park nomination acceptance festivities for the Democratic vice presidential nomination, August 9, 1920. FDR LIBRARY

substantial fare to hungry Democrats in the house. Most locals had never before seen the interior of Springwood.

Faithful to his promises, in his acceptance speech Franklin declared, while Eleanor sat conspicuously on a balustrade to listen, that the League of Nations was "a practical solution of a practical situation," and he conceded to stubborn advocates of treaty reservation clauses that the Constitution had to remain supreme. He attacked Republican nitpicking about the conduct of the war, although he had been one of the sharpest internal critics, asserting, "We have seen things on too large a scale to listen in this day to trifles, or to believe in the adequacy of trifles." He proposed budgetary simplification, more professionalism rather than politics in the civil service system and more efficient use of the nation's natural resources, including its people—as the military draft had exposed vast tracts of illiteracy and impoverishment. He wanted something better for the future than Harding's promise of a return to "normalcy." Rather, he insisted, "We must see that it is impossible to avoid, except by monastic seclusion, those honorable and intimate foreign relations which the fearful-hearted miscall by the Devil's catchword 'international complications.'" And with a buoyancy that would be his trademark whatever the outlook, he added, "We can never go back. . . . We cannot anchor our ship of state. . . . We must go forward, or flounder."

Without mentioning either former president, he was combining reformist themes from Theodore Roosevelt and Woodrow Wilson, but all of his years under Wilson suggested that the role model for his future would be his Uncle Ted. The cold, ascetic arrogance of Wilson had paled in the glare of the energy, optimism and zeal of the elder Roosevelt. Franklin recognized that he was not a facsimile of the hearty, happy political warrior that he had known. TR had emerged from a different era now destroyed by war, with its consequences still to be played out. Gifted with a magic surname he would need to establish as his own, FDR would have to create his buoyant presidential persona out of the ashes of certain defeat for the vice presidency that only through accident had catapulted the earlier Roosevelt into the White House.

Accompanying Franklin on his campaign train west would be his former Navy public relations assistant Marvin McIntyre, much later a White House staffer, and Louis Howe, who was taking a month's leave to circumvent Civil Service rules about politicking. Charles McCarthy staffed a campaign office in Washington, bringing in Marguerite A. ("Missy") Le Hand, twenty-three, as secretary. Her life to its end would be devoted to FDR.

As politicians must, Roosevelt radiated confidence, but when McIntyre asked him bluntly whether he had any illusions about the outcome, Roosevelt conceded, "Nary an illusion." He recognized the disappointment and apathy pervading the postwar electorate. Eleanor, who joined some stages of the campaign to suggest a working marriage, found party exuberance artificial and, privately, useless and even sad.

From left, Louis Howe, unkempt as usual; Thomas Lynch, Franklin's longtime Poughkeepsie friend; FDR; and Marvin McIntyre, vice presidential publicist in 1920 and later a White House aide. Washington, DC, August 1920. FDR LIBRARY

From Hyde Park she wrote to Franklin, then on the campaign trail, on August 27, "So far the Republican papers having nothing very bad against you[,] have simply been trying to treat you like an amiable, young boy; belittlement is the worst they can do." The TR family, she reported in a later letter, was out in force for the Harding-Coolidge ticket. "Did you see that Alice is to go on the stump for Harding and that Auntie Corinne is to speak for him in Portland, Maine? . . ."

Theodore Roosevelt, Jr., was dispatched by the Republican campaign as a one-man truth squad to trail Franklin. "He is a maverick," cousin Ted charged in Sheridan, Wyoming, disowning the wrong party's Roosevelt. "He does not have the brand of our family."

Following the expected Republican landslide on November 2, 1920, largely a rejection of the failing Wilson, and a reaction to the accumulation of postwar discontent, Warren Gamaliel Harding, before his inauspicious inauguration on March 4, 1921, named Ted, Jr., Assistant Secretary of the Navy.

FDR in Washington in August 1920, appearing ebullient as Democratic vice presidential nominee. FDR LIBRARY

Sources

The key resource for all matters FDR is the Franklin D. Roosevelt Presidential Library at his family home in Hyde Park, New York. As have earlier biographers noted below, I have foraged in its wealth of documents, images and memorabilia. Its holdings keep expanding as collections by former FDR intimates are acquired and accessed. The plethora of books about Roosevelt employed in this narrative of his prentice years as Assistant Secretary of the Navy range from single-volume biographies to multi-volume length, and include books by his immediate family and his extended political family. Where some information is unique to a particular source not identified in the text, I have cited it in the appropriate chapter.

ROOSEVELT FAMILY BOOKS USED
THROUGHOUT INCLUDE THE FOLLOWING:

Eleanor Roosevelt, *Autobiography* (New York: Harcourt, Brace, 1961); *This I Remember* (New York: Harper, 1949)

Elliott Roosevelt, ed., *FDR: His Personal Letters, I* (New York: Duell, Sloan & Pearce, 1947); *An Untold Story: The Roosevelts of Hyde Park*, with James Brough (New York: Putnam, 1977)

James Roosevelt, with Sidney Shalett, *Affectionately, F.D.R.* (New York: Harcourt, Brace, 1959)

Roosevelt family intimates include the following:

Joseph Alsop, *A Centenary Remembrance* (New York: Random House, 1982)

Blanche Wiesen Cook, *Eleanor Roosevelt, I, 1884–1933* (New York: Viking Penguin, 1992)

Jonathan Daniels, *The End of Innocence* (New York: Da Capo Press, 1954); *Washington Quadrille* (Garden City, NY: Doubleday, 1975)

Josephus Daniels, ed. David E. Cronon, *The Cabinet Diaries of Josephus Daniels, 1913–1921* (Lincoln: University of Nebraska Press, 1963; *[The Letters of] Roosevelt and Daniels: A Friendship in Politics*; ed. Carroll Kilpatrick (Chapel Hill: University of North Carolina Press, 1952); *The Wilson Era: Years of Peace 1910–1917* (Chapel Hill: University of North Carolina Press, 1944); *The Wilson Era: Years of War and after 1917–1923* (Chapel Hill: University of North Carolina Press, 1946)

Joseph P. Lash, *Eleanor and Franklin: The Story of Their Relationship* (New York: Norton, 1971)

BIOGRAPHIES, MEMOIRS AND EDITED DOCUMENTS (OTHERS REFERRED TO IN PASSING ARE CITED WHERE THEY ARE UTILIZED):

Bernard Asbell, ed., *Mother and Daughter: The Letters of Eleanor and Anna Roosevelt* (New York: Coward, McCain & Geoghegan, 1982)

Conrad Black, *Franklin Delano Roosevelt, Champion of Freedom* (New York: Public Affairs Press, 2003)

H. W. Brands, *Traitor to His Class: The Privileged Life and Radical Presidency of Franklin Delano Roosevelt* (New York: Doubleday, 2008)

Kenneth Davis, *FDR: I, The Beckoning of Destiny, 1882–1928* (New York: Putnam, 1972)

Julie M. Fenster, *FDR's Shadow: Louis Howe, the Force That Shaped Franklin and Eleanor Roosevelt* (New York: Palgrave Macmillan, 2009)

Frank Freidel, *FDR: I, The Apprenticeship* (Boston: Little, Brown, 1952)

Nathan Miller, *FDR: An Intimate History* (Garden City, NY: Doubleday, 1983)

Stephen O. Muskie, *Campobello: Roosevelt's "Beloved Island"* (Camden, ME: Down East Books, 1982)

Joseph E. Persico, *Franklin and Lucy: Mrs. Rutherfurd and the Other Remarkable Women in Roosevelt's Life* (New York: Random House, 2008)

Janice Pottker, *Sara and Eleanor: The Story of Sara Delano Roosevelt and Her Daughter-in-Law, Eleanor Roosevelt* (New York: St. Martin's Press, 2004)

Alfred B. Rollins, Jr., *Roosevelt and Howe* (New York: Knopf, 1962)

Jean Edward Smith, *F.D.R.* (New York: Random House, 2008)

Lela Stiles, *The Man behind Roosevelt: The Story of Louis McHenry Howe* (Cleveland: World Publishing, 1954)

Geoffrey Ward, *A First-Class Temperament: The Emergence of Franklin Roosevelt* (New York: Harper & Row, 1989); ed., *Closest Companion: The Unknown Story of the Intimate Friendship of Franklin Roosevelt and Margaret Suckley* (Boston: Houghton Mifflin, 1995)

PREFACE

"Navy man": see chapter 8, "The Service Vote," in S. Weintraub, *Final Victory: FDR's Extraordinary World War II Presidential Campaign* (New York: Da Capo Press, 2012). Robert R. McCormick's belittlement of FDR is in Richard Norton, *The Colonel: The Life and Legend of Robert R. McCormick* (Boston: Houghton Mifflin, 1997). The James Roosevelt visit with young Franklin to President Cleveland is in Black (above) and other biographies. D. D. Guttenplan in "One Uncompromising Vision," *TLS*, London, October 12, 2012, described the ship's prow apex of the Roosevelt Memorial at Four Freedoms Park.

CHAPTER 1

FDR is pictured in derby as new Assistant Secretary in *The American Review of Reviews*, April, 1913. For Daniels's accounts of selecting FDR, and the Assistant Secretary appointment delays, see Daniels, *Cabinet Diary*, above, and Daniels and Kilpatrick, above. FDR's early career and background is described in the Roosevelt family sources above. His basic income came from his father's $120,000 trust fund for him. Kermit Roosevelt's "Pop is praying for Clark" is expanded absurdly in a biography of Wilson. Quotes from letters to Howe and from Howe are from Rollins and Stiles (both above), here and hereafter from the FDR Library. Fenster (above) adds little that is new. The closing quotation, borrowed from General Grant in many biographies but here taken from Geoffrey Perret, *Ulysses S. Grant: Soldier and President* (New York: Random House, 1997), was identified for me by Richard E. Winslow III.

CHAPTER 2

Theodore Roosevelt's letters to Franklin are in the FDR Library, as is FDR's 1918 letter to Randolph Marshall. Alice Roosevelt Longworth's involvement in FDR's early months in office is from her *Crowded Hours: Reminiscences* (New York:

Scribner, 1953); Michael Teague, ed., *Mrs. L.: Conversations with Alice Roosevelt Longworth* (Garden City, NY: Doubleday, 1981); and Stacey A. Cordery, *Alice* (New York: Viking, 2007). Wilson's retention of the Adams quotation placed by TR is in Mildred Dewey's letter to her stepson on FDR, undated, in the George Dewey Papers, Naval Historical Center, Washington. Howe's failures to be ship-shape and his file copy about the burial of a cow at Mare Island are from Rollins, above. Daniels's comment on the photo with FDR looking out at the White House is from Jonathan Daniels, above; the photo is in the FDR Library. Adm. Fiske's diary entries here and following, including memos to FDR, are from his autobiography, *From Midshipman to Rear Admiral* (New York: Century, 1919). FDR on Fiske at a press conference is from *Complete Presidential Press Conferences of Franklin D. Roosevelt* (New York: Da Capo, 1972). Further press conference quotations are from this edition. The Roosevelt home life on Campobello, the "cottage" and travel details about access to the island are from Jonas Klein, *Beloved Island: Franklin and Eleanor and the Legacy of Campobello* (Forest Dale, VT: Paul S. Eriksson, 2000). Other details about Campobello are from Lash (above). Other contemporary details about access are from Baedeker's *The Dominion of Canada: Handbook for Travellers* (London: Fisher Unwin, 1922).

CHAPTER 3

TR's letters to FDR on *The Outlook* letterhead are in the FDR Library. Spring-Rice's pervasive anti-Semitism is described by Edmund Morris in *Colonel Roosevelt* (New York: Random House, 2010). ("Springy's" hall of infamy also included Adolph Ochs of *The New York Times* and banker Jacob Schiff, among others.) The history of the Ralph Stackpole female image at San Francisco which FDR craved to possess was reported to me by Michelle H. Frauenberger, Museum Collections Manager at the FDR Library, November 8, 2011. She furnished photos of the vanished miniature and Stackpole's oversized replacement now at Hyde Park. FDR's "The Problem of Our Navy" appeared in the February 28, 1914, issue of *Scientific American*. Details of the ceremonial keel-laying of the *Arizona* appeared in *The New York Times* on March 17, 1914. FDR's press conference reminiscence of the blinkered Wall Street response to the war is from *Press Conferences* (above). Count Kessler's typical German response on the likely duration of the war is from his diaries, *Journey to the Abyss* (see below, chapter 5). "Americans Are Hurrying Home" and other dispatches from early wartime Europe appeared in Associated Press articles across the nation in August 1914.

Hoover's role is recollected in his *Memoirs* (New York: Macmillan, 1951), and in George H. Nash, *The Life of Herbert Hoover: The Humanitarian 1914–1917* (New York, W. W. Norton, 2010). Hoover's August 21, 1914, statement urging Americans to conserve food by returning home was in an AP dispatch. Ambassador Page's misguided gratitude to Heaven for the Atlantic Ocean, in a letter to Wilson, appears in most biographies of the President.

CHAPTER 4

Press dispatches widely reported the internment of German and Austrian vessels in American harbors. For Fiske, see above, chapter 2. Wilson's State of the Union address on December 8, 1914, was widely quoted in the American press. TR's letters to FDR are in the FDR Library. The satiric cartoon on the *Lusitania* sinking appeared in the *New York American*, in March 1915. Daniels's jumping the co-opted Captain Benson over thirty-one more senior officers to be CNO is footnoted in the Daniels *Diaries*, above. As always FDR's letters to Eleanor are in *Personal Letters*, above. For FDR's losing primary campaign, see Ward and Davis, above. TR's kind refusal to visit Sara at Springwood during the campaign season is quoted in James MacGregor Burns and Susan Dunn, *The Three Roosevelts: Patrician Leaders Who Transformed America* (New York: Atlantic Monthly Press, 2001). Henry Adams's Christmas 1914 letter to Elizabeth Cameron, and his later letter to her daughter, Martha Cameron Lindsay, are in *Letters of Henry Adams*, ed. J. C. Levenson (Cambridge, MA: Belknap Press of Harvard University Press, 1988).

CHAPTER 5

Eleanor's receipt of the telegram from Howe about Franklin's hospitalization is in Elliott Roosevelt and James Brough, *An Untold Story*, above. The anticipated launching of the *Arizona* was reported in detail in *The New York Times* for June 13, 1915, and the event itself on June 20, 1915. Roosevelt's preparedness publications at this time were "The Future of the Submarine," in the *North American Review*, October 1915; "The Naval Plattsburg," in *The Outlook*, June 28, 1916; "How Can I Serve My Country?" in *The World's Work*, March 1917; and "On Your Own Heads," in *Scribner's Magazine*, April 1917. Count von Zeppelin, Ludwig Stein and Hans von Haeften are quoted by Count Harry Kessler in his diaries, *Journey to the Abyss*, ed. and trans. Laird M. Easton (New York: Knopf: 2011). Spring-Rice's January 16, 1917, memo is quoted by David F. Trask in *Captains and Cabinets: Anglo-American*

Naval Relations, 1917–1918 (Columbia: University of Missouri Press, 1972). FDR's junket to Haiti is described in all the Roosevelt biographies. Smedley Butler's earlier career and postwar disillusionment are detailed in his *War Is a Racket* (New York: Round Table Press, 1935), and in Adam Parfrey, ed., *War Is a Racket: The Antiwar Classic by America's Most Decorated General, Two Other Anti-Interventionist Tracts, and Photographs from the Horror of It* (Los Angeles: Feral House, 2003). Wilson's steadfast and continuing comments on strict neutrality were quoted widely in the press. Quotations from *Life* which appeared as relations with Germany reached the breaking point are from Edward S. Martin, ed., *The Diary of a Nation: The War and How We Got into It* (Garden City, NY: Doubleday, Page, 1918). Alice Roosevelt Longworth's undated recollection of Eleanor's returning alone and unhappy from a party is quoted in *Mrs. L.: Conversations . . .* , above. Colonel House's recommendation about removing Lindley Garrison and later about removing Baker, Daniels and Lansing are from Edward Mandell House, ed. Charles Seymour, *The Intimate Papers of Colonel House* (Boston: Houghton Mifflin, 1926).

CHAPTER 6

TR's impromptu visit to the bedrooms of his great-nephews as war began is described by Geoffrey Ward in *A First-Class Temperament* (above) from interviews with James Roosevelt and Franklin D., Jr., who were too young to remember the episode (James may have had a vague memory of it) and must have been told about it later by their mother. TR's appeal to Wilson to serve abroad is most fully described in Morris, *Colonel Roosevelt*, above, and Daniels, *The Wilson Era*, above, which recalls TR's cajoling of Tumulty. FDR's snarky "web-footed" message to a general at Camp Upton is quoted in Rollins, above. FDR's letter to Major Philip Little on periscopes is reproduced in facsimile in the Swann autograph catalog for April 17, 2012. Executive Order 2651, June 30, 1917, requisitioning interned enemy vessels is U.S. Official Bulletin 51, July 10, 1917. It includes a complete listing of the ships under the order. The use of American flag transports otherwise returning from France empty to carry salvaged period furniture for use in film sets by movie moguls is described by Claude Lanzmann, Frank Wynne, trans., in *The Patagonian Hare: A Memoir* (New York: Farrar, Straus, 2012). FDR's indictment of yacht owners is detailed in *The Literary Digest* for May 26, 1917. The original proposal of a "mine barrage," taken by FDR to Wilson in October 1916, is recalled by Daniels in *The Wilson Era*, above. Count Kessler's diary entry, October 17, 1917, on the alleged folly of the United States leaving the Pacific open to Japanese greed and the U-boat commander's claim that the mine barrage was "irrelevant" are both in Laird M. Easton, ed. and trans., *Journey to the Abyss: The Diaries of Count Harry Kessler, 1880–1918* (New York: Knopf, 2011). Eleanor's "watch over Father" (and Lucy) on the *Sylph* after first declining to sail is from Roosevelt and Brough, *An Untold Story*, above.

CHAPTER 7

FDR's warning to the *New York Sun*, March 18, 1918, to publish nothing further about an "aerial torpedo," and his ordering scrutiny of letters dealing with chess problems as possible covert communications, are from James R. Novak, *Censorship 1917* (New York: Da Capo, 1972). One of FDR's many entreaties to the public to offer "binoculars, spyglasses and telescopes" to the Navy is in *The Literary Digest* for February 2, 1918. His article warning "U-Boats Off Shore!" was published in *The New York Times* on June 9, 1918. A detailed account of the new Main Navy Building is *Main Navy Building: Its Construction and Original Occupants* (Washington, DC: A Naval History Publication, Series 2, Number 14, August 1, 1970). The prophylaxis stations at naval bases (Daniels saw them as "invitations to sin") are described in many FDR biographies. That he acted to authorize them during a Daniels absence is from Byron Farwell, *Over There: The United States in the Great War* (New York: Norton, 1999). Livingston Davis's diaries including the trips to England and France are Box 33 in the FDR Library. FDR's accounts of his travels in the war zone are from his letter-diaries—fifty printed pages beginning July 9—in *Personal Letters* (above). He intended the accounts for a book he would never write. Daniels's reports from FDR's inspections abroad are from his Cabinet diaries (above) and in *Roosevelt and Daniels* (above). Paul von Berger's comment and the showing of the navy play in Berlin are from Kessler (above). Capt. (Later Rear Adm.) Schofield's complaint about sharing office space in London with FDR is from a letter to his wife, Claribel, furnished by Lannie Liggera. FDR's visits to Italy and Britain were reported in *The Times* under dates indicated in the text. Howe's letter to Eleanor, August 23, 1918, while FDR was abroad, that the Services would be accepting "no new volunteers," is in the FDR Library. Wilson's remark about the efficacy of Adm. Plunkett's naval guns is quoted in Daniels's Cabinet diaries, February 25, 1919. Influenza deaths are on record at the U.S. Army Military Institute in Carlisle, PA. Franklin's arrival "at an Atlantic port . . . suffering from a light attack of pneumonia" was reported in *The New York Times* in a dispatch dated September 19, 1918. Livy Davis's diary also reports FDR's return, and Elliott Roosevelt describes the medical embarkation and subsequent circumstances in his *An Untold Story*, above.

CHAPTER 8

Early hints in print about the Lucy Mercer affair appeared in 1954 in Jonathan Daniels's *The End of Innocence* (above), and more explicitly (as Eleanor had died in 1962) in his *The Time between the Wars: Armistice to Pearl Harbor* (Garden City: Doubleday, 1966). *The New York Times*, in "Roosevelt Romance Reported," August 12, 1966, was followed the next day by "Kin Deny Account of F.D.R. Romance," but Drew Pearson's nationally syndicated columns on August 16 and August 22, 1966, gave the affair additional credence. Joseph P. Lash, a close friend of Eleanor, and the biographer who refers to her seeing *Candida*, followed with an account of the affair from her point of view in *Eleanor and Franklin* (above) in 1972. The Elliott Roosevelt-James Brough *An Untold Story* (above) in 1977 continued opening up the affair. Joseph Alsop, a family connection, reporter and columnist, wrote further about the Mercer relationship in his *FDR: A Centenary Remembrance* (New York: Viking, 1982), after which the floodgates opened. Murray Kempton, reviewing the Alsop book in "The Kindly Stranger," *New York Review of Books*, April 15, 1982, closed with a wry, "fugitive fantasy" about how the affair might have continued if FDR had left Eleanor for Lucy. The Virginia Moore poem clipping dated by Eleanor as "1918" and found at her death in 1962 was published by Blanche Wiesen Cook (above) in 1992, and later biographies, including Pottker's *Sara and Eleanor* (above), enlarged on the affair via interviews and speculation. The first book-length account was Joseph Persico's *Franklin and Lucy: Mrs. Rutherfurd and the Other Remarkable Women in Roosevelt's Life* (above), in 2009. New York State divorce law in the period of the affair, and how the law had developed from its beginnings, was outlined for me by Mark Weintraub, February 9, 2012.

TR's late 1918 letter to Franklin is in the FDR Library. Harry Truman's reminiscence of the Armistice is quoted by S. Weintraub in *A Stillness Heard Round the World: The End of the Great War* (New York: Dutton, 1985). Events following the Armistice and through the close of 1918 are detailed in FDR's Annual Report to the Secretary, 1919, FDR Library; Daniels's *Cabinet Diaries*; *Roosevelt and Daniels*; and *Wilson Era* (both above); FDR's letters are quoted in biographies above, and *Personal Letters* (above).

CHAPTER 9

Eleanor's lonely visits to the Clover Adams memorial in Rock Creek Cemetery are described by Joseph Lash and Blanche Wiesen Cook (both above) and noted also by such later FDR biographers as Ward and Persico. Many studies of Adams, "Clover" and St. Gaudens deal with the cryptic memorial; the most recent is Natalie Dykstra's *Clover Adams: A Gilded and Heartbreaking Life* (Boston: Houghton Mifflin, 2012). Franklin's calling TR "the greatest man I ever knew" is in Morris, *Colonel Roosevelt* (above). FDR's letters to film producer William Fox were offered on sale by Swann Galleries (see under chapter 6). Cook and other biographers also deal with race riots and the Red Scare in Washington in 1919. *An Untold Story* (above) also quotes Eleanor's letters to Sara on the European voyage with FDR, and her diary entries afterward such as "Dined alone." Livy Davis's diary is quoted from the original in the FDR Library. Mrs. Wilson's spin on the voyages and on Wilson's illnesses is drawn from her autobiography quoted by Phyllis Lee Levin in *Edith and Woodrow* (New York: Scribner's, 2001) and from Gene Smith, *When the Cheering Stopped: The Last Years of Woodrow Wilson* (New York: Morrow, 1964). The history of the Washington replica desk desired by Edith Wilson was reported by Michelle Frauenberger, FDR Library, June 8, 2012. FDR's involvement in postwar dirigible and aircraft flight attempts are reported in *Personal Letters*, in *Wilson Era* and in photographs in the FDR Library. Aircraft radio technology at the time is from a site visit to the Sparks Museum of Radio and Electricity in Bellingham, Washington. FDR's "against Navy regulations" is from *Wilson Era*, and the details of radio transmission of the fight and FDR's involvement are from *The Wireless Age*, July, 1921. FDR's letter to Salazar, November 4, 1943, on the Azores bases in 1918–1919 from *Foreign Relations of the United States* is quoted by John Lewis Gaddis in *George F. Kennan* (New York: Penguin Press, 2011). The flights of the C-5 and the NC-4 are drawn from *Personal Letters* and from org/wiki/C-5 and org/wiki/NC-4, which include period photos. The Prince of Wales's visit to Annapolis is described by Daniels in *Wilson Era* (above). The account of Wilson's aborted speaking campaign is largely from Conrad Black and Gene Smith (both above). FDR's ceremonial retirement in Main Navy is described by Alfred Rollins, Jonathan Daniels and later Roosevelt biographers.

CHAPTER 10

Bertie (Mrs. Charles) Hamlin's diary entry is quoted by most later FDR biographers. The Newport sailors' sex scandal and its embarrassing repercussions, several years in the making, is described by Blanche Wiesen Cook, Geoffrey Ward, Kenneth Davis, Jonathan Daniels and other biographers (above), including *Woodrow Wilson* by H. W. Brands (New York: Times Books, 2003). FDR's abortive effort to buy Curaçao from the Dutch is in Conrad Black (above). Associated Press dispatches throughout July 1920 carried details of the Democratic convention in San Francisco, including exaggerations of the scuffle for the New York standard. Geoffrey Ward (above) quotes purported eyewitnesses who saw, for the press, more brawl than tussle. *The Literary Digest's* "Another Roosevelt Headed for the White House" appeared on July 31, 1920, following the convention. Sara and Eleanor's responses to the FDR nomination, and the scene in Hyde Park, are best seen in Lash and in Pottker (above). The Campobello dimension, including the shipment there of the *Vireo*, is in Klein, *Beloved Island* (above). FDR's ceremonial resignation as Assistant Secretary is described by Daniels, who quotes the exchange of letters (including a ghost-written one from Wilson) in *The Wilson Era* and *Roosevelt and Daniels* (both above).

CHAPTER 11

FDR on the attractions of public life is quoted from Nasser Ghaemi, *A First-Rate Madness: Uncovering the Links between Leadership and Mental Illness* (New York: Penguin Press, 2011). Details of the Hyde Park public greeting and FDR's acceptance address are in all major FDR biographies; Eleanor's letters are quoted by Joseph Lash (above). FDR's concession, "Nary an illusion," to Marvin McIntyre is from Jonathan Daniels, *The End of Innocence* (above). Ted, Jr., on FDR as "maverick" is from Cordery, *Alice*, but appears in other biographies as well.

Acknowledgments

Credits for illustrations used have been posted with captions for the illustrations themselves. I appreciate the good offices of those who have assisted me in the searches and procurement of these images. The staff at the FDR Library has been especially generous.

I am grateful, too, for information, good offices, and assistance, to Bruce Austin, Timothy Baker, Robert Clark, Charles Creekman, Jonathan Crowe, Pat Daly, Robert C. Doyle, Timothy L. Frank, Michelle Frauenberger, Robert Guinsler, Kay Li, Lannie Liggera, Michael Lipschutz, Rafik K. Mansour, Mark Mollen, Christopher G. Palmer, Michel Pharand, Robert L. Pigeon, Martin R. Quinn, Valerie F. Raphael, Mark Renovitch, Peter Sayers, Cisca Schreefel, Richard Swain, Karen Turner, Lissa Warren, Mark T. Weber, Mark Bennett Weintraub, Rodelle Weintraub, Martha Whitt, David Winkler, Richard E. Winslow, and Philip Zimmer.

Index